OTHER PEOPLE'S MONEY

Also by Peter Foster

The Blue-Eyed Sheiks
The Sorcerer's Apprentices

OTHER PEOPLE'S MONEY

The Banks,
the Government
and Dome

PETER FOSTER

Collins Toronto

First published 1983
by Collins Publishers
100 Lesmill Road, Don Mills, Ontario

Canadian Cataloguing in Publication Data

Foster, Peter, 1947-
  Other people's money

Includes index.
ISBN 0-00-217122-8

1. Dome Petroleum Limited — History.   I. Title.

HD9574.C24D65   1983   338.7'6223382'0971   C83-099047-X

Printed and bound in Canada by John Deyell Company

For Jane

Contents

''We weren't really successful in exploration, but the important thing is that we did it with other people's money . . . That's a bad quote, isn't it.''

BILL RICHARDS

Acknowledgements

As with my other two books, the bulk of the Dome story was obtained through personal interviews, of which I conducted more than a hundred in New York, Toronto, Montreal, Ottawa, Calgary, Edmonton and Vancouver. Given the delicate and controversial nature of the subject matter, almost all of these were given on a non-attributable basis. Nevertheless, I take this opportunity to thank all those who took the time and trouble to give me their versions of the extraordinary events here described.

Among those who gave me less controversial, but nonetheless valuable, information, help or advice, I thank Charlie Dunkley, Bill Mooney, Walt Dingle, Carlyle Dunbar, June Tattle of the Toronto Stock Exchange, the staff of the *Financial Post* library and Bernie Maas of the American Stock Exchange. Particular thanks are due to Calgary's petroleum writers' "mafia" — Dunnery Best of the *Financial Post*, David Hatter of the *Calgary Herald*, Tom Kennedy of the *Calgary Sun* and David Yager and Delton Campbell at *The Roughneck.* Thanks also to Alex and Donna and the Masons. Last but far from least, I feel no acknowledgements would be complete without mentioning both the Howse and the Osler families.

Dome itself was probably as co-operative as any company could have been in its trying circumstances. They made clear to me that they would rather I was not writing the book but that since I was, they would help me as far as they could. Bill Richards, in particular — and true to his character — was both a good deal more frank and more generous with his time than most men would have been in his position.

Once again I have to express may sincerest thanks to my editor, Colleen Dimson, for all her efforts. I also wish to thank Grace Deutsch for attempting to rectify both my copy and my male chauvinism. At Collins, I wish to thank Margaret Paull, Linda Pellowe and Jenny Falconer.

In terms of published sources, apart from the normal corporate reports, proxy statements and releases and filings with the U.S. Securities and Exchange Commission, I also looked through a huge volume of clippings and articles on Dome. In particular, I would like to note just three that I do not mention elsewhere in the text but which I found extremely useful. They are "Conoco" by Steven Brill in *The American Lawyer*, November, 1981; "How Dome Petroleum Got Crunched" by Shawn Tully (with research assistant Ford S. Worthy) in *Fortune*, January 10, 1983; and finally the stories by John Ridsdel about Dome and super-depletion in the *Calgary Herald* of August 22, 1979, entitled "Tax Manoeuvres Mean Profits for Dome Drillers" and "Public Foots Most of the Exploration Bill." I also have to thank Peter Newman for his excellent account of Dome's Kaiser acquisition in *The Canadian Establishment. Volume Two: The Acquisitors*, published by McClelland and Stewart, 1982. Finally, although I make reference to it in the text, I feel I should acknowledge my debt to Anthony Sampson's excellent account of the road to the international sovereign debt crisis, *The Money Lenders*, published by Hodder and Stoughton, 1981.

1
The End-
of-the-World Party

*"There must be something wrong with a world
banking system which cannot afford to cease lending
to a bad debtor."*

DENIS HEALEY

FORMER BRITISH CHANCELLOR OF THE EXCHEQUER

In September, 1982, bankers, politicians and money mandarins from all over the globe descended on the city of Toronto for the annual meeting of the International Monetary Fund (IMF). It was perhaps the fund's most significant gathering since its inception, for the world was teetering on the brink of financial disaster.

To outside observers, the affair looked like a gigantic party. Dignitaries drank and danced beneath a massive blue and white striped marquee at Queen's Park, home of the Ontario provincial legislature; they attended select cocktail parties in the massive downtown towers of the major Canadian banks; virtually every limousine in the province was commandeered to ferry bankers out to gatherings in the mock-manorial splendour of the Old Mill in the city's west end, or aboard the paddle-steamer *Mariposa Belle* on Lake Ontario, or in the Art Gallery of Ontario. But while the champagne flowed and the jazz bands played, the spectre of international collapse, like Banquo's ghost, loomed over the proceedings. "It was," said one of the Canadian bankers participating, "a little like an end-of-the-world party, because people were frightened that that was what might just happen."

Mexico's delegation was not seen at as many social gatherings as the others. There was a good reason for this low profile. Less than a month before, the country had startled and horrified its foreign bankers by informing them that it could no longer make payments on its $80 billion foreign debt. Shortly afterwards, Argentina, owing almost $40 billion, and Brazil, with a debt close to $90 billion, would declare that they, too, could not meet existing debt schedules.

Within months, Yugoslavia, Romania, Ecuador, Chile, Cuba and Uruguay would join the list of heavily indebted countries requesting international help and debt rescheduling.

The crisis, once again, was related to the commodity that had fueled most of the economic turmoil of the previous decade: oil. But it was also due to an enormous increase over the same decade in international lending by major banks. Some, if not most, of that lending now appeared to have been the height of imprudence. The banks — including the major Canadian banks, which had become major lenders in international markets — were now calling on the International Monetary Fund to bail them out.

The IMF, set up under the Bretton Woods agreement in 1944, which erected the framework for postwar world financial relationships, had originally been considered a millionaire's club. Its concerns were international financial discipline, co-ordinating national monetary policies and the prevention of self-defeating economic warfare. It was also the "lender of last resort" which would come to a country's aid if it got into severe financial problems.

The arrival of the people from the IMF usually meant hardship for a country's population and sometimes curtains for its government. In return for its aid, the fund always demanded tough economic measures — usually devaluation and deflation — with their attendant economic suffering. As a result, the IMF was often the subject of abuse that perhaps more appropriately should have been directed at the national governments whose policies had forced the IMF to be called in.

But the reason the IMF was so important now was that paradoxically, throughout the 1970s, its role, and that of other organizations of financial aid such as the World Bank, had been usurped by the commercial bankers, which had doled out money in ever increasing amounts to countries that had little hope of paying it back. The total external debt of the developing countries had, in the previous decade, grown to over $600 billion. Well over half of this was owed to the banks. The sums were mind-boggling, the implications were frightening.

In 1852, in the preface to his book *Memoirs of Extraordinary Popular Delusions and the Madness of Crowds*, Charles Mackay wrote: "In reading the history of nations, we find that, like individuals, they have their whims and their peculiarities; their seasons of excitement and recklessness, when they care not what they do. We find that whole communities suddenly fix their minds upon one object, and go mad in its pursuit; that millions of people become simultaneously impressed with one delusion, and run after it, till their attention is caught by some new folly more captivating than the first."

During the decade leading up to the IMF meeting in Toronto, it appeared that the entire world banking "community" had suddenly

16

fixed its mind on the object of lending to impecunious developing countries.

Mackay also wrote that "men ... think in herds; it will be seen that they go mad in herds, while they only recover their senses slowly, and one by one." Now the herds of international bankers were very quickly recovering their senses. The problem, however, was how to rectify what they had done.

John Maynard Keynes, the economic genius behind much of the Bretton Woods structure, had always been disparaging about bankers and their so-called prudence, and had also noted their tendency to herd-thinking. "A 'sound' banker, alas! is not one who foresees danger and avoids it," he once wrote, "but one who, when he is ruined, is ruined in a conventional and orthodox way along with his fellows, so that no one can really blame him."

In retrospect, throughout the 1970s the bankers' behaviour most resembled that of lemmings, those unfortunate rodents with a predilection for swimming out of their depth.

The Bankers' Exposed Assets

Banking assets are an unusual form of wealth, for they consist primarily of a bank's loans. The measure of what a bank "has" is thus mainly the volume of money it has loaned to others. These assets are of course the source of profits, chiefly via the spread between the interest rates the bank pays for deposits and the rates it charges on loans. Nevertheless, a bank's own risk capital is a small proportion of the funds it lends. For Canadian banks, for example, assets are around 30 times capital — one of the highest ratios in the world. It therefore takes a relatively small percentage of a bank's loans to go sour to endanger its capital base, and thus its very existence. Bankers perform a much more precarious balancing act between lenders and borrowers than they ever care to admit. The precariousness of the act, however, depends very much on the quality of the borrowers.

The crisis that faced the world's bankers in Toronto was so horrifying because of the sheer volume of loans to countries that suddenly appeared unable to meet their debt obligations.

The U.S. banking system was the most exposed to the crisis in absolute terms. Its nine largest banks had more than 100% of their risk capital loaned out to Argentina, Brazil and Mexico. But the five major Canadian chartered banks — the Royal Bank of Canada, the Canadian Imperial Bank of Commerce, the Bank of Montreal, the Toronto-Dominion Bank and the Bank of Nova Scotia — collectively had about $6.5 billion loaned to Mexico, $5.5 billion to Brazil, $3.5 billion to Venezuela and $2.2 billion to Argentina. That total, too, represented more than their combined capital base.

The Canadian banks, like their U.S. counterparts, had engaged in an enormous surge of foreign lending in the previous decade and their total foreign assets, that is, mainly overseas loans, had grown to $140 billion, or 40% of their total assets. The 1982 edition of "Bank Facts," put out by the Canadian Bankers' Association before the international crisis broke, noted: "The Canadian chartered banks have been so successful internationally that they are recognized as world leaders in the field."

Suddenly international lending was a bad field in which to lead.

The key questions were: why had international lending to developing countries expanded so dramatically; and why had the crisis not been foreseen?

The enormous growth in international lending had been a direct offshoot of the growth of the trillion-dollar Eurodollar market, based in the square mile of the City of London. Originally the home for expatriate currency, London had become a centre for unprecedented expansion of world credit. All the world's major banks had come to get a piece of the action. To these select banks, money was available in the market at a small premium over the fluctuating LIBOR (London Interbank Offered Rate), and they made their profits by lending it out at a higher premium, usually a fraction of 1%, above that rate. This spread might only be $^3/_8$ of a percent, but $^3/_8$ of a percent of a billion-dollar loan was a lot of money. Moreover, since the loan fluctuated with LIBOR, the interest rate risks for the banks were minimal. For the borrower, however, they were potentially large should the LIBOR suddenly jump. These huge slabs of money sought large lenders. The largest borrowers — and the ones that needed the money the most — were sovereign countries. These massive needs were accommodated through banking syndicates. As a result, there was a fundamental change in the nature of banking. These loans weren't usually for anything specific; they were "wholesale" money. By 1970, bankers were actively selling these loans. Preferred lenders were developing countries that needed funds for economic development, like Mexico and Brazil. However, there was an air of unreality about the whole procedure. Because of increasing competitiveness, rates in no way reflected the real risks involved.

An enormous increase in the funds available followed the first OPEC crisis in 1973–74 and the quadrupling of oil prices. Petrodollars, the huge volumes of oil income that the OPEC nations like Saudi Arabia were unable to spend themselves, began looking for a home. They found a home in the banks, and the London interbank market. But

18

of course the banks, in order to make profits on these huge new deposits, had to lend them out again. By 1976, the OPEC nations of the Middle East and North Africa had deposits of more than $11 billion with the six largest U.S. banks, and there was fear that money might be used as a weapon to influence foreign policy just as oil had been. But the real problems weren't to come from the money's source but from where the OPEC money eventually wound up.

There was something comforting about the concept of recycling petrodollars, as if the banks were performing some enormously necessary and responsible act of re-balancing a world economy skewed by the sudden increases in oil prices. However, in so doing, they were performing acts of quite unaccustomed generosity. They were indeed lending money to countries that needed it. What wasn't so certain was how these countries were ever going to pay it back. Apparently, the bankers just chanted to themselves that old refrain: "Countries can't go bankrupt."

The notion of the non-bankruptability of countries derived partially from the fact that no bank or group of banks could move in and seize a country's assets and sell them off. That was hardly a comforting thought for lenders. However, the bankers never tired of telling each other that no sensible government would dream of defaulting on its international commitments, because then it would be blacklisted by the international financial community. What they seldom mentioned publicly was that they also believed that ultimately a nation's workforce would have to pay the price for economic mismanagement on the part of its government. In the end the people would have to pay because they were the only ones who *could* pay. Nevertheless, although sensible governments might well wish at all costs to avoid default, sensible governments were also quite likely, in the heat of the electoral moment, to borrow more funds than they could reasonably hope to repay in order to finance politically popular economic expansion. And then there were the loans to governments that weren't terribly "sensible" in western bankers' eyes.

The whole concept of recycling had a conceptual balance to it that was highly spurious. As oil prices rose, OPEC had more funds and the oil-consuming developing nations needed more funds. Recycling was meant to link that supply with that demand. But because of the economic impact of higher oil prices, the non-oil countries were borrowing more at the same time as their ability to repay was declining.

Paupers and Bankers: A Strange Dance

Recycling seemed to make a lot of sense from the perspective of international aid. It made much less sense from the perspective of prudent traditional banking. Nevertheless, bankers were mesmerized by the short-term benefits from this new business. In general terms, the poorer the borrower, the higher were the interest rates on loans and the greater the profits. The profitability of loans went hand in hand with the borrowers' fundamental insecurity. Moreover, when it came to loans for smaller and poorer countries, although the funds might be vaguely committed to a dam or a highway project, they were as likely to finish up buying a Boeing 747 jet for some tyrant, or financing a dictator's palace.

" ... In the more corrupt countries of the world, like Zaire or Indonesia," wrote Anthony Sampson in *The Money Lenders*, "selling loans was like offering crates of whisky to an alcoholic." In Zaire, the story circulated that President Mobutu went around with the country's gross national product in a briefcase chained to his wrist. In most cases, however, the loans finished up simply financing consumption, thereby merely delaying the wolf's inevitable arrival at the national door.

Over time, the large banks and the impecunious developing countries became locked in a dance from which neither could afford to become disengaged. The more the banks lent to countries, the more reluctant they would be to declare default. Since all increasingly feared panic, they would much rather simply lend more money in order to avert a crisis.

This present crisis — following earlier banking scares in Turkey, Zaire, Korea and, most recently, in 1981, in Poland — had once again been precipitated by oil. But the financial implications proved vastly different from those of the first crisis. When the second OPEC crisis was sparked by the revolution in Iran in 1979–80, it seemed, as oil prices soared again, that the cycle of the earlier crisis might play itself out again. However, the flood of petrodollars was not so great this time. The oil-producing countries had developed massive development programs that led them to retain far more of their oil revenues. Indeed, so ambitious were some of the programs that major producers, too, were now taking massive loans. Mexico was the outstanding example. Meanwhile, higher oil prices also greatly increased the demand for funds from the non-oil developing countries, such as Brazil. However, although the sharp increases of 1979–80 had their adverse impact on non-oil countries, projections for both petroleum demand

20

and world prices soon proved to be grossly exaggerated — to the detriment of the ambitious oil producers.

Brazil and Mexico were at opposite ends of a paradox. The commercial banks had loaned huge amounts to them both, but the conditions under which the loans were viable for Mexico — continuously rising real oil prices — were potentially disastrous for Brazil. Meanwhile, if oil prices slumped, as they were now doing, then that indicated lower commodity values everywhere — once again to the detriment of commodity-rich Brazil. Bankers insisted that they were behaving in a commercial fashion, but the whole system of credit, as Sampson pointed out, "had mythical assumptions at the heart of it."

Moral Hazards

There could be no doubt that many billions of dollars of rash loans had been made. The question was: who was to bear the consequences? Conceptually, the issue boiled down to that of "moral hazard," a term derived from the insurance business. "Moral hazard," in the definition of George Gilder, "is the danger that a policy will encourage the behaviour — or promote the disasters — that it ensures against." In his book *Wealth & Poverty*, Gilder was writing primarily about the moral hazards of social insurance and welfare schemes. The most obvious case of moral hazard in the case of fire insurance would be the temptation to arson. In the social insurance field, it might be that unemployment benefits would lead some individuals deliberately to seek unemployment.

International financial institutions like the International Monetary Fund and the World Bank had certainly not been set up as giant insurance agencies for the banking system, but that, effectively, is what they had now become. Helping countries out of their debt problems meant inevitably helping the bankers who had loaned them money. The key issue was how far many of the rash loans to developing countries had been made with a tacit belief that, if things went wrong, the IMF could always be counted upon to bail the countries out: "Countries can't go bankrupt." Sampson saw this problem as: "how to have a system safe enough to rescue banks from collapse, but not so visibly safe that it encouraged banks to be rash and imposed no sanction on them?"

Ironically, commercial lending to the Third World had originally been welcomed as a way of introducing greater financial discipline to underdeveloped countries. But in fact the hectic competition for business had achieved exactly the opposite result. As Sampson wrote:

21

"Ever since the oil crisis of 1973 had built up the OPEC surpluses these flows had been drastically privatised, until two-thirds of the money now came through the banks. And these bank loans had ended up in wastage on a far greater scale than the most incompetent aid agency could have dreamed of — whether they went to the private coffers of President Mobutu in Zaire, in bribes to Indonesian officials, or to Communist Party funds in Warsaw."

The international loan problem was exacerbated by increasing financial difficulties among the industrialized nations. In the U.S., three financial institutions — Drysdale Government Securities, Penn Square Bank and Lombard Wall — all failed in 1982, while Europe was rocked by the liquidation of the Banco Ambrosiano. In Canada, as elsewhere, the economy was severely depressed and the Canadian dollar had come under heavy selling pressure in the middle of the year. In June alone, Canada had been forced to borrow U.S. $2.35 billion to replenish reserves that had been heavily depleted by the defence of the dollar. In the depths of the midsummer gloom there was even a suggestion that Canada itself might have to apply to the IMF for aid.

Dome: The Skeleton in the Vault

It was against this depressing background that the chief executives of the major Canadian banks held their parties in Toronto. There, potentates and finance ministers of indigent countries sought audience with the big bankers who for years had been almost thrusting funds upon them but were now threatening to cut them off. But four of the five CEOs — Russell Harrison of the Commerce, Bill Mulholland of the Montreal, Dick Thomson of the Toronto-Dominion, and Rowland Frazee of the Royal — had another big problem on their minds. It was a lender as potentially damaging to their corporate empires as any foreign sovereign loan. But the lender was not a country; it was a single company. The company was Dome Petroleum. Moreover, they weren't in the Dome problem alone. Walter Wriston, the towering head of U.S. banking giant Citicorp (parent of Citibank), was also deeply embroiled in Dome, although his bank's concern was less for exposure than for the embarrassment and possible legal consequences of having led a major syndicate of bankers to loan Dome $2.1 billion without full awareness of the company's desperate financial condition. Wriston, a focal figure at the meeting, had guided Citicorp into the position of being one of the largest and most aggressive banks in the world. A large part of that aggressiveness had involved leading the bankers' charge into the Third World. For him, Dome was a relatively minor problem, but for the Canadian bankers it loomed over all else.

22

By the end of the month, Dome had to come up with $1.3 billion for the four banks. It clearly could not do so. For most of the preceding summer, the bankers had been locked in bailout negotiations with the Canadian federal government over Dome.

The Dome situation ranked right up there with the problem countries. Dome's debt, at around $8 billion, was approximately one-tenth that of megadebtors Brazil and Mexico. It was half that of Chile. It was more than that of Cuba and Uruguay combined.

Even before the Mexican crisis broke, the Dome situation had already caused a ripple of panic through what had always been considered one of the soundest banking systems in the world. The Bank of Nova Scotia had made a public statement that concerns about its stability were unfounded. But then the Scotia had no exposure to Dome. Rowland Frazee of the Royal had sent letters to his branch managers earlier in the year assuring them that it was nonsensical for anyone to imagine that the bank was in any difficulties. But then the Royal was the largest Canadian bank, and its exposure was just a third of that of each of the other big three. The Commerce, the Montreal and the T-D each had close to $1 billion out to Dome. Suggestions that the CIBC might be in trouble over its Dome exposure had earlier in the summer caused a sharp drop both in its share price and that of its outstanding Eurobond issues. Small runs on a number of banks' deposits had been reported. The Dominion Bond Rating Service, a Toronto-based credit rating company, had cut the long-term bond ratings of all the major banks.

The Dome situation bore a close relationship to what was happening on the world stage. Its borrowings had been based on highly optimistic growth forecasts and expectations about the continued rise in world oil prices. Its bankers, jostling with each other to increase their asset growth, had vied to see who could lend it the most. And now that the crunch had come, the issue of moral hazard had raised its head. Some of the banks were turning to the federal government to help bail out Dome on the basis that the company simply owed too much to be allowed to go bankrupt. However, Dome's situation had an angle that was unique to Canada, for the rapid expansion-through-acquisition that was at the root of its problems had been vociferously encouraged by a fiercely economic-nationalist Liberal government. That thrust had been embodied two years previously in the National Energy Program, a complex policy that sought, among other things, to encourage "Canadianization" through greater government intervention and a combination of financial discrimination against, and partial expropriation of, foreign-owned and controlled oil companies.

The NEP had turned into a policy disaster. Dome — which had

23

been hailed as a "chosen instrument" of the Liberal government —
was its most conspicuous casualty.

However, the OPEC background, the banks' unaccustomed generosity and Canada's political direction explained only part of Dome's
situation. How had the company become the "chosen instrument"?
Why had the banks lent it such a massive volume of money? To answer
those questions, one had to turn to the unique nature of the company,
and the two extraordinary men who headed it.

2
The Men
for the Times

"This turbulent and heavily politicized environment appeared to create unique opportunities for Canadian oil people. No company looked to be as skillful at taking advantage of the situation as Dome Petroleum."

Most companies start as the inspiration of one person with a business vision to which he or she attracts the investments of others. The vision may fail or succeed. The company may pursue no more than its original mandate — possibly on a larger and larger scale — or it may diversify into new businesses; it may change its products or its goals completely as new partners or executives produce new visions.

Emerson wrote that an institution is the lengthened shadow of its founder. However, over time as that shadow grows longer it may become amorphous. Most of the world's great corporations have long outlived their founders and become faceless pyramids of power programmed by professional managers as self-perpetuating organisms pursuing profits and growth.

A corporation can be viewed in myriad ways. For the economist, it is a group of people co-ordinated for the profitable process of goods or production of services. Its activities and objectives can all be subsumed within graphs that plot demand, costs and break-even points. But such naked common denominators do no more justice to companies' infinite variety than the definition of a human being as "a two-legged creature without wings or feathers."

For its employees, a company may merely represent an office in a building, a physical location where they turn up on weekdays to perform some mundane task in return for a salary. For its executives, too, it may represent just a job, some function of financing or marketing or production within an overall corporate strategy.

For investors or investment analysts, a publicly quoted corporation is a vehicle to increase wealth and security. If the analysts are "technical," their sole concern may be the spidery course of the corporation's share price on a chart. For these analysts, that line will distill all that is relevant. With price registered along its vertical axis, and time along its horizontal, all the analyst, or any investor, will want from the chart is a rightward diagonal rise, and the sharper the better.

But a company can also be infinitely more: the focus of personal ambition, the source of "belonging," the route to fame. Egos can become inextricably wound up with corporations; corporations can appear inseparable from one person or a group of people.

The oil business has always attracted a rare breed of individuals: gamblers, visionaries and empire builders. Of the Seven Sisters, the corporate giants that still significantly dominate world oil, three — Exxon, Mobil and Standard Oil of California — are the offshoots of the one man whose shadow still stretches down from the last century, John D. Rockefeller. Rockefeller's corporate children and their other four sisters — Royal Dutch Shell, Gulf, BP and Texaco — almost totally dominated world oil until the early 1970s. But then came the OPEC crisis of 1973 and a whole new set of economic and political parameters. In Canada, as elsewhere, it seemed there was now an opportunity for a new type of corporate vision.

The Corporate Odd Couple

In the decade after the first OPEC crisis of 1973, the Canadian oilpatch threw up a whole firmament of new business stars. Two men, and one company, outshone and outgrew all others. The company was Dome Petroleum; the men were its chairman, "Smilin'" Jack Gallagher, and its president, Bill Richards. They were deified by their staff, consulted by government, idolized by investors and courted by the banks.

Between 1976, when it started drilling high above the Arctic Circle in the Beaufort Sea, and 1981, when it ran corporate rings around U.S. oil giant Conoco en route to its $4 billion acquisition of Hudson's Bay Oil & Gas (HBOG), Dome Petroleum was a phenomenon with few parallels in recent corporate history. In those five years, its share-price soared from $1.58 to $25.38. It dominated the Toronto and American stock markets, and caused frenzied trading on the floor of the London Stock Exchange as investors from Geneva to Tokyo were caught up in its corporate dream.

Dome's 33-storey black tower in the heart of Calgary — a city that exceeded all North American growth records in the latter half of the 1970s — became the focus of an empire that far surpassed its home town's expansion. And yet Dome was a company of paradoxes. Built on U.S. investment, it was being feted as the "chosen instrument"

26

of a highly nationalist Canadian federal government at the same time as its shares were surging over the border to eager American investors. Although it borrowed money like an unrepentant Mr. Micawber, boasting in its annual reports about how much more the company spent than it earned, yet it became the darling of Canada's supposedly ultra-conservative banking community, which engaged in an unseemly scramble to give it more and more money.

Nevertheless, for five golden years, Dome put on a dazzling display of corporate footwork. Its annual summer exploration sorties in the Beaufort were portayed as crusades in the national hydrocarbon interest; its megaproject proposals were seen as daringly original displays of corporate thinking; its acquisition of HBOG drew paeans of praise both from the government and the investment community.

But in October, 1980, when the Liberal government of Pierre Trudeau announced its revolutionary National Energy Program (NEP), it seemed that Dome must finally face an insurmountable challenge. The whole program was designed to syphon revenue from the industry, expropriate frontier landholders — of which Dome was one of the largest — and discriminate against foreign-owned and controlled companies. Dome was discovered to be more than 60% foreign-owned. The NEP looked like a disaster for Dome, but far from slowing down, Dome used the policy as a springboard. To take advantage of the NEP's new discriminatory system, a subsidiary, Dome Canada, was created — with the biggest share sale in Canadian history. In May, 1981, seemingly sanctifying the federal government's controversial plans for "Canadianization," Dome set out after HBOG, the biggest acquisition in Canadian corporate history, and one of the largest in the world.

Then, suddenly, things began to go terribly, terribly wrong. In a single year, between the spring of 1981 and the spring of 1982, the tides of fortune turned for both Dome and the two men who headed it. Like the heroes of classical tragedy, Gallagher and Richards had seemed more than mere mortals, but each had a fatal flaw. An almost obsessive belief in the petroleum potential of his beloved Beaufort Sea, along with a corresponding reluctance to dilute ownership of Dome by issuing new shares, was Gallagher's flaw. An addiction to "deals," particularly takeovers, supported by his belief that world oil and gas prices would continue to soar, was to be Richards' downfall.

Smiting Former Heroes

Nevertheless, it was only because the two heroes had been borne so high on the willing shoulders of the banking community that they could ultimately fall so far. When the financial crunch came, the success with which they had sold — and the banks had bought — their joint vision became apparent. If Dome had gone under, it would have been the biggest bankruptcy in the history of the world. The banks — the gods that were to indulge and ultimately undo Gallagher and Richards — proved, like their classical Greek counterparts, to be an argumentative and bitchy lot. On Canada's financial Olympus, situated in the five bank towers gathered around the intersections of King and Bay Streets in downtown Toronto, there were scenes reminiscent of Homer, with bitter disputes about how the former heroes should be brought down. The disputes were all the more bitter because the heroes threatened to bring down Olympus with them.

Gallagher and Richards had always seemed the odd couple of Canada's oilpatch. Two men more different in appearance and style would be hard to imagine. Gallagher was tall, slim and elegant; Richards was short, stocky and scruffy. While Gallagher's tie would sport a diamond stud, Richards' — sitting beneath a collar whose ends pointed off at rebellious angles — was more likely to feature some indeterminate food stain. Gallagher was a fitness fanatic, jogging each morning and occasionally astonishing travelling companions by taking off around airport perimeters while waiting for Dome's executive jet to be refuelled. He would gently chide people who were overweight, or smoking, and give brief fatherly lectures to anyone he found riding an elevator for only two floors. Long before the advent of present diet fads, Gallagher had been immortalized within the exclusive portals of Calgary's Petroleum Club by having a lunch (consisting of a turkey salad sandwich, fruit cup and cottage cheese) named after him. He never drank coffee and seldom took alcohol. By contrast, the word "exercise" appeared to have no place in Richards' vocabulary. He enjoyed vintage wines (and had an extensive cellar at his ranch outside Calgary) and puffing on fat, Montecristo cigars. He seemed most in his element digging into a fast-food snack in the boardroom late at night while slapping another hundred million onto his latest takeover offer.

It wasn't merely in style and habits that the two men differed. They also had arguments about corporate strategy. Nevertheless, these rows, witnessed only by senior management, were seen as a type of creative diversity. And however serious the disagreements might have seemed at times, they certainly didn't put any brake on Dome's growth.

28

It was in promoting that growth that the visions of Gallagher and Richards coincided. Although they believed in different routes, their ultimate joint goal was to make Dome one of the greatest — if not the greatest — oil companies in the world.

There was another approach they also shared. Their entrepreneurial visions gave them a remarkably scant regard for traditional financial constraints. The important consideration for them both was the world of their visions, the company as they could *make* it. This resulted in a disdainful view of the traditional accountants' and bankers' world of numbers, where a company is laid out neatly as two sets of figures: a balance sheet, showing what it owns and owes — its assets and liabilities — and a profit and loss account, showing what it earns and spends. Although both sets of figures are subject to considerable flexibility in presentation, they are supposed to show all necessary evidence of a company's success, prudence and bankability. It was when these numbers were compared year-on-year that Dome's magic showed through. Dome's accounting methods might be far from conservative, but nevertheless its assets and profits soared throughout the 1970s. And so did its debt.

In the eyes of Jack and Bill, that trend was merely an indicator of bigger and better things to come. For Jack Gallagher, the most important set of numbers about Dome were the ones that never appeared on the list of its assets. They were the billions of barrels of oil he saw waiting to be plumbed miles beneath the sea-floor of the Beaufort. For Bill Richards, numbers were simply tools which could always be stretched to suit higher corporate goals. Richards had an unshakable belief that there was no creature smarter, or more deadly than himself in the corporate jungle. In the end, some believed that Gallagher's visions divorced him from hard financial realities. But Richards was not so much divorced from reality as a believer that certain kinds of reality were changeable, and that all hurdles were temporary. In Richards' view, lots of businessmen, particularly bankers, were just too damned serious. After all, he used to say: "It's only money." Agreements were just words written on a piece of paper. They could be changed. Bids for other companies or proposals for multi–billion dollar megaprojects "only cost saliva," said Richards.

Both Gallagher and Richards thought investors and bankers were far too cautious. They believed that investors who weren't prepared to put their money on the line in the Dome cause simply lacked vision. And certainly, in the latter half of the 1970s, judging by the amount of money being put on the line, the vision *was* spreading.

Gallagher's quiet, low-key presentation on the potential of the Beaufort, with its magic-lantern show of accompanying slides, never failed to intoxicate those who heard and saw it for the first time. After 1976, each summer saw pilgrimages of investment dealers, politicians, bankers and journalists flown north to Dome's exploration base at Tuktoyaktuk and then helicoptered out to the drillships. There they were told that they were sitting just a couple of miles above some of the greatest petroleum deposits in the world: "One, maybe two Middle Easts," Gallagher was fond of saying in a matter-of-fact way. And each year, stock prices would rise in anticipation that this would be the year of the big one, the discovery of that hydrocarbon "elephant." The necessarily hard-hearted guardians of billions of dollars of investors' and depositors' funds would come away from the Beaufort, or from lunch with Gallagher at the Petroleum Club, in something approaching a trance.

Gallagher dreamed of being remembered as Canada's greatest oilman, the man who brought oil self-sufficiency to the North American continent. He wanted to be known as one of the great oilfinders, an almost mystical brotherhood within the oil fraternity, whose names and discoveries have been remembered down the years.

For Bill Richards it was different. He wasn't really an oilman at heart. First and foremost he was a doer of megadeals, a one-day-at-a-time, heads-up, single- or multiple-combat corporate warrior, a business warlord. "Bring 'em all on" was his motto. He dreamed of conquest, of scrambling to the top of the pile. For a while, it looked as if both men would pull it off.

The Turbulent Decade

But of course the talents and failings of Dome Petroleum's chiefs could not by themselves account for the company's spectacular rise and messy fall. Dome was the product of a turbulent decade, a decade ruled by the politics and economics of petroleum. Dome took advantage of two great economic and political waves — waves caused by the oil "crises" of 1973–74 and 1979–80. Everywhere, as oil prices rocketed, similar trends emerged: increased distrust of multinational oil companies; increased government intervention; and increased desire for access to "safe" — preferably domestic — supplies. Dome cast itself perfectly to take advantage of these trends, and draped in the Maple Leaf flag, was a politically "sensitive" and voracious explorer within Canada.

In the latter half of the 1970s, as Bill Richards' vision came to dominate the company, Dome also became an enormously active corporate acquisitor. This trend reflected an emerging feeling within the policy-heart of the Liberal government: that foreigners should be bought out and the oil industry Canadianized. When the second oil crisis occurred, the Liberals hatched their NEP, declaring that acquisition of foreign companies was of paramount national interest. Dome's expansion increased. But when the second OPEC wave came crashing, Dome, which had borrowed to the hilt, came close to crashing too. The only reason it didn't was that it had become so heavy a borower, and so pervasive a presence within the oil business, that if Dome sank, a business armada would sink with it.

The first oil crisis of 1973–74, when world oil prices quadrupled within a matter of months, sent economic shock waves around the globe. Consumers suddenly realized how much petroleum had come to dominate their lives. It fuelled their cars, heated their homes, ran their factories, and — through the petrochemical industry — appeared in a million synthetic forms. Now the 13 nations of the Organization of Petroleum Exporting Countries — an unlikely collection of desert sheiks, despots and dictators — seemed to be holding a knife to the world's economic jugular.

In Canada, the impact of the OPEC crisis was complicated because the country was both a major producer and consumer of petroleum. Moreover, production was concentrated in the West — overwhelmingly in the province of Alberta — while consumption was centred in the industrial heartland of central Canada, in Ontario and Quebec. It now seemed ironic that since the 1947 major oil find at Leduc near Edmonton had started a string of significant oil discoveries in the province, Alberta producers' main problem had been to find a market for their oil. Massive postwar discoveries in the Middle East combined with the low cost of tanker transportation meant that imported oil was cheaper than Alberta's in Eastern Canada. Under a policy introduced by the Diefenbaker government in 1960, markets west of the Ottawa Valley were reserved for Albertan oil, while exports to the U.S. were encouraged. Nevertheless, the federal government resisted efforts by Albertan producers to have an oil pipeline built into Montreal.

One important source of friction between the Canadian independent producers like Dome and the foreign-owned majors was that the multinationals also opposed putting Alberta oil into Montreal. For purely economic reasons they favoured putting cheaper foreign oil — acquired from their parent companies — into their Montreal refineries. Of course, Quebec consumers — who reaped the economic benefits — agreed with them

The OPEC crisis produced an immediate change in the perspectives of the eastern consumers and the western producers. Faced with unpredictable foreign supplies at quadrupled prices, the East suddenly found new charms in western oil. It was secure, and of course

31

Alberta would sell it far cheaper than OPEC, wouldn't it? But Alberta had other ideas. Despite the fact that Ontario, for more than a decade, had paid higher than international prices so that Alberta might have a market, Alberta saw little reason for gratitude. The province considered central Canada an exploiter of the West's resources while forcing it, through tariff barriers, to purchase its own more expensive industrial products. Alberta suddenly saw the sun. It also perceived the East's desire for Alberta oil at less than world prices as a further attempt at exploitation. Under the Canadian constitution, Alberta owned its natural resources. The federal government, however, had the right to set prices outside the province, where most of Alberta's oil was sold. OPEC set the stage for a battle-royal between the Alberta and federal governments.

Led by Peter Lougheed, the iron-willed corporate lawyer who had swept his Conservative party to power in 1971, the Albertans' fight with Pierre Trudeau's federal Liberals over petroleum prices became much more than an economic debate. In Albertan eyes it was a struggle for provincial self-assertion against a distant and arrogant federal government. Bumper stickers appeared in Alberta bearing the legend: "Let the Eastern Bastards Freeze in the Dark." For more than a year the two sides fought over prices, using the blunt weapons of royalties and taxes to carve off large chunks of the revenue cake. But the oil companies emerged as the main victims of the fight. In 1974, drilling rigs began to head for the border in increasing numbers as exploration budgets were slashed and opportunities appeared in the U.S. Both federal and provincial governments suddenly realized they were in danger of killing the goose that laid the golden eggs.

It was agreed after further negotiation that Canadian oil and gas prices would gradually rise towards world levels, while generous tax allowances and incentives would be introduced for exploration and development. The result was one of the greatest economic booms in Canadian history. Moreover, it was a boom in which, for a number of political and strategic reasons, Canadian companies would take a clear lead.

The Nationalist Surge

In the wake of the OPEC crisis, consumers everywhere railed not so much against OPEC as against those whom they believed had led them into this economic ambush, the major oil companies.

The twentieth century had seen the Seven Sisters develop vast commercial empires that now spanned the globe. Their revenues matched those of many medium-sized countries, and their tanker fleets were larger than most navies. In the quarter-century after the end of the Second World War, these companies, five American, one Dutch-British and one British, seemed to have completely tamed the unpredictable substance in which they dealt.

As the 1970s opened, no other developed country had as large a degree of foreign ownership of its industry — and in particular its oil industry — as did Canada. According to government figures, almost 80% of oil industry assets were foreign-owned, while almost 90% were foreign-controlled. Given the proximity of the U.S., the similarity of markets and the domination of world oil by U.S. companies, this was almost inevitable. And indeed, it had seemed a benevolent dictatorship. Four of the Seven Sisters, Exxon, Gulf, Shell and Texaco, had Canadian subsidiaries that dominated the oil industry. Their gas stations blanketed the country from coast to coast. They saw themselves as the apolitical agents of technical excellence and the better corporate way, parts of worldwide organizations dedicated to finding oil, producing profits and generating growth. In particular, Imperial Oil, the subsidiary of Exxon and by far the largest oil company in Canada, typified the attitudes of these companies. There was no doubt in the minds of Imperial executives that their company's best interests and the best interests of Canada were synonymous. Imperial's history went back to 1881. It had, in its own corporate mind, demonstrated an unchallengeable dedication to Canada, drilling 133 dry holes before it made the strike at Leduc that heralded the modern era of Canadian oil.

Over the years, many outstanding independent Canadian oilmen had appeared, and, indeed, had made some of the major discoveries in Alberta after Leduc. But many had willingly sold out to the big bucks of foreign oil. In general, the smaller, independent Canadian companies lived in the corporate shadow of the foreign-controlled majors. However, even before the OPEC crisis broke, other forces were at work in Canada that seemed to signal the end of the Seven Sisters' rule.

Throughout the 1960s in Canada, there was a significant increase in economic nationalism. The major thrust of that movement was the claim that the enormous degree of foreign — principally U.S. — investment in Canada was ultimately detrimental to the country. Canadian branch-plants were portrayed as companies vulnerable to the whims of their parents; not enough research was done in Canada; Canadian interests were claimed to be subordinated to the uncertain multinational marketing plans of foreign corporate giants. The arguments, although ostensibly based on objective analysis, were emotional and contained much thinly disguised anti-Americanism. Canada was portrayed as a second-class resource hinterland to the U.S., and Canadians as mere "hewers of wood and drawers of water" whose progress was in some way retarded by their resource wealth and its exploitation by foreign capital.

Due to the high profiles of the foreign-controlled majors in Canada, they had always been a focus of resentment for the economic nationalists. For Walter Gordon, the Liberal cabinet member and patron saint of economic nationalism, the mere mention of Imperial Oil was enough to raise his blood pressure. He called them pirates and said they should be nationalized. Few in government shared his extreme views. However, the OPEC crisis did bring about an enormous increase in public suspicions about big oil, particularly when oil company profits subsequently soared.

The most important result of the economic nationalist movement was the creation of the Foreign Investment Review Agency (FIRA) to oversee, among other areas, further acquisitions of Canadian companies by foreign interests. FIRA became an effective restraint on foreign acquisitions of Canadian oil companies, and it was able to achieve this while initially maintaining a low profile. Its mere existence frequently prevented foreign companies from even attempting bids for their smaller Canadian counterparts. However, after the first OPEC crisis, foreign oil had a lot more problems than coping with FIRA.

Both OPEC and politics threw wrenches into the carefully laid corporate plans of the majors in the 1970s. In the late 1960s, seeking large petroleum finds to replenish their reserves, and believing that the province of Alberta was largely played out, they had shifted their exploration activities towards the "frontiers," off the east and west coasts and around the Mackenzie Delta, east of Prudhoe Bay, where a massive find had been made in 1968. The east and west coasts proved initially disappointing. Significant amounts of gas were discovered in the Mackenzie Delta, but plans to exploit it were temporarily sterilized by the decision in 1977 to kill the proposal to build a pipeline down the Mackenzie Valley. Moreover, as domestic prices started to rise, it became apparent that Alberta was far from played out. A number of companies, in particular the mightiest of them all, Imperial Oil, had to pay handsome prices to buy their way back into the province. Meanwhile, the refining and marketing operations of the majors were to be severely disrupted by slumping demand in the face of rising prices. This turbulent and heavily politicized environment appeared to create unique opportunities for Canadian oilpeople. No company looked to be as skillful at taking advantage of the situation as Dome Petroleum.

3
Starting
from Scratch

"Their skill at getting their way, and earning sweet financial deals, earned them a grudging nickname from their opponents. They were dubbed Butch Cassidy and the Sundance Kid."

Dome Petroleum is a striking example of the schizophrenia at the root of Canadian economic nationalism. It was to be touted as a "chosen instrument" to seize back the Canadian oil business from foreign control, yet it would never have been created without Wall Street money. Dome was conceived between the Wall Street offices of investment bankers Loeb Rhoades and the Park Avenue home of Loeb's managing partner, Clifford Michel. One of the last of New York's great paternal investment bankers, Michel was a brilliant and kindly man whose door was always open to employees. He was the product of an age when dealings in the financial canyons of lower Manhattan were more personal and ownership less faceless. For Dome Petroleum's first 25 years, Michel was the company's chairman and a commanding figure on its board of directors.

Michel was born in New York City in 1911, the son of a railroad executive. After attending Columbia University and Dartmouth College, he started working on Wall Street as an investment analyst. In 1937, he married one of the granddaughters of Jules Bache, the great industrialist and investment banker. By the time of his death in 1944, Bache had built J.S. Bache & Co. into a major finance house, with 37 branch offices in the U.S. and a staff of 800. Outside the company, Bache's principal interests lay in the Chrysler Corporation, of which he was a vice-president, and in Dome Mines, the Canadian gold producer over which he presided between 1918 and 1943.

For American investors during most of this century, the great attraction of gold mining companies was that holding their shares was the closest they could come to owning gold itself, which was prohibited under federal law. Dome Mines, and its corporate predecessors, had operated a mine at South Porcupine, Ontario, since 1910. With its subsidiaries Sigma Mines, which started production at Val d'Or,

Quebec, in 1937, and Campbell Red Lake Mines, which opened its first shafts at Balmertown, Ontario, in 1949, it was to become Canada's largest gold-mining concern.

Jules Bache had no sons, and took a great liking to the young man who had married his granddaughter. In 1938, Bache took Michel into his investment business as a partner. In the same year, Michel went onto the board of Dome Mines, and eventually became its chairman. (The Bache-Michel family interest in Dome Mines continues to this day. After Clifford Michel's death in 1976, his seat was taken by his son, Clifford L. "Mickey" Michel, a prominent Wall Street lawyer. When Mickey Michel left the board in 1980, he was succeeded by Alan McFarland, a partner of investment bankers Lazard, Frères and husband of Clifford Michel's youngest daughter. In 1982, Mickey Michel returned to replace McFarland. A family trust still holds about 2% of Dome Mines' equity.)

Dome Petroleum was created as an offshoot of Dome Mines, as a corporate gamble in the new and exciting oilfields of Alberta, where Imperial's strike in 1947 had heralded not only a scramble for land and profits but also the modern age of Canadian petroleum.

Jim McCrae, the Canadian operating brains behind Dome Mines, had travelled out to see the boom first-hand, and had returned convinced that Dome Mines should become involved. McCrae thought the smug, elitist Toronto investment community was slow in responding to the western opportunities. He put a proposal to Michel, and Michel agreed, to farm-in to some lands controlled by lawyer Eric Harvey. (A farm-in is an agreement to bear drilling costs on someone else's land in return for a share in the land rights.)

However, Dome Mines needed someone to manage its Albertan interests and it was then that McCrae came across a young geologist in his early thirties who seemed ideal. His name was Jack Gallagher.

A Globetrotter Comes Home

Gallagher was born in 1916, the son of an Irish immigrant railroad worker, in Winnipeg. In 1937, he graduated in geology from the University of Manitoba in the same class as Jack Armstrong, who would one day become the chairman and chief executive of Imperial Oil. On graduation, Gallagher joined the Shell Oil Co. in California as a field geologist. He then moved back East to join the biggest company of them all, Standard Oil of New Jersey (later renamed Exxon), the heart of John D. Rockefeller's trust-busted corporate empire. For the next ten years, Gallagher became a cog in the gigantic

36

Standard machine, roaming the globe in search of oil. It was a life of high adventure, probing the deserts of Egypt, hacking through the rain forests of Central and South America, and criss-crossing the Andes at the head of a string of native bearers.

In 1948, when Gallagher was manager for exploration in the head-waters of the Amazon in Peru, Standard pulled him out of South America and sent him to Harvard for the Advanced Management Course. Seen as a potential rising star by the head office in New York, he was given a choice of two jobs: chief geologist for the Far East, or assistant production manager for Standard's Canadian subsidiary, Imperial Oil. Since Leduc the previous year, Imperial had been rapidly expanding its exploration and production capabilities. Canada was suddenly a new and exciting place to be within the Standard empire, and so Gallagher, jaded with a decade of globe-trotting, decided to return home. With his dashing good looks, natural charm and exotic foreign experiences, he came to Calgary as the personality boy of the company. This did not sit well with his immediate boss, V.J. "Tip" Moroney, who felt that young Mr. Gallagher should be cut down to size. Gallagher was given the job of supervising construction work on a townsite Imperial was developing. The international highflier suddenly found himself grounded in mundane bricks and mortar. Discouraged and depressed, he decided to quit Imperial. Then he met Jim McCrae and Clifford Michel.

Like McCrae, Michel was very impressed by Gallagher, and soon decided that there was scope for expanding Dome Mines' petroleum interests in Alberta. Michel, who had after Bache's death moved to Loeb, Rhoades, made a proposal to Bill Morton, a vice-president with Boston-based State Street Investment. He suggested that if Morton could come up with some money at fixed rates of interest, they might raise some equity capital and put together a Western Canadian ex-ploration company. The scheme was particularly appealing to U.S. investors because of generous U.S. tax allowances for exploration at home or abroad. Michel also suggested to Loeb, Rhoades' senior partner, John Loeb — the aristocratic and autocratic scion of the family business — that he, too, should put some money into the venture. Morton subsequently solicited endowment funds of $7.5 million for the venture from Harvard, Princeton and the Massachussets Institute of Technology — at the princeley initial rate of 2% — while $250,000 of share capital of the private company was distributed to its founders. Dome Mines wound up with 24% of Dome Petroleum, while Loeb, Rhoades controlled 16%. Public offerings in 1951 and 1955 raised $10 million of equity.

For the next 25 years, Jack Gallagher engaged in the long, uphill slog to build a company from scratch in the shadow of Canada's foreign-controlled giants.

Early on, Gallagher developed his corporate strategy, which was to spread investment between relatively certain, cash-flow building ventures and the occasional rank wildcat well, an exercise in "drilling for the moon." Dome's earliest bread-and-butter activities were concentrated in the Redwater and Drumheller fields of Alberta. Its earliest rank wildcat was one of the deepest wells drilled in British Columbia. The Buckinghorse well probed more than two miles beneath the Earth's surface. It was dry. Moreover, it set the pattern for Dome's overall exploration success in those early years. Nevertheless, Gallagher retained the complete confidence of his New York backers. He'd turn up at Cliff Michel's home on Park Avenue after flying all night from a production test somewhere in the wilds of Alberta, his young wife, Kathleen, having met him at Calgary airport with a suit to swap for his oil-stained coveralls. For Michel and his partners Dome was really just a crapshoot, made attractive by generous U.S. tax provisions. But they'd sit up late at night in Michel's library listening to young Gallagher telling them of his exploration and corporate plans, delivered in his low-key way and punctuated with his devastating smile.

Strong Ambitions

From the beginning, Gallagher attracted unusual talents to Dome. His first employee was a brilliant and consumingly ambitious young man named Maurice Strong. Strong was a Prairie child of the Great Depression. Born in Oak Lake, Manitoba, once the western terminus of the Canadian National Railway, in 1929, he was the eldest of four children. He had run away from a desperately poor home when he was 13, first working his passage to Vancouver by washing dishes on a train and then signing up as a cabin boy on a troop ship. By the time he was 20 he had spent a year with the Hudson's Bay Company at Chesterfield Inlet in the Arctic, had dabbled in prospecting and stock promotion, been a minor functionary at the United Nations, flirted with the idea of a career in the Royal Canadian Air Force and finally returned to his home province to work for James Richardson & Co. in Winnipeg as a stock analyst. The Albertan oil boom had just started and Strong was involved in mining and petroleum shares. Strong knew that Richardson & Co. was about to appoint a full-time Calgary analyst and he desperately wanted the job. But then he heard that someone else had been appointed and that he hadn't been considered because he was too young. (In fact, he was even younger than they thought. He'd falsified his birth certificate when he was 13 in an attempt to get into the armed forces during the war.)

Strong had to deliver a package to Ralph Baker, the head of the company and an enormously tough man feared by all. Strong screwed up his courage and blurted out: "Excuse me, but my department's sending someone else to Calgary because I'm too young, but I've been following the oils closely and I really want that job." Baker didn't look up from what he was reading. "And if I didn't do well, I'd expect to be fired in six months." Still not looking up, Baker said gruffly: "Well, we'll see about that." Two weeks later, Strong was told he'd be going to Calgary.

Richardson's office on Eighth Avenue saw a constant stream of oilmen coming through to see what was happening on the stock market. One of these, with whom Strong became friendly, was Gallagher. When Gallagher left Imperial and linked up with Dome Mines, he asked Strong along to become his assistant. A bustling factotum, Strong was eager to learn all Gallagher could teach him about the oil business.

After only a couple of years, the restless young Strong took a globe-trotting sabbatical. He learned Swahili, helped develop a graphite mine in Tanzania and set up gas stations in Kenya and Zanzibar. After two years, he returned to Canada, determined to get a job in the field of international development, but he was turned down — because of lack of qualifications — by Ottawa's Department of External Affairs, the YMCA and a number of other foundations. The rejections stung.

Nevertheless, Gallagher was glad to take him back. The organization bustled on, but after another couple of years Strong's personal drumbeat demanded that he once more move on. Shortly before he left Dome Petroleum, Gallagher made him a vice-president. When Strong told him he was going to set up his own oil business, Gallagher felt both hurt and a little used. He had even offered Strong the presidency of the company in an attempt to persuade him to stay. Strong's restless vision was to drive him on to one of the most varied careers in recent Canadian history. First he put together an oil company, Canadian Industrial Gas and Oil (CIGOL). Then he was invited to Montreal to become executive vice-president and then president of Power Corporation. At Power, Strong melded CIGOL, which Power now controlled, with two natural gas distributors, to form the basis of Norcen Energy Resources. From Power Strong went to work for the federal government in Ottawa as head of the Liberal government's foreign aid program. Then he became undersecretary general of the United Nations, responsible for the 1972 UN Conference on the Environment.

Eventually, he returned to Canada in 1975 to become the first chairman and president of the state oil company, Petro-Canada.

Strong by then had become a strange hybrid, a wheeler-dealer, self-made millionaire, international do-gooder and powerful proponent of government intervention in the economy. He tended to make businessmen suspicious. They muttered that he was an opportunist. But if he was, his opportunism had taken him, by the time he became chairman of Petro-Canada, to a position where he was a rival of his old mentor Gallagher.

Ironically, considering what Dome was to become, in those early days Strong found Gallagher a little cautious in his corporate approach. He had been disappointed when Gallagher had turned down the chance to move to Toronto to manage Dome's parent, Dome Mines. Gallagher in turn thought that Strong wanted to grow too fast and that he was obsessed with size. Gallagher wanted a more gradual approach and one where he could be sure of retaining control. Strong had also been keen to do a deal with the Bronfmans when they offered to merge their much larger Royalite Company with Dome and make Gallagher chief executive. But Gallagher told Sam Senior, the Bronfman's irascible patriarch, that he wasn't interested in getting into Royalite's refining and marketing interests.

Towards the end of the 1950s and early in the 1960s, all the majors were courting Dome. British Petroleum, Shell, Amoco and Mobil all came along with offers of takeovers or mergers, as did Glenn Nielson, head of Husky Oil, and Ian Sinclair of Canadian Pacific, but Gallagher turned them all away and persuaded his board to support his independence. It wasn't that Gallagher was overcautious. Indeed, Dome's aggressive exploration led it consistently to overspend its budgets, but Gallagher wasn't a believer in the benefits of size for its own sake, or a great fan of corporate acquisitions or mergers.

One of Strong's ultimately most significant acts at Dome was to hire the man who would become Canada's most aggressive corporate acquisitor, Bill Richards.

Butch Cassidy and the Sundance Kid

Bill Richards was another child of Manitoba's Depression years. His father had died when he was eight and he was brought up by his mother, "a woman of remarkable determination." Unlike Strong, Richards had managed to squeeze in military service towards the end of the war, and wound up taking an arts degree at the University of Manitoba before going into law. While still at law school, Richards was already displaying entrepreneurial aggressiveness. He and a partner ran a "dreadfully unsuccessful" lumbermill that at one time employed 20 people, but finished up a financial fiasco. When Richards graduated, Manitoba was still economically depressed. As there were lots of young lawyers around, Richards decided to head for Alberta's oil boom. By this time he already had a wife and two children and couldn't afford to move to Alberta "on spec." So when a job opportunity came along with a company he had never heard of called Dome Petroleum, he decided to use it as a springboard. Richards enjoyed the oil business so much he never found any need to jump off.

Richards was to rise to stardom through Dome's supposedly less exciting "cash-flow building" activities. These activities, centred in the exploitation of natural gas and natural gas liquids, were to prove the company's main source of growth. The man behind the evolution of this side of the business, and with whom Richards was to work for many years, was another of Dome's diverse geniuses, Don Wolcott.

Wolcott was a great sandy-haired bear of a man who gave the initial impression that he had arrived straight from the farm. But Wolcott was a technical genius and a penetrating conceptual thinker.

Dome's involvement with the natural gas business began with a successful exploratory gas well in the early 1950s in the Provost area of Alberta. Subsequent drilling was to result in the development of the Provost field, with over 1 trillion cubic feet of gas reserves. Wolcott, an engineer, was hired from Gulf in 1957 to bring the field into production. During the following 20 years, he was to play a seminal role in making Dome the leading natural gas liquids producer in Canada, as well as making it a key player in the development of Alberta's petrochemical industry.

Natural gas liquids, or NGLs, including liquid petroleum gasses (LPGs) such as propane and butane, are recovered from field-based facilities or "stripped" through straddle plants that sit across main gas arteries.

The year after he joined Dome, Wolcott persuaded Gallagher that they should build a $17 million NGL recovery system at Steelman, Saskatchewan, to collect LPGs from essentially all the southeastern Saskatchewan oil fields. In 1962, he masterminded the first straddle plant in Canada, just outside Edmonton. In 1970, LPG supply took a further leap when a second straddle plant was built jointly with Amoco at Cochrane across the Alberta and Southern pipeline, which took the province's gas to California.

This end of the business, featuring myriad deals with producers and extensive government approvals, proved ideal for Richards' talents. He could negotiate tough agreements and draw them up quickly, and he positively relished the cut and thrust of regulatory hearings, particularly competitive ones where Dome had to face rival schemes. Richards' legal brilliance allied with Wolcott's superb technical mastery enabled both men to shine at regulatory hearings. Their skill at getting their way, and earning sweet financial deals, earned them a grudging nickname from their opponents. They were dubbed Butch Cassidy and the Sundance Kid.

In the late 1960s and early 1970s, Dome's outstanding achievements were made in NGLs. The straddle plant at Cochrane was just part of a scheme involving an NGL pipeline to Edmonton that picked up LPGs from other plants along the way. These LPGs were then "batched" for transportation through the Interprovincial Pipe Line to the East. Nobody had attempted to move natural gas liquids through an oil pipeline before, and the scheme, which involved a total expenditure of $200 million, was both a technical and an economic *tour de force*. Previously, LPGs had been moved from Edmonton to Sarnia in southwestern Ontario by railroad tankcar at a cost of 10¢ a gallon. Moving them through the Interprovincial line cost 1.5¢ a gallon.

The Cochin Line: A Technological Marvel

Dome's biggest and boldest NGL scheme started with the construction in 1972 of an additional straddle plant at Empress, Alberta. The plant, jointly owned with PanCanadian, the oil and gas arm of Canadian Pacific, was designed to produce 17,000 barrels a day of propane and heavier LPGs, and 18,000 barrels a day of ethane. The ethane was extracted via a revolutionary turbo expander plant which was the first in Canada and the largest in the world. Because there was no Albertan market for ethane, Dome's typically daring solution was to build a 1,900-mile pipeline — the Cochin line — to Green Springs, Ohio, where the ethane would be used by Columbia Gas Systems to make synthetic natural gas. However, for the following five years, the scheme was to become bogged down in a regulatory process greatly complicated by the increasing heat of oil politics, both between the federal and Alberta governments, and between Canada and the U.S.

Late in 1971, Wolcott and John Beddome, another Gulf engineer that he had attracted to Dome, met with the Canadian petrochemical companies (most of whom were headquartered in and around Sarnia, Ontario) about the possibility of using some of the ethane shipped down the Cochin line as a petrochemical feedstock. Ethane can be turned into ethylene which in turn can be converted into derivatives yielding products from camera film through synthetic fibres and detergents to adhesives.

Previously, the Canadian petrochemical industry in the East had used oil-based feedstocks. Dome was suggesting this alternative not merely as a way of making more money out of its extraction and proposed pipeline system, but also because the National Energy Board (NEB) in Ottawa had recently declared it would not be allowing any additional natural gas exports. Dome was concerned that this ban might extend to its plans to export ethane, and so was seeking to find additional Canadian benefits for its planned pipeline in the shape of providing chemical feedstock to Eastern producers.

However, the issue was further complicated because Peter Lougheed's Conservative Party had just swept to power in Alberta. One of Lougheed's major concerns was eastern exploitation of western resources. He was also very keen on the notion of "upgrading" resources within the province. Stripping ethane from Albertan natural gas and then shipping it east for use as a petrochemical feedstock jarred both these concerns. Suddenly a new player entered the fray, Bob Blair, president of Alberta Gas Trunk Line (AGTL), the company set up by the Albertan provincial government in 1954 to hold the monopoly on gas collection within the province. Why not, Blair suggested to Lougheed, build a world-scale petrochemical industry within the province, upgrading the stripped ethane and derivative ethylene via a massive series of large new petrochemical plants? The idea was appealing to Lougheed but highly problematic for Dome.

Dome, over the ensuing five years, was thus to face a number of major hurdles: federal concerns — loudly backed up by eastern consuming provinces — about ethane exports; Alberta's demands for the upgrading of ethane within the province; and chemical industry opposition from those companies with a vested interest in the continued use of oil-based feedstocks.

Wolcott and Richards, with numerous provincial regulatory hearings behind them, were now an established double act. Richards would slice up intervening lawyers while Wolcott, with a combination of technical knowledge and country-boy humour, kept opponents off balance and had observers occasionally rolling in the aisles.

Dome was eventually joined in its application by one of the eastern chemical companies, Dow Canada, subsidiary of the mighty Dow Chemical Corporation of Midland, Michigan. The NEB hearing determined that ethane exports should, like natural gas, require a permit, and stated that they were only prepared to allow the export of limited quantities. This in turn damaged the economics of the Cochin line. The NEB then decided that the ethylene produced from the ethane required a permit too. That meant another hearing.

Meanwhile, Bob Blair's Alberta Gas Trunk Line had evolved its rival scheme. Since it planned to use all stripped ethane in the province, it threatened the whole Cochin pipeline.

In order to expedite the hearings on ethylene exports, the NEB decided that intervenors would not be able to cross-examine Dome and Dow. However, the move was successfully challenged in the courts by AGTL and a number of provinces. Meanwhile, Peter Lough-eed publicly declared that he preferred the AGTL scheme to that of Dome and Dow. Some Dome and Dow executives now felt like giving up. The only answer was felt to be an accommodation with Blair. Wolcott, who had known Blair for many years (and had negotiated the straddle plant at Cochrane while Blair was president of the Alberta and Southern pipeline which the plant straddled) was designated as marriage broker. Neither Richards nor Dow's president, Cliff Mort, with whom Richards had formed a firm friendship, had much stomach for the arrangement. They considered Blair to be an opportunist who had stolen their idea and now they were forced to invite him in on their scheme. After further games of musical chairs with other chemical companies, and further negotiations with the Alberta government, a detailed letter of intent was finally signed in September, 1975, between Alberta, Dome, Dow and AGTL to link up ethane-gathering plants at Edmonton, Cochrane and Empress via gathering lines to an ethylene-manufacturing plant at Joffre, near Edmonton, and to the proposed Cochin line. Excess ethane and ethylene would then be shipped down the Cochin line, where the ethane would be used by Columbia to manufacture synthetic natural gas, while the ethylene would go to Sarnia to be used in the manufacture of petrochemicals. The whole scheme would cost $1.5 billion.

The transportation of ethylene, particularly batched sequentially with propane, butane and ethane, had never been attempted over a distance as great as that of the Cochin line before. Dow's U.S. engineers didn't believe it could be done and thought that the ethylene would be contaminated by the other products. However, the scheme was to work — and be classified as a technological marvel — after the Cochin line was opened in 1978.

In 1976, Wolcott, miffed that his undoubted contribution to Dome's reputation and earnings had not — in his opinion — been adequately recognized, left the company, shortly after to join Petro-Canada and the man who had disappointed and upset Gallagher by leaving Dome 17 years before, Maurice Strong.

Meanwhile, the young lawyer that Strong had hired, Bill Richards, had climbed to the top of Dome. Gallagher had made him president in 1974 and had sometime before that begun to step back from the day-to-day running of the company. There was one element of the business, however, in which Gallagher kept a full-time interest, and that was in finding oil. And although Dome's successes had been relatively sparse, he still believed that he was destined to make the big find. In particular, he believed that his destiny lay in the Far North.

4
Selling
the Northern Vision

"Oil is found in the minds of men."
WALLACE PRATT
GEOLOGIST

*"I sometimes feel Dome may be drilling in Ottawa
rather than the Beaufort Sea."*
IAN WADDELL
NDP ENERGY CRITIC

The mental stance of the oil explorer has to be somewhere between inveterate gambler and eternal optimist. Like the bold gambler, the oil seeker always finds the odds stacked against him. The odds against drilling a successful wildcat well are longer than those against rank outsiders in horse races. Apart from technical ability, therefore, the prime requirements of the successful explorationist are supreme self-confidence, skill in selling his ideas, the ability to bounce back from disappointment and, perhaps most important of all, luck. Dome was particularly short of this last requirement.

The man responsible for overseeing Dome's uphill exploration activities for most of its history was Charlie Dunkley, a young engineer who had previously worked for Standard of California before he became Dome's second employee. Dunkley's dry sense of humour compensated for his declining optimism over the years. His definition of a pessimist was someone who had worked for an optimist for five years: "And," he'd say, tongue-in-cheek, when he was close to his retirement in 1979, "I've been working for Jack Gallagher for 25 years!".

Not surprisingly, the history of the oil industry is littered with the frustrated visions and bankruptcies of oilmen, although it is a tribute both to their indomitable spirit and the unique hold of petroleum that the dreams frequently survived the bankruptcies. As the American oil historian Ruth Sheldon Knowles wrote in *The Greatest Gamblers*: "When a man is exploring for oil, the only reality is the next wildcat, the one that will come in. He lives so completely in his undiscovered wealth that the struggle to pay his bills is what seems like a dream."

47

The best way to pay those bills has always been to persuade others of one's hydrocarbon dreams, to be able to paint alluring pictures of petroleum bonanzas that leave investors salivating. The answer has always existed in three magic initials: OPM, Other People's Money. No other company in Canadian history, and few in world oil history, would be as successful in attracting OPM to pursue its exploration dreams as Jack Gallagher's Dome. That was all the more remarkable because of Dome's dearth of luck.

In 1950, Gallagher, having explored literally millions of acres in exotic regions for Standard, now had to struggle to accumulate just a few of his own. He had to build up a position, sometimes almost acre by acre, from wily prairie farmers. He bought production lands at Crown sales and farmed-into lands near production. Like the other independents, he, for many years, scrabbled for petroleum pickings on the fringes of the majors' successful finds. Nevertheless, Gallagher always believed he had a date with geological destiny, and over time he became convinced that the tryst would take place in Canada's Far North.

Gallagher had first encountered the Canadian North as a summer student while at the University of Manitoba in 1936, working with the Geological Survey of Canada. He formed part of a two-man team trekking the wilds and travelling by canoe for weeks on end without seeing another soul. For $2.50 a day, he mapped and surveyed rugged terrain seen by no white person before. If that was the seed of Gallagher's northern vision then it was to lie dormant for a long time, for Gallagher's interest in the North would not be jogged for more than 20 years, when he became interested in the potential of the Arctic Islands. Over the following two decades that seed was to grow slowly until it was transplanted west to the Beaufort Sea. Then it sprouted and flowered under almost unprecedented financial fertilization.

The great American geologist Wallace Pratt had declared shortly after the war that the Arctic Islands might be an area of great petroleum potential, but his assessment was strictly hypothetical. The Islands were a great frozen desert where biting winds swept thousands of miles of arid plains sitting on permafrost a half-mile thick. Moreover, even if oil and gas could be found in such hostile conditions, transportation seemed to present insurmountable difficulties. Frozen seas or roving icebergs — nature's most picturesque form of destruction — waited for tanker traffic, while no pipeline technology existed to cope with such conditions.

Nevertheless, in the late 1950s, interest was stirred by a Geological Survey of Canada report that there was enormous hydrocarbon potential in the area. Also, the passages of the U.S. nuclear submarines

Nautilus and *Skate* beneath the ice at the North Pole prompted science fiction notions of submarine tankers transporting crude oil.

Gallagher was at a cocktail party at a Mines ministers' conference in Nova Scotia in 1959 when he met a scientist from the Geological Survey who told him about the enormous geological structures in the Arctic Islands. Gallagher returned to Calgary brimming with enthusiasm and told the exploration staff that Dome had to file for land in the Arctic Islands as soon as possible. He went to Dome's board of directors with his proposal. They turned him down. He filed anyway and two years later, in 1961, Dome was the operator of the first well in the high Arctic, 1,000 miles from the North Pole at Winter Harbour on Melville Island. The well was dry but Dome had established the feasibility of year-round drilling in the unprecedently hostile climate.

Gallagher was to remain an ardent fan and continue to operate exploration wells in the high Arctic for the next decade, but the man who really kept the whole Arctic Islands "play" alive was J.C. "Cam" Sproule, another visionary geologist. Although he had to scale down his plans and had to herd a large number of companies — ultimately 20, including Dome — into his drilling consortium, Sproule eventually formed Panarctic Oils with $11 million of corporate money, and $9 million of government money put up by Ottawa.

Through Panarctic, Gallagher became recognized by the Ottawa political and mandarin establishment, an element of which was attracted to the Arctic Islands not merely because they offered resource potential but because the major, foreign-owned companies refused to express interest in the area. Gallagher, despite the large U.S. ownership in Dome, was — if there had ever been any doubt about it — firmly stamped as a "good Canadian."

For the next decade, Gallagher's relationship with Ottawa would flourish as he made frequent visits to the nation's capital, cultivated contacts and developed a sensitivity for subtle political winds.

The Birth of the Beaufort Dream

In 1968 the enormous U.S. discovery at Prudhoe Bay on the North Slope of Alaska multiplied enthusiasm for the Far North. Prudhoe Bay was the largest field ever found in North America, with over 10 billion barrels of oil (more than Canada's entire established reserves). It sparked a land-rush both in the Arctic Islands and nearer to Prudhoe Bay in the Beaufort Sea. In fact, Imperial Oil had already tied up land offshore of the Mackenzie Delta in less than 60 feet of water, where drilling from artificial islands was possible. Dome, and other companies, found themselves filing for interests in deeper waters, where it would be more difficult, if not impossible, to drill.

For most of the year, the Beaufort is a slow-moving sheet of ice, moving to the north with the permanent polar ice pack, which grinds clockwise around the pole at about three miles a day. As the 24-hour blackness of winter gives way to the 24-hour sunlight of summer, the ice melts, allowing a brief three-month marine drilling season. However, nobody had attempted to drill under such circumstances before, and there was doubt that anyone could.

The bidding for Beaufort land took the form of work bonuses, by which oil companies were committed to spend money on exploration activity. If they failed to spend the agreed amount, they had to hand it over to Ottawa. The companies with deeper offshore lands formed a loose consortium but soon recognized the enormous problems facing them. What kind of drillships would they use? Would they pool their lands? If so, where would the wells be drilled? Some of the Canadian managers of the foreign-owned companies involved were concerned that their head offices might approve what they considered to be crazy Beaufort expenditures. And then along came Dome.

Dome had held discussions with drilling contractors on its own behalf, but when Richards' corporate staff had run the numbers, it was discovered that the contractor — at going rates — would have paid for his specialized marine drilling equipment and earned a respectable rate of profit within five years. The solution was typical of the kind of bold corporate thinking that was beginning to characterize Dome: why not build the drillships themselves?

Dome had no knowledge of this kind of drilling, so the obvious answer was to find someone who did. Charlie Dunkley heard of a Canadian offshore specialist, Gordon Harrison, working for Mobil in England. Dunkley phoned Harrison and explained what Dome had in mind — the construction of a new type of drilling fleet to operate in Arctic waters, for which they needed to develop a technology. Harrison's initial reaction was that it was a pretty wild scheme. Nevertheless, he agreed to meet Jack Gallagher, who happened to be in England at the time. Gallagher gave him a glimpse of his vision and Harrison was hooked. He joined the company in 1974 and for the next nine years the soft-spoken scientist was to be at the heart of Dome's thrust into the untried field of offshore Arctic drilling, which was to be carried out through a new Dome subsidiary, Canmar, of which Harrison became president.

To adapt and fit two ships for Arctic drilling, Dome had to go to Galveston, Texas. A third ship was brought from Norway. Legal entanglements delayed the program, but eventually the Galveston ships were ready in early 1976 to sail to the other end of the continent.

Not everyone was as gung-ho as Gallagher. Don Wolcott, the senior vice-president and brains behind the company's main money-spinner, its NGL system, at one point refused an appropriation for $2 million worth of steel for the ships. He thought the company was paying too much, and that there was no great hurry since the ships' instrumentation hadn't been built. After Jack Gallagher was told, Wolcott wasn't involved in the Beaufort program again. In fact, he left Dome in 1976 as the first Beaufort drilling season was being prepared.

The larger companies with deeper Beaufort acreage, like Mobil, Gulf, Canadian Superior, Texaco and Aquitaine, were originally surprised when Dome came along with its bold proposals, but soon they realized that Dome's drilling fleet was the only hope of fulfilling their work bonuses. From Dome's point of view, Canmar would not only earn money but also — and more important for Gallagher's dream — increase the company's Beaufort acreage by accepting mineral rights as part payment for drilling services.

In the fall of 1975, four icebreaker supply ships were completed, and one moved into the Beaufort to help with site preparation. In 1976, Dome's three drillships, *Explorer I*, *Explorer II* and *Explorer III*, made their historic passages to the top of the world.

Explorer I and *Explorer II* met up in Victoria, B.C., the first having come from Galveston via the Panama Canal, and the second from Norway via the Straits of Magellan. In the early summer, these two ships, with the remainder of the support craft, set off on the 3,000-mile voyage around Alaska, through ice-infested waters, to arrive in the Beaufort under the blazing Arctic sun and begin drilling operations in August. The third drillship became the first vessel to undertake the voyage from Galveston via Halifax and the Northwest Passage to the Beaufort. It arrived in September.

In that first season, two wells were drilled, the Tingmiark K–91 and the Hunt Dome Kopanoar D–14. According to Dome, Tingmiark, located 30 miles offshore, encountered a high-pressure gas zone at 10,000 feet, while Kopanoar, drilled 90 miles northwest of the tiny hamlet of Tuktoyaktuk, had to be plugged and abandoned after encountering a high-pressure flow of fresh water at a shallow depth.

The first Beaufort drilling season was significant not for what it found but because it had taken place at all. In the style of the classic entrepreneur, Dome had seen the opportunity and acted upon it. Through hiring Gordon Harrison, through contracting with shipyards, through securing a $120 million consortium loan with a group of Canadian banks, the concept had been realized in the form of a sophisticated marine drilling fleet. But Dome also discovered by the end of that first drilling season that if they carried on under existing circumstances, Canmar would go broke. For Dome, that merely represented a temporary obstacle. The solution was obvious: if present circumstances were unprofitable, change the circumstances. That corporate approach had been instilled by Bill Richards. In 1974, when Clifford Michel had vacated the chairmanship in favour of Jack Gallagher, Gallagher had ceded the presidency of Dome to Richards, although Gallagher had retained the title of chief executive officer, and thus continued to hold responsibility for Dome's corporate direction.

Using the Ottawa Connection

Gallagher had groomed Richards for more than a decade. He liked Richards' ability to spin off ideas, his aggressiveness and his total dedication to Dome. Richards was no yes-man, but Gallagher didn't like yes-men. The two frequently argued, but what counted was results, and each year the results looked better and better. For several years, Gallagher had been transferring more and more power and responsibility to Richards.

Richards, in turn, had assembled a very bright corporate staff and introduced a brainstorming approach to corporate problems and the evolution of corporate strategies. When faced with the realization that Canmar could easily prove to be a white elephant, Richards' corporate raiders came up with the simple solution: persuade Ottawa to change the tax system in order to make Arctic drilling more attractive to investors. Instead of being able to write off your investment against taxation, why not write off 200% of your investment, said Richards. That seemed a little rich, but if anybody could sell it to Ottawa, Jack Gallagher could.

During the formation of Panarctic, Gallagher had got to know key Liberals and Ottawa mandarins, men — like Mines and Resources Minister Art Laing, and Jack Austin, Laing's tall, rosy-faced young executive assistant — who would have enormous influence on Canadian energy policies in the coming decade. He also met Donald Macdonald, who would be energy minister when the OPEC crisis broke and then finance minister when Gallagher went seeking tax concessions.

In 1971, Gallagher had agreed to serve on the board of the Canada

Development Corporation (CDC), a controversial new holding company set up by the Liberals to promote Canadian industrial development. CDC was the brainchild of Walter Gordon, the ardent economic nationalist, and Maurice Strong, who had helped write the CDC legislation before taking off for the United Nations. Gordon's original intention was that the CDC would be government controlled. However, after much debate it was agreed that the CDC would be set up with government money but then transferred to public ownership. Despite this modification, however, to take a CDC board membership was still seen as a controversial step, particularly by western businessmen. Nevertheless, one of the side benefits of that directorship was that Gallagher was once again plugged into Ottawa thinking — at least until the CDC began to take a much more independent stance. Gallagher also accepted a position on the Science Council.

But Gallagher was also careful about the form of his Ottawa connections. It was significant that he was invited — but refused — to sit on the National Advisory Committee on Petroleum (NACOP), a group of leading oilmen set up by Liberal Energy Minister Joe Greene to give the government advice on energy policy matters. Jack Gallagher was a lone wolf. He did not want to travel in a pack.

One lesson that Gallagher learned from his visits to Ottawa was to appreciate the practical power of the bureaucracy. He saw that in an increasingly complex society, where politicians, and in particular cabinet ministers, tended to be snowed under by work, their senior public service advisors had enormous power in moulding public policies.

Gallagher's most respected convert to the Beaufort vision was one of the most powerful mandarins of all, Finance Deputy Minister Tommy Shoyama. Shoyama was a quiet, low-key public servant who started his bureaucratic career working for the CCF government of Tommy Douglas in Saskatchewan. Like all bureaucrats who flourished under the Trudeau regime, Shoyama was academically brilliant; unlike most of the others, he also had widespread practical administrative experience. He was in fact to grow increasingly uneasy as the policy-making initiative in Ottawa was seized in the latter half of the 1970s by ivory-tower thinker Michael Pitfield, Clerk of the Privy Council, and Jim Coutts, Trudeau's principal secretary and devout follower of opinion polls. When Dome started drilling in the Beaufort, Shoyama was one of the most influential public servants in Ottawa, mandarin overlord of its traditionally most powerful department, which, in hatching budgets, controlled the fiscal flow of the nation.

Shoyama had first become acquainted with Gallagher when Gallagher had joined the board of the CDC, a fact which had in itself impressed Shoyama. Subsequently, Dome's chairman had made sure that Shoyama was always on his list of calls when he visited the nation's capital, and Shoyama always kept an open door for Gallagher. Shoyama was impressed by Gallagher's courteous approach, and by the fact that he always seemed to have time to pay attention to Shoyama's departmental staff.

The finance deputy minister found Gallagher's approach refreshingly different from that of the multinationals operating in Canada. Those who had traditionally cultivated Ottawa relationships still held the undisguised belief that they knew what was best for the country. Those foreign-controlled companies now making contact with Ottawa for the first time — suddenly awakened to the fact that the political process was increasingly important to their operations — often displayed a remarkably inept and sometimes insulting approach. They would send public relations men to suggest to the deputy minister that he fix up a meeting for their president with the minister. Of course, Shoyama was nobody's fool, and was wary of being "stroked" by the private sector, but the big oil companies never attempted such an obvious approach. They tended to be self-righteous, blunt and insensitive. Gallagher's visits were quite different. Shoyama's staff would smile and fluster when Dome's chairman arrived. He'd stop to have a word with them all before being led in to take Shoyama's outstretched hand in that two-handed grasp that was his trademark. In fact, Gallagher's two-handed grasp originated in an accident in the Andes when he had put his back out. He did it so that people wouldn't shake his hand too hard and jar his back. Nevertheless, it was typical of Gallagher that even an ailment should wind up as part of the charming image. Shoyama never even considered that Gallagher was "stroking" him, possibly a tribute to how skillfully Gallagher did it. There was no doubt that Gallagher's personal approach and his professions of national energy concern were attractive. But most of all for Shoyama, what Gallagher said seemed to make so much sense.

Before becoming deputy minister of finance, Shoyama had served as deputy minister of energy under Donald Macdonald. He was thus not only well aware of the great potential of Canada's frontiers but also that drilling results to date had been extremely disappointing. The Arctic Islands had so far failed to live up to their earlier promise; Shell Canada and Mobil had pretty much given up on the Atlantic offshore; and Shell had been disappointed again offshore British Columbia. As deputy minister of energy, Shoyama had also been intimately involved in the bitter battle with Alberta in 1974 over oil revenues. That battle had greatly increased the federal government's desire for commercial frontier oil as a counterweight to Alberta's petroleum clout. The Far North was particularly attractive because oil found there would be free of any dispute over ownership with jealous provinces.

Gallagher was well aware of this when he brought his siren song to Ottawa.

Once in a minister's or mandarin's office, Gallagher would pull out the maps of the Beaufort and spread them on the desk. Then he'd point out the globular shapes of the 40 or so potential oil-bearing structures that had been identified by seismic work — bouncing soundwaves off the rocky strata beneath the Beaufort's seabed. The potential, he said, was enormous. He explained how drilling further offshore made more sense because in the traditional river delta oil-bearing regions of the world — like the Mississippi, the Niger and the Persian Gulf — the thickness of the oil-bearing sand increased as you moved offshore. It looked just like that in the Beaufort. But of course, Gallagher pointed out, the deeper offshore you drilled, the more expensive it got. Moreover, drilling in the Beaufort was particularly expensive because the weather made the drilling season so short. This was federal oil and would produce billions of dollars of tax revenue. It seemed only reasonable that there should be some form of tax incentive to explore in this hostile region, particularly when you remembered that exploration costs were such a small proportion of the enormous overall development costs for the Beaufort. Billions would be spent, but many more billions would be earned for the federal government, while at the same time the very desirable objective of becoming independent from uncertain world oil markets would be achieved.

The "Dome Budget"

This vision appealed to Shoyama, although not everyone in Ottawa found it as plausible. Shoyama had been appointed one of the founding directors of Petro-Canada, the state oil company. This was one place where he did not find his Beaufort enthusiasms reciprocated. Nevertheless, he was converted to Gallagher's suggestion — thought up by Richards and his corporate tax wizards — that there should be additional allowances for expensive offshore wells. As a result, a measure giving an additional write-off on all wells costing more than $5 million was introduced in the 1977 budget. Since Dome was the only company drilling $5-million wells at the time, the provision was quickly dubbed the "Gallagher Amendment" in the "Dome Budget." When this new measure, known as super-depletion, was combined with provisions allowing individuals to write off petroleum exploration expenses against private income, it was to create a more than generous tax allowance. In certain cases, it became possible for high-bracket taxpayers to make money out of financing the drilling of dry

55

holes. Needless to say, these provisions aroused resentment in the rest of the industry, and led to dark mutterings about Dome being the "second national oil company." That accusation, in turn, was none too popular with the first national oil company, PetroCan, and went part of the way to explaining PetroCan's lack of enthusiasm both for the Beaufort and for Dome.

Super-depletion, whose official name was the Frontier Exploration Allowance (FEA), worked like this: the FEA was a tax deduction of $66^2/_3\%$ of any expense in excess of $5 million made on a single well. It was applicable against the income of a company or individual from any source at any time. It was given in addition to two other allowances: the Canadian Exploration Expense (CEE), under which any company or individual investing in petroleum exploration was permitted to write off 100% of expenditures against income from any source; and the Earned Depletion Allowance (EDA), under which a further $33^1/_2\%$ of the amount invested — over and above the CEE — could be deducted from up to 25% of profits from the resource sector.

Somewhat paradoxically, Dome itself was not in a position to benefit from super-depletion because it was in a non-taxable position, having consistently reinvested all its profits and built up tax allowances it would be able to use far into the future. Nevertheless, it used this position brilliantly in a tax manoeuvre thought up by Richards' tax team to "sell" super-depletion to other companies and individuals. Since super-depletion only applied to the amount spent *after* the first $5 million on a well, that $5 million — attracting fewer tax allowances — was relatively more expensive, so Dome volunteered to pick it up. The tax authorities ruled that this was permissible and that tax allowances could be split "horizontally," meaning that those who only invested funds over the $5-million mark could claim all three allowances, CEE, EDA and FEA.

In other words, investors with resource income (enabling them to take the Earned Depletion Allowance on top of the other two allowances) who invested only in the post-$5 million portion of the well would be able to claim 100% of their investment under the CEE, $33^1/_2\%$ of their investment under the EDA, and $66^1/_2\%$ under the FEA, for a total tax deduction of 200% of their initial investment. If the investors were in a tax bracket higher than 50%, this would mean that they could actually make a profit on the investment whether or not oil or gas was ever found! The most extreme example was the case of a Quebec investor with resource income and a total taxable income of $100,000 a year or more. With a 69% marginal tax rate, the investment would return him or her $1.38 for each $1 invested. Even without resource income, the same investor could still turn a profit.

This arrangement meant of course that many high tax rate investors wound up investing in the Beaufort purely for tax reasons, with the prospect of an oil strike as a little icing on the cake. Dome, never one to give away too much in any deal, made sure that it was, indeed, a *little* icing. Much of this private investment came to Dome through a burgeoning form of financial arrangement called a drilling fund.

A drilling fund is a collection of private investors brought together by a promoter to funnel their investments through an operator into exploration for petroleum. In the early 1970s, German drilling-fund money began seeking a home in Alberta. The impetus came from German tax laws that enabled write-offs even greater than super-depletion for investment in oil and gas exploration anywhere in the world. These laws were eventually dubbed "tax-pornography." Some of the funds' West German promoters were also fast-buck artists, taking huge commissions — or "front-end loading" — the funds. Some of these West German funds, in turn, found their way into Dome's exploration, but the funds really took off when super-depletion was introduced along with the provision allowing individual Canadians to write off exploration expenditures. Dome quickly saw that it could raise large sums of money for drilling without having to give very much away in return. For example, its 1978 fund of $53 million was gratefully donated by investors in return for a $1/2$% profit interest in just 1,000 acres surrounding successful wells drilled with the money. This interest was considered very small. Nevertheless, since most investors were interested primarily in tax allowances, they didn't really care. Not surprisingly, super-depletion became widely regarded both in Ottawa and even in the industry as an abuse.

As for most of Dome's corporate partners, super-depletion allowed them to "compensate" Dome for taking the more expensive first $5 million of exploration expense on a well by granting Dome, or farming out to it, a relatively larger percentage of their mineral rights. In some cases companies, like individuals, could come away from Beaufort drilling with a profit simply on tax allowances. The fact that these companies were foreign-owned made the provision even less popular.

"Manitoba Calm"

Nevertheless, super-depletion led to an enormous burst in Beaufort exploration expenditure, and also — and not just incidentally — a great change in the prospects of Canmar, which suddenly became a great money spinner. By 1978, Canmar was estimated to be responsible for 10% of Dome's profits. From a standing start, Dome was virtually single-handedly responsible for hundreds of millions of dollars being ploughed into the Beaufort. It was seen as a feat of corporate genius. The shrewder analysts in the investment communities both north and south of the border had been impressed already with the technological brilliance and profitability of Dome's natural gas liquids gathering system and its Cochin pipeline proposal. Now suddenly the Beaufort drew a great deal more attention to Dome, and the spotlight fell on Jack Gallagher.

Gallagher had long had a reputation around the oilpatch for his silver tongue and for driving hard bargains. The classic — though obviously apocryphal — story about Gallagher told of another oilman visiting the Dome chairman to negotiate a deal. Before the visit, the oilman asked a friend for advice about approaching Gallagher. The friend told him that Gallagher was a really smooth talker, so he'd better make sure he held onto his shirt. So the oilman went to see Gallagher, and throughout the negotiations he made sure he kept a tight grip on his shirt. Even when the negotiations were over he continued to keep a firm hold on his shirt as he said goodbye. It was only when he'd left the Dome building that he realized that he didn't have any trousers on! But of course, that story dated back to the good old days when Jack got much more involved with the nitty-gritty of the business. Throughout the 1970s, he had involved himself less and less with the day-to-day operations of Dome, leaving all that to Bill Richards. However, he still enjoyed the status that came with being chairman and chief executive, and he particularly enjoyed selling the Beaufort dream.

A decade before, Gallagher had won many converts to his enthusiasm for the Arctic Islands. In 1967, he had given an address at New York University about the potential of the Arctic Islands. His speech was not specifically for the investment industry, but a number of Wall Street analysts had come along. They had been spellbound. Gallagher's presentation didn't take a tub-thumping evangelical approach. It was delivered in a soft, sometimes almost hesitant, low-key way that was all the more devastatingly effective.

Historian Michael Bliss wrote that Gallagher possessed "a tone of speech and gesture conveying utter sincerity and self-confidence. There is nothing of the rural twang of western oil in Gallagher's speech; but with the dropped 'g's, as in drillin' and biddin', the way of talking is not exactly big city sophistication. Actually it is mid-Canadian spoken at its best, a style and mood that could be called Manitoba Calm."

Gallagher's "Manitoba Calm" really knocked them dead in Manhattan. Of course it wasn't only his style, but his effortless and striking way of making his geological dreams comprehensible to the layperson.

Over the years, Gallagher's presentations to the investment community became almost a ritual, but he'd always have a new twist, a new addition to his armoury. After the Beaufort came along, he'd still include the Arctic Islands in his presentation. To emphasize their extent, he'd point out casually that the sedimentary basin — the potential oil-bearing area — was just slightly larger than the total land area of all the five largest U.S. oil-producing states. He'd present slides showing that many of the 40 or so potential oil-bearing structures identified in the Beaufort were individually bigger than the Prudhoe Bay field.

After Beaufort drilling started, there were always slides of Canmar's advanced drilling equipment and of bold new plans for satellite-controlled drillships that swivelled into oncoming ice, or super-dredgers reinforced against ice, or Class 10 icebreaker tankers more powerful than any in the world.

The presentations were always a *tour de force*, and few who saw Gallagher's magic-lantern show for the first time came away without having been infected by a little of Gallagher's belief. It made acolytes to the Dome cause feel good. There was something for everybody: the promise of oil self-sufficiency to protect North America from the political uncertainties of OPEC; the promise of stock market profits; and the vision of a technology where Canada was at the leading edge.

Most important of all, few doubted that Jack Gallagher believed what he was saying. His pronouncements took on an oracular form. He also became a little like a Homeric poet, repeating a favourite tale, making little additions from time to time but relying on a basic stock of facts linked by well-seasoned verbal formulae. What was perhaps surprising was that Gallagher never tired of presenting the case for his Arctic vision, and was capable of producing it word-perfect three or four times in a single day. Moreover, he never lost an opportunity of presenting it.

The Super-Salesman

On one occasion, Jack Gallagher and Loeb, Rhoades partner Mark Millard, a courtly investment banker several years Gallagher's senior, were due for an appointment with the then U.S. energy czar, James Schlesinger. Schlesinger, who was head of the U.S. Energy Department during its massive expansion under Jimmy Carter, had a reputation for being arrogant and autocratic. He seldom asked his staff to sit when they entered his office, and even his most senior officials

— men of considerable stature in Washington — were usually kept on their feet in his presence. Visitors were expected to be on time for their appointments, to keep to the point and to leave after their allotted 15 or 30 minutes. Gallagher and Millard were in Washington to discuss the Northern Border gas pipeline — part of the proposed system to bring Prudhoe Bay gas to the lower 48 states. The two men were ushered into the energy secretary's office. Schlesinger greeted them curtly and invited them to sit down. To Millard's amazement, Gallagher had maps of the Beaufort out on Schlesinger's desk before their bottoms hit their chairs. The Wall Street banker was horrified, but the truly amazing aspect of the situation was that Gallagher carried it off without being thrown out. Again, during his first meeting with Ben Branch, head of mighty U.S. chemical giant Dow Chemical, Gallagher spread out his Beaufort maps on the bemused Branch's desk and began to deliver his Arctic vision.

Gallagher, in fact, hardly ever passed up an opportunity to recount his vision to influential people that he met. And he also tried to persuade them to visit the Beaufort. After 1976, each summer saw aerial convoys heading north to touch down at the growing hamlet of Tuktoyaktuk, thence to be helicoptered to Dome's drillships for half-heard explanations amid the thunder of the drilling equipment. Gallagher enticed Pierre Trudeau to the Beaufort, along with a large number of cabinet ministers, while bankers and influential investment analysts were accompanied each year by other senior Dome personnel. The courting of investment analysts was not wasted. The brokers' recommendations for Dome were strong and the share-price soared. Dome's drilling in the Beaufort became, in the late 1970s, the dominant feature of Canadian summer stock markets. On September 1, 1978, the Toronto Stock Exchange's oil and gas share-price index leaped 91 points — its largest ever one-day rise — as a result of rumours of a big strike in the Beaufort. Almost exactly a year later, on September 7, 1979, the same index rose even higher, with a jump of 186 points, as the word spread down Bay and Wall Streets that Dome had at last struck big oil in the North. In 1978, as the great Albertan oil boom gathered momentum, more than half of the top 50 stocks traded on the Toronto Stock Exhange were oil or oil related, but by far the heaviest trading was in Dome Petroleum, whose dollar volume was $472 million. Once Montreal and the American Exchange were included, the total value of Dome stock changing hands in 1978 rose to $792 million. The following year, that total was almost to quadruple, to $2.8 billion.

And each year the Dome share-price marched relentlessly on. In 1976, its high had been $45. In 1977, it rose to $60.38; in 1978 to

$106.75; and in 1979 (when the stock was split four-for-one) to the equivalent of $223.52.

Dome — and Jack Gallagher in particular — performed brilliantly in promoting the Beaufort, but there were problems on the horizon. Super-depletion was due to run out in 1980, and although each season's results were presented with a maximum of fanfare and enthusiasm, and indeed orchestrated to look somewhat more impressive than they actually were, everybody at Dome knew that the Beaufort was a long-term exploration venture where the skill would be in keeping up the flow of OPM with little hope of return in the short-term. Gallagher and Richards talked of producing 500,000 barrels of oil a day by 1985 and 1 million barrels a day by 1990, but most industry observers regarded that as wildly optimistic. At some stage, credibility was going to become a problem, not because the oil wasn't there, but because Dome knew that it was likely to take a lot longer to find and bring out than most investors believed.

Gallagher and Richards were obviously eager for the government to extend super-depletion, but within the mandarinate there was a growing feeling that too much had been given away to Dome and its partners, both corporate and private. Moreover, there was growing concern — particularly after the accession of the Ayatollah Khomeini in Iran and the subsequent rise in OPEC prices — about the degree of foreign ownership of the Canadian oil business. Dome's problem was that the more it seemed to be blessed by Ottawa, the more eagerly U.S. investors clamoured for its shares.

Throughout the 1970s, corporate executives who could most becomingly drape themselves in the Maple Leaf flag, or develop the best political and bureaucratic connections in Ottawa and Edmonton, were the new stars of the Canadian oil industry. The name of the game was to win government concessions or approvals by establishing that your corporate ambitions were clearly aligned with the national interest, or to think up schemes *because* they appealed to the government of the day.

Suddenly, political sensitivity became as important as an MBA, and indeed took precedence over it, since a great many of the daringly new, politically aware schemes made little economic sense. However, with lavishly donated public funds available, good old straight economics became regarded as something of a blinkered bore.

61

5
The Blessed Trinity

"Geologists find you oil and gas. Politics makes you money."

CALGARY OIL TYCOON

Super-depletion indicated the corporate benefits to be gained both from political connections and sensitivity to political goals. But Dome was not the only company to seek corporate advantage, or to flourish, in the new, complex environment.

Petro-Canada, the national oil company, was obviously the most political creation of the post-OPEC period, but another company, Alberta Gas Trunk Line, run by Bob Blair, also proved particularly adept at operating in a much more nationalist and heavily politicized atmosphere. Indeed, in the second half of the 1970s, these three companies engaged in a subtle — and sometimes not so subtle — contest for corporate supremacy, a contest made all the more fascinating because it involved the clash of massive corporate egos.

Bob Blair became a potent symbol of the ascendancy of western businesspeople in the latter half of the 1970s. While Alberta premier Peter Lougheed was taking on the federal political establishment, the dour and aggressive Blair was squaring up to, and beating, some of the eastern corporate establishment's biggest names, including the major oil companies. Within just a few years, Blair leaped from provincial obscurity to national prominence. He defeated the Arctic Gas consortium — a who's who of eastern and U.S. corporate clout — by gaining regulatory approval in 1977 to build a natural gas pipeline from Prudhoe Bay to the lower 48 states. Then a year later he snatched control of Husky Oil from under the noses of Petro-Canada and Los Angeles-based oil giant Occidental Petroleum in what was, at the time, Canada's largest takeover battle.

Blair was an enigma to many of his corporate colleagues and counterparts, but he inspired fierce loyalty in his staff, who were to become — like their counterparts at Dome — caught up in something approaching a corporate religion.

Blair had been a precocious youth. Born in Trinidad, where his father managed a refinery, Blair attended the exclusive Choate School — where young Rockefellers and Mellons spent their formative years — at nine, two years ahead of most of his classmates. (Blair's father went on to become president of Canadian Bechtel and was credited with much of the research into developing the economic feasibility of the tar sands.)

When he was only 16, Blair went to Queen's University at Kingston to study chemical engineering. Subsequently, his entire working life was spent in the pipeline business. He rose to become president of Alberta and Southern Gas and then in 1969 he joined Alberta Gas Trunk Line, becoming its president the following year.

AGTL had been set up in 1954 "to gather and transmit gas within the province of Alberta," but it had also had a political purpose — to assert provincial control over production, pricing and marketing of Alberta gas in the face of any federal challenge. When Blair joined AGTL, it seemed like a company in decline since the province's natural gas was inevitably a finite resource. Blair pursued twin strategies to reverse this decline: revitalization of the pipeline system by directing natural gas from the Arctic through the province and diversification away from the basic pipeline business.

Blair's plan for diversification dovetailed perfectly with the desires of Peter Lougheed, who was concerned about Alberta's resource dependence and lack of manufacturing industry. However, Blair's first successful attempt at diversification — into petrochemicals — was believed by Dome to be at its expense. It was the beginning of an intense rivalry between the two companies.

Pipeline Politics

Blair's next corporate coup — related to his strategy to bring northern gas through Alberta — was also far from pleasing to Dome.

When Prudhoe Bay had been discovered, the top priority had been to bring the field's oil into production. That priority appeared much more urgent when the OPEC crisis struck in the winter of 1973. In November, President Richard Nixon certified a trans-Alaska oil line that would carry the oil through an 800-mile pipeline to the port of Valdez on Alaska's southern coast. From there, it would be shipped south by tanker.

The field's natural gas — more expensive to transport and not in such a great demand — was treated as an afterthought, despite the fact that half of America's homes and about 40% of its factories were heated by natural gas. Then, in the winter of 1976–77, a natural gas crisis struck the northern U.S. states. Its impact was every bit as severe as that of the OPEC oil crunch. Factories, schools and businesses were closed in 20 states as more than two million workers were laid off. Suddenly, Prudhoe Bay gas seemed much more important.

Until then, the front runner to build the pipeline through Canada was the Arctic Gas consortium, consisting in 1977 of 15 members including Imperial Oil, Gulf Canada, Shell Canada and a raft of major U.S. and Canadian gas transmission companies. The consortium planned to build a giant 48-inch-diameter pipeline more than 2,500 miles long to pump 4.5 billion cubic feet of natural gas a day to the United States. On the way, the line was to take a detour to the east to pick up Canadian gas found by Imperial, Gulf and Shell in the Mackenzie Delta, south of the Beaufort Sea. Some of this gas would initially be exported to the U.S., but in the longer term, Delta gas would be transferred to Canadian domestic use as demand increased. It seemed like a masterpiece of corporate logic. Politically, the plan was more troublesome.

Blair had at one time been a member of the consortium, but had never been happy with it, contending that it was dominated by U.S. interests, which he knew might not be politically acceptable in the prevailing climate. Blair was also aware that there were potential problems both with environmentalist and northern native groups. He decided that flexibility was the answer. He left the consortium and proposed first an all-Canadian line down the Mackenzie Valley, and then a completely new route for Alaskan gas down the Alaskan Highway, the Alcan line, with a spur line to link up Mackenzie Delta gas.

The Arctic Gas sponsors saw this as annoying opportunism. They had spent over $100 million on a presentation of the most comprehensive submissions ever seen by regulatory bodies. When they had filed their applications in Ottawa and Washington in March, 1974, each had been accompanied by 100 pounds of supporting documentation. Blair's schemes, by contrast, appeared to be little more than hastily drawn lines on the map of the North. While they had their project tied down in virtually every respect, Bob Blair just appeared to be floating with the political winds. But it was those political winds that would blow Arctic Gas away.

In May, 1977, the report on the environmental and social impact of a Mackenzie Valley pipeline — prepared by the radical Justice Thomas Berger — was published. It dealt not one but two potentially crushing blows to Arctic Gas. It recommended a ten-year delay in any development of the Mackenzie Valley, and it condemned altogether a pipeline across the Arctic National Wildlife Refuge, which was on the route from Prudhoe Bay to the Mackenzie Delta and which was essential if Mackenzie Delta gas was to be piggybacked.

Two months later, the National Energy Board dealt Arctic Gas its deathblow when it recommended the Canadian federal cabinet choose

Blair's Alcan line. But if it was a stunning upset for the three major companies who had expended huge amounts of money exploring for petroleum in the Mackenzie Delta and whose reserves now seemed in danger of being sterilized, it was an even greater blow for Dome, which had assumed that oil and gas found in the Beaufort would be piped down the Mackenzie Valley. Blair had once again thrown a wrench in Dome's plans.

Nevertheless, the gas pipeline decision hardly caused Dome to break its corporate stride. Almost immediately, Dome started talking about icebreaker tankers as the "preferred" means of transportation in the earlier phase of Beaufort exploration.

Blair's next piece of corporate aggression was to leave egg on the face of the other member of Canada's dynamic nationalist trio, Petro-Canada. PetroCan was the favourite child of the nationalist forces unleashed by the OPEC crisis and the distrust of big oil. First announced by Pierre Trudeau in December, 1973, it finally came into existence in January, 1976. PetroCan was declared to be merely a mild-mannered catalyst, primarily in existence to stimulate frontier exploration and certainly not to compete with the industry. However, that orientation soon changed.

In 1976, PetroCan took over Atlantic Richfield Canada, and in 1978 drew a bid on Husky Oil, a company rich in heavy oil lands. As a defence, Glenn Nielson, the man who had started Husky 40 years before and built it to a company with revenues of over $600 million, solicited a counteroffer from Armand Hammer, the hawklike octo-genarian head of Occidental Petroleum. For two weeks PetroCan and Occidental jousted, making offers and counteroffers, but Petro-Canada was quietly confident that the Foreign Investment Review Agency would never permit the Occidental offer to go ahead. Then, however, Bob Blair had quietly entered the fray and, with a strategic master-stroke, gained control of Husky by simply going into the market and buying up 35% of the company.

For Petro-Canada the blow was a bitter one. It was particularly bitter for Bill Hopper, who had succeeded Maurice Strong as head of the Crown corporation and was eager to prove himself as dynamic as his predecessor. Instead, Blair had made him and his advisors appear inept. Not only had Petro-Canada drawn criticism for attempting to bring another private-sector business under state control, but by failing, it had also attracted ridicule.

Rival National Oil Companies

But if there was little love lost between Dome and AGTL, and even less — in the wake of the Husky takeover — between AGTL and PetroCan, perhaps the coolest feelings of all lay between the occupants of the corporate suites at Dome and Petro-Canada. When Donald Macdonald had been looking for a president for PetroCan, he had approached Jack Gallagher. Gallagher had come right out and told the energy minister that he just didn't believe in it. Relations hardly improved when Maurice Strong was appointed the national oil company's first chairman and president.

General opprobrium was heaped on the state oil company by most of Calgary's oil community. Its headquarters were quickly dubbed "Red Square" and those who joined the company quite often found themselves ostracized by previous friends. Jack Gallagher used to tell a joke about Ann Landers receiving a letter from a man who had a problem telling his fiancée about his family. His mother was a hooker, his father was a lush and his sister worked for the mother. All that wasn't so bad, however. The thing was how could he tell his fiancée that his brother worked for PetroCan! All the Dome employees at the company barbecue would slap their sides when they heard the joke.

Nevertheless, despite political and personal distaste for PetroCan, it couldn't be ignored. After all, it was a potential source of OPM. Dome tried to entice Petro-Canada into investing in the new Class 10 icebreaker, but as usual Dome drove a terribly hard bargain and PetroCan said no deal.

The state oil company was also unhappy about Gallagher's skill in selling the concept of super-depletion, especially since PetroCan's geological staff was far less enthusiastic about the Beaufort than either Dome or Dome's Ottawa converts. PetroCan executives lost no time in calculating the tax losses to Ottawa as a result of super-depletion and then giving off-the-record briefings to the press. Wasn't it unfair, they'd tell reporters, that Canadian taxpayers were funding the exploration of a private company and could hope for only a royalty, whereas if the funds were channelled through Petro-Canada then everything would be owned by the people of Canada. Sympathetic reporters, oblivious to the Marxist semantics of PetroCan's suggested alternative, would go off and write the story.

Sometimes the attack was more direct. Joel Bell, one of the founding super-bureaucrat whiz kids of PetroCan, found himself once on the same platform as Jack Gallagher at an energy conference in Mexico. Gallagher presented the usual Beaufort magic-lantern show and left his Mexican hosts suitably stunned with the potential of the Far North.

At the next intermission there was a buzz of conversation among Mexican officials: here were the Americans forcing Mexico to produce oil faster than they wanted while in the North there was this vast amount of oil and no pressure was being applied to export it to the States. The officials came to Bell and expressed their concerns. He told them not take everything Gallagher said at face value. In fact, he said a lot of it was crap. Well, why don't you say that, they suggested. So Bell got up and said it.

He went up to the podium and, while noting that he wasn't a technical expert, proceeded to tear into Dome's projections. Gallagher got up from his seat on the platform and went and sat down in the front row of the audience where he attempted to pierce Bell with a laser stare for the rest of his speech. Bell hadn't just offended Gallagher, he had dared to mutter heresy, to cast doubt on the dream.

Other confrontations were sometimes more humorous. The diminutive, paunchy figure of Bill Hopper would run into the equally paunchy figure of Bill Richards as the PetroCan president emerged from the energy minister's office. "'Sorry, Bill," Hopper would say with a smile, "you're too late. I just got all the money." And Richards would chuckle and say: "Well, I hope not because we really need some too."

Dome executives never missed an opportunity to take a shot at the state oil company, while Petro-Canada executives tended to get pretty angry about the con-job they thought Dome was pulling off.

In Ottawa, Petro-Canada's attitude towards Dome was regarded as sour grapes. A number of powerful deputy ministers who sat on PetroCan's board — Tommy Shoyama, Mickey Cohen and Ian Stewart — all at various times took Hopper to task for his negative attitude towards Dome and the Beaufort. Hopper, Bell and other PetroCan executives meanwhile were astonished at what they regarded as Ottawa's naivete. In 1977, Michael Pitfield, the tall, professional Clerk of the Privy Council and mandarin overlord, called Hopper after Jack Gallagher had spent a couple of hours with Pierre Trudeau. Pitfield expressed the opinion that Petro-Canada had "missed out" by not joining Dome in the Beaufort exploration. "But we don't think there's anything there," snapped Hopper. "Oh no, you're wrong," said Pitfield. "Jack Gallagher has shown us the pools." Gallagher had shown Pitfield and Trudeau his Beaufort maps with the myriad blobs drawn in that were meant to be potential oil-bearing structures — "They look like a dose of acne," Hopper had once said, sourly — and persuaded them that they were all brimming with oil. Hopper got mad with Pitfield. "They're ripping you off," he said, and hung up.

It was inevitable that the three companies' corporate ambitions and corporate strategies — involving acquisitions and new project proposals — would bring them into conflict. But in the case of new projects, it also meant that, due to the size of the projects, they found themselves in partnership. The boom of the latter half of the 1970s is frequently linked primarily to oil, but in fact the real boom surrounded natural gas. Alberta's fastest growing empires were built on natural gas, as were its fastest growing personal fortunes. Dome's NGL system, and AGTL's 6,500 miles of gas-gathering pipeline, were the bedrock on which their companies were built. For the future, too, natural gas seemed to offer the most promise. From the producers' point of view, the price received for natural gas went up much faster than oil in the 1970s. In particular, the export price, which was linked to the price of oil, rocketed. The result was an exploration boom and the availability of large new supplies. Finding new markets for these supplies suddenly became the name of the game. This meant getting into the gas transmission business. In Canada, the gas transmission business meant first and foremost TransCanada PipeLines.

The TransCanada Coup

TransCanada PipeLines (TCPL) is the giant gas transmission company that carries Alberta supplies to the East, and also ships considerable export volumes. The decision to build the line was made in the mid-1950s amid a storm of controversy. The Liberal government of the day was forced to build the portion of the line through Northern Ontario at public expense in order to get the whole line completed (the section was later sold to TCPL), but the Liberals' attempts to force the financing of this portion through the House led to their electoral downfall. Nevertheless, the company developed into one of the world's largest gas transmission systems, shifting by the late 1970s 3 billion cubic feet of gas a day through its 5,800 miles of underground pipe.

Over the years, however, it came to be seen as a prominent symbol of the East's resource rape of the West. It was always viewed in Alberta as a tool of the Ontario and Quebec consumer, and indeed it had a vested interest in keeping gas prices low. Since it was a regulated utility, whose income depended on the volume of throughput, it wanted to spur as much consumption as possible, and cheap gas was the most obvious stimulus.

TCPL was doubly disliked in the West because it fell under the control of Canadian Pacific Investments, the investment subsidiary of the Canadian Pacific Railway. The CPR had always been a prime target for western resentment against eastern-dominated transportation systems, the systems that took away cheap resources and brought back expensive manufactured goods. That feeling was comically, but graphically, embodied in the classic story of the Prairie farmer standing soaked beneath a monumental thunderstorm that is in the process of wiping out his crops. Shaking his fist at the cruel elements he shouts: "Goddamn the CPR!"

CP Investments held just 13% of TCPL's shares but it dominated the pipeline's board of directors, primarily in the hulking shape of Ian Sinclair, CP's powerful Winnipeg-born chief executive. Also on the board were Robert Campbell and John Taylor, respectively chairman and president of CP's oil subsidiary, PanCanadian Petroleum.

Under the dominance of Sinclair, and the chairmanship of the diminutive and haughty chairman, James Kerr, TransCanada was considered to have become staid and unadventurous. Sinclair had squashed any attempts at diversification, while Kerr had confirmed the idea that TCPL was in no other business than running an East-West pipeline.

TransCanada PipeLines and the CPR were, perhaps not surprisingly, two of Alberta Premier Peter Lougheed's pet hates. Shortly after he came to power, Lougheed had attempted to renegotiate with TCPL what he considered a ludicrously low price for Alberta gas. Kerr's attitude had caused the Albertan premier to storm out of the meeting, leaving embarrassed Alberta and TCPL officials to bring it to a close.

TCPL was also one of Bob Blair's pet hates. TCPL had been a vigorous supporter of Arctic Gas, Blair's rival to build a gas pipeline from Prudhoe Bay. But it had also attempted to keep him out of a previous group studying a northern pipeline. He had never forgiven the company.

After the great federal-provincial dispute over pricing in 1974, responsibility for both oil and gas pricing outside Alberta had been taken over by the federal government. However, this didn't increase Alberta's affection for the pipeline. Towards the end of the 1970s, as more gas was found, higher gas prices and competition from fuel oil and coal caused eastern markets to flatten. TransCanada did not handle the situation well. Announcing that it could not take contracted volumes of gas from producers in 1978, it declared that it would cut them back by rigidly enforcing contracts if they did not agree to a "voluntary" plan. Why, asked the producers, were they not looking for new gas markets instead of threatening them? It was then that Bob Blair came onto the scene and appeared to run rings around his big, sluggish eastern counterpart. Blair hatched a scheme called the Quebec and Maritimes (Q&M) pipeline to carry Albertan gas beyond Montreal to Quebec City and then to the Maritimes. Like a clever chess move, the Q&M scheme seemed to achieve many objectives at once. It promised an additional domestic outlet for gas production; it promised to displace some of the increasingly expensive imported oil that provided most of the energy in Eastern Canada; and it also seemed to offer an additional commercial link to increase the tenuous bonds of confederation with Quebec. Blair seemed to be outflanking TCPL, both literally and metaphorically. In fact, Blair's line made little economic sense, but it made lots of political sense. Moreover, he even managed to entice PetroCan into the scheme as a partner.

PetroCan in turn hatched another elaborate new scheme — the brainchild of former Dome executive, Don Wolcott — to liquefy natural gas in the Arctic Islands and then ship it south via tanker. This plan seemed to challenge TCPL since TransCanada was the sponsor of the Polar Gas pipeline, which was a proposal to build a pipeline to the Arctic Islands. Blair became a partner in the Arctic LNG project.

Finally, when the National Energy Board (NEB) had given Blair's Alcan line from Prudhoe Bay approval, the board had suggested that TransCanada, since it was the largest transmission company in the country, should be brought in as a partner. The idea was repugnant to Blair, and after several months of desultory discussions, it was announced that TCPL would not be joining the scheme after all. Even so, the Alcan line began running into problems soon after approval. Not only were there significant doubts about the financeability of the line, but the growing Albertan gas surplus presented a potential problem. Why bother to ship expensive gas all the way from Prudhoe Bay if much cheaper gas was closer at hand? AGTL came up with a brilliant solution, based on a little semantic sleight of tongue. The solution was to "pre-build" the southern portions of the Alcan line, that is, those from Alberta into the U.S. These portions would initially carry additional Canadian exports but then would switch to Prudhoe Bay gas when the remainder of the Alcan line was built. The key question was: what guarantee was there that the remainder of the northern pipeline would ever be built?

TransCanada, at last convinced that it had to appear to be demonstrating some sort of initiative, came up with a rival to the Q&M, a modified pipeline extension beyond Montreal. This angered Blair who claimed that this rival of the pre-build threatened the financeability of the whole Alcan line. Corporate relations sunk to an all-time low.

And then an unexpected development took place. Towards the end of the summer of 1978, Canadian Pacific announced that its block of shares in TransCanada was up for sale. AGTL would have liked to take control, but federal Energy Minister Alastair Gillespie publicly stated that he would not like to see the shares fall into Alberta government hands — and for all intents and purposes that meant AGTL.

PetroCanada — in particular Joel Bell — also desired the TCPL stake, but that, in turn, would have encountered stiff opposition from Peter Lougheed. And then along came Dome.

Dome had never come into open conflict with TransCanada or CP, although in private Bill Richards was every bit as scathing as Blair was of CP's stewardship. Speaking of CP Richards had said: "They can't run a railway, they can't run an airline, they can't run a goddamn company. The disaster is that they're just too Canadian."

But in fact, when the CP block came up for sale, neither Richards nor Gallagher was originally that enthusiastic. It was Senior Vice-President John Beddome who saw the greatest potential in the move.

Beddome was a rotund, quiet-spoken gas engineer who had been a classmate of Don Wolcott's and who had worked with Wolcott at Gulf Canada. Wolcott had recruited him to Dome and he had risen quickly, ultimately being promoted past Wolcott himself, which was rumoured to be one of the reasons why the disgruntled Wolcott left Dome and wound up at PetroCan in 1976. Beddome pressed Richards on the wisdom of the TransCanada purchase, and after running it through Dome's newly created acquisition staff, the pair took the scheme to Gallagher.

Richards pointed out that financing was the key. If they could get a good deal on some term-preferred shares, he noted, then the dividend paid to them by TCPL might easily cover financing costs. So Gallagher phoned the Canadian Imperial Bank of Commerce and got his deal. In August, Dome announced that it had bought CP's stake in TCPL for $97 million.

The purchase was seen as a tactical masterstroke. If TCPL's problems arose from lack of dynamism and poor relations with western producers, then who better to take control than Dome, the most dynamic of western producers?

On October 4, 1978, a highly symbolic board meeting of Trans-Canada took place. Canadian Pacific's representatives took their seats for the last time and then rose and were replaced by Gallagher, Richards and Beddome. The change of personnel indicated not just a change of minority control, but also a critical shift of power from a staid bastion of eastern corporate supremacy to the new, restless western business phenomenon that was Dome.

It also raised fascinating possibilities about the relationship between TransCanada and AGTL. Dome had already suggested that Blair's Q&M scheme was uneconomic and had proposed a rival plan to serve the Maritimes with propane. The winter of 1978–79 was one of intense behind-the-scenes negotiations between AGTL and Dome. In April, 1979, Dome, AGTL and TransCanada jointly announced a new era of sweetness and light. An agreement had been reached about major natural gas transmission planning, while the three would also work together to deal with Alberta's natural gas surplus. TransCanada would, after all, have a part to play in the Alcan pipeline, while Dome and TransCanada would join the effort to expedite the pre-build of the line's southern sections. There was even mention of joining PetroCan's Arctic LNG scheme.

Indeed, TransCanada not only became involved in AGTL's pre-build, it also replaced PetroCan as AGTL's partner in the Q&M Line, while Dome joined the Arctic LNG scheme.

All now seemed cosy between Canada's triumvirate of new corporate stars. Each had enjoyed a hectic period of growth. Petro-Canada, frustrated in its attempted acquisition of Husky, fell upon a bigger prize at the end of 1978 in Pacific Petroleums, which was 48%-owned by Oklahoma-based Phillips Petroleum. In March, 1979, the national oil company completed its $1.46 billion takeover, the largest in Canadian history. AGTL increased its stake in, and control of Husky, while its pre-build scheme was given approval and it forged ahead with its plans for Alberta petrochemicals. But Dome — although it had now completed the Cochin line, expanded its operation in the Beaufort and controlled TransCanada — showed no signs of slowing down. In fact, it was about to enter its most frenetic stage of expansion. And the architect of that expansion was the man who, unknown to the public, had been effectively running the company for several years, Bill Richards.

6
Richards' Vision: Teamwork and Takeovers

"Richards joked to his acquisition team that Dome's next acquisition should be Brink's, so they'd have an armour-plated way of bringing back all the money from Ottawa."

When Dome made its symbolic entry into TransCanada's board-room in October, 1978, the company seemed synonymous with Jack Gallagher. The Beaufort had brought the company into national prominence, and the Beaufort was clearly Jack's baby. Gallagher's broad and beneficent smile was becoming almost a national heritage. It appeared on platforms as he launched into his well-practised sales pitch; it gleamed under a hard hat set at a jaunty angle as he guided the prime minister around Dome's Arctic drillships; it beamed over dinners for select Ottawa mandarins and politicos at Ottawa's Rideau Club; it seemed to assist the floodlights at home games of the Calgary Stampeders football team; it shone on bankers; and down jogging tracks and on the golf course and in the Petroleum Club. Smilin' Jack symbolized Dome as a geologist's vision and an investor's dream.

Within Dome, however, there had been significant changes in authority and control. In particular, although Gallagher retained the title of chief executive as well as chairman, effective day-to-day management and corporate decision making had passed to Bill Richards, its bustling president. Gallagher's main function was now to liaise with the upper echelons of the financial community — in particular the CEOs of the major banks — and to represent Dome's public face. The ultimate PR man, Gallagher appeared like an imposing figurehead on the prow of a ship. But after 1978, the ship was in the process of constantly being rebuilt and enlarged behind him. The man doing the building, while rushing between the wheelhouse and the engine room, was Bill Richards.

Significant changes both in management and Dome's overall autonomy had already occurred earlier between 1974 and 1976. Clifford Michel, the New York investment banker who had organized the company's original financing, ceded the chairmanship to Gallagher in 1974 and left the board in 1975. He died unexpectedly the following year. Michel had always been a great fan and supporter of Gallagher, but he had also placed a restraining hand on some of Smilin' Jack's more expansive schemes. He also knew and understood financial markets intimately, a strength lacking in the company after his departure.

There was also an important change in Dome Petroleum's relationship with Dome Mines, of which Michel had also been chairman and which was, effectively, Dome Petroleum's parent. This change was partly the result of the introduction of the Foreign Investment Review Act, which restricted "ineligible" companies — that is those deemed by the act to be non-Canadian — from making acquisitions or entering into new businesses without the approval of the federal government. Under the act, both Dome Mines and Dome Petroleum found themselves classified as "foreign."

Dome managed, however, to persuade FIRA to reclassify both itself and Dome Mines via a corporate rearrangement that seemed — as far as the act was concerned — highly cosmetic. During 1976, Dome Petroleum acquired 1.9 million shares of Dome Mines (29.5% of its equity). Of this total, 1.3 million were bought from the public for $40 a share, while the other 600,000 were acquired through a share swap between the two companies. Over the following three years, Dome Petroleum increased its stake in Dome Mines to 38.5%, while Dome Mines continued to hold about 25% of Dome Petroleum. This incestuous relationship meant that each, through the other, effectively held 10% of itself.

Dome Petroleum's purchase of Dome Mines shares was far from cosmetic as regards the relationship between the two companies, however. On the one hand, it protected Dome against the possibility of being taken over via Dome Mines — a prospect about which Jack Gallagher was particularly sensitive. On the other, it meant that the aggressive Dome Petroleum now effectively controlled the staid and conservative Dome Mines, which in turn controlled Campbell Red Lake Mines and Sigma Mines. The Dome Mines group was to find itself inexorably drawn into the corporate vision, and then the deep corporate troubles, of Dome Petroleum.

The fact that Gallagher remained in the limelight while Richards — at least as far as the public was concerned — remained in the shadows was partly a matter of policy. It was felt that Richards was, at times, too outspoken, an uncut diamond not quite ready to be put on public view. But despite the great differences in appearance and approach between Richards and Gallagher, there were also similarities. Both were broad conceptual thinkers rather than detail men. Both had a penchant for taking big risks. Both believed in stretching the company to the limit financially. Both firmly believed in paying no taxes, no dividends, and in borrowing to finance expansion. Both held lots of Dome shares.

One major difference in approach, however, was the route to corporate growth. Gallagher preferred to grow internally; Richards became increasingly convinced that acquisitions were the only way to go, that with oil and gas prices set to rocket faster than interest rates, it made abundant sense to go out and borrow money to buy oil and gas reserves in the ground. It was Richards' view that was to dominate the company for the next two and half hectic years; and if Gallagher was uneasy with it, he certainly wasn't uneasy enough to stop it.

While Gallagher concentrated on new converts in government and the financial community, Richards was most effective within Dome in assembling a fiercely dedicated workforce, and, in particular, a tight-knit corporate court around himself. The TransCanada deal would mark the beginning of the ascendancy of this group as Dome, under Richards' leadership, entered what became known as the "acquisition phase."

The theoretical rationale for a corporate takeover is simple: the acquisitor believes his target is worth more than he will have to pay for it. The target may be undervalued because of poor management, or because the market simply does not realize its worth. Or it may be that when the acquisitor and the target are merged they will form a whole that is greater than the two parts, so-called "synergy." But this rather antiseptic microeconomic approach ignores the role of corporate ego and naked ambition in takeovers. Even when takeovers are "friendly," and the target sells out willingly, there is still a strong element of management machismo in an acquisition. Bill Richards and his corporate raiders were to develop the biggest machismo in the Canadian oilpatch.

The Human Pinball

Through the 1970s, Jack Gallagher had been seen less frequently by the rank and file at Dome. It wasn't that he was aloof, just that he was less and less involved in Dome's day-to-day management. It was Richards who set the style of total 365-days-a-year devotion to Dome, a corporate ethos that spread to Dome's lowest ranks. Richards made sure that he met new employees and the company started holding cocktail parties at the Petroleum Club for them. At these gatherings he would bustle between groups of the newly appointed, asking their names and which group they had joined. He had a prodigious memory for names, and would always crack little jokes and pleasantries such as: "Gee, it's tough being a lawyer among all you engineers."

Richards was admired as a human and caring man. If a young geologist had to make a presentation on a new exploration play to the management committee and was obviously shaking with fright, Richards would calm him or her down and lead the neophyte through the presentation until the geologist forgot that the room was filled with senior executives.

Whenever Dome did a new deal, Richards would hold a "meat and potatoes" barbecue at his ranch, and there were a lot of barbecues at the end of the 1970s. But Richards was also a hard taskmaster. He gave 100% and demanded the same of those he saw had potential. Senior staff *could* go on holiday, but they had to let the switchboard know where they were. Working late became the rule, working on weekends became the norm. While other oil companies in the fat years of the late 1970s started giving workers Fridays off or instituting flexi-hours, Richards scoffed at such ideas. Indeed, Dome employees had a little joke about getting every third *Sunday* off. A premium was put on originality. New employees were given psychological tests to ascertain their skill at abstract thinking, their lack of prejudice and their ability to take risks. Richards loved stretching ideas to the limits, taking notions all the way to their logical extremes, examining all possible avenues and by-ways to get the jump on the opposition. Some of the company's older executives noted that this frequently led to a lot of chasing down blind alleys, but Richards' approach was to leave no conceptual stone unturned.

Dome's president had an intense dislike for hierarchical corporate structures. There may have been organizational charts, neatly laid out boxes with discrete departments and clear lines of management-reporting relationships, but Dome didn't *work* like that, particularly near the top. Dome wasn't like those corporate diagrams in the books on management theory, showing neat static pyramids or wheels with information flowing up to, and decisions being handed down from, the apex or the hub. Those were for companies that simply *ran* a business. Dome was in the business of taking over business, of going boldly where business had never been before. Bill Richards wasn't an apex or a hub, he was a pinball. Only the quickest and the smartest could keep up with him. And even then, no one executive could ever hope to keep up completely. His young lions marvelled as he'd keep three project meetings going at the same time, darting from one to the other like a juggler keeping plates spinning, or a grandmaster playing simultaneous games of chess.

If Richards wanted someone for a project, he didn't send a memo to be passed through four levels of management; he just called the person up. His greatest enjoyment came from bouncing ideas off four or five of his brightest young recruits, lawyers or engineers or corporate financiers.

Part of this corporate style came from a concept he had encountered in his hobby, cattle breeding. It was called "hybrid vigour," and it referred to the phenomenon that when two breeds of cattle were crossed, the resultant calf was usually a strong one. Richards' style was to bring together talented, hard-working people from different backgrounds in the belief that intellectual cross-fertilization would produce new and fruitful ideas. And it seemed to work. But the most important ideas always came from Richards himself. And in the latter half of the 1970s, the idea that prevailed in Richards' mind was acquisition.

Apart from Richards' growing belief in the cheapness of oil and gas reserves and the expanding thrust of the company's corporate aggressiveness, Dome's other rationale for moving into the takeover field was its tax position. Its bold exploration program and relatively large capital expenditure program, which always tended to be greater than its cash flow, had given it a large store of tax write-offs. These could be transferred to takeover targets if they were in a taxpaying position. So Dome was effectively in a position to make more generous offers than other companies lacking its considerable write-offs. This, and similar constant seeking for "tax angles," was to be a critical feature of Dome's highly original expansion phase. However, the approach was not to endear it to the guardians of the nation's fiscal system in Ottawa, who were already miffed about the enormous advantages Dome had wrung out of super-depletion.

Typical of Richards' young lions — and a central figure in the whole acquisitions phase of Dome — was Wayne McGrath. McGrath was a personable young man who, after taking a science degree from the University of Saskatchewan and doing some postgraduate research in operational research in the U.S., had returned to Saskatchewan to join the Federated Cooperatives conglomerate. He had worked there seven years and then moved to Calgary to join Thorne Riddell as a management consultant. After two years with Thorne Riddell, during which he put in more flying time than his brother, who was a pilot for Air Canada, McGrath decided to "drop out." He moved his family to Sparwood, B.C., where he bought a service station, but he soon became bored pumping gas and had already decided to sell out when he received a call suggesting he return to Federated Cooperatives. Flying back to Saskatchewan for an interview, McGrath had two hours to kill at the airport in Calgary, so he phoned another old friend who had joined Dome.

The friend suggested that he fix up an interview at Dome for McGrath on his way back to B.C. McGrath forgot all about it, only remembering when he got a call from Dome in Sparwood. So he returned to Calgary the following day and was interviewed by Dome vice-president of business development, Bob Gillanders, an ambitious and hard-working executive with an eye for recruiting talent. McGrath was told that his responsibility would lie in takeovers, in which Dome had not previously been prominent. Within three years, McGrath would be at the core of the most aggressive acquisition team in Canada. Within five years, he would be part of one of the biggest corporate takeovers in the world.

Siebens: The Brink's Job

The first of the big acquisitions, that of Siebens Oil & Gas, was the sweetest of all, and perhaps the most brilliant. It had started at the beginning of 1978 with a call from the CN pension fund, announcing to Richards that the fund was interested in investing in oil and gas. Did Dome have any suggestions? The team got to work. One of the key players in evolving the eventual form of the deal — and many others — was Don Gilley. Gilley was the head of corporate planning and carried a number of other functions, including finance. Gilley was from an old Ontario family, but despite his establishment background, his corporate style was far from conventional. His slow, methodical, meticulous approach would occasionally drive colleagues to distraction, but the mental process always produced brilliant results. He was regarded within the company as a one-man think tank. But the most unusual thing about him was his working hours. He could never be found in the office at 9 A.M. but would wander in at mid-morning and not begin to get into his stride until others were going home. Then it was not unusual for him to work all night. On more than one occasion, as he was going home he bumped into staff on the way in. Other key players were McGrath, Jack Pirie, another highly regarded corporate planner who had in fact left Dome four years before but whom Richards had persuaded to work part-time for the company, and Vic Zaleschuk, the tall, quiet controller of the company, who had previously worked for Siebens.

The first feature of a deal with a pension fund that occurred to the Dome team was the fund's tax-free status. A brilliant scheme was worked out whereby the CN pension fund would bid for a target company and then sell most of its assets to Dome. The assets could be sold tax-free while Dome's purchase would qualify for tax write-offs. The target company chosen was Siebens Oil & Gas. Siebens had

80

been started in 1965 by Bill Siebens, whose father, Harold, had come to Alberta after Leduc and made a very large amount of money specializing in dealing in oil and gas lands. Bill, a tough petroleum engineer and former United States Air Force pilot (who had once landed his jet at night with a jammed undercarriage because he claims he was "too frightened" to bail out!) had proved every bit as successful as his father at spotting "hot" land plays and filing ahead of the pack. Bill had not only picked up land in the West and the Far North, he had also moved into the international field, acquiring interests from South Vietnam to the North Sea. In 1973, Siebens had a visit from executives of the Hudson's Bay Company, the venerable trading institution and now nation-wide retailer. The Bay still had 4.5 million acres of mineral rights in the western provinces left over from lands granted to it in its original charter. For tax reasons, and also because it sought more aggressive management of these lands, the Bay offered to inject these lands into Siebens in return for a chunk of the company. So Siebens finished up with the mineral rights on the 4.5 million acres, and the Bay received 2.8 million Siebens shares.

Siebens, as the Bay wanted, then proceeded to manage the mineral rights more aggressively, which meant jogging Hudson's Bay Oil & Gas — which in turn held the leasing rights on the same lands — into greater activity.

From Dome's point of view — and that of the CN pension fund — the attractions of Siebens were not only its fine land-spread, but also that, although it was a public company, there were three large blocks of shares available. The Bay and Bill's father, Harold, both held 34.8%, while Bill held 10.9%. It was soon established that they were willing sellers.

The deal was originally to be concluded in February of 1978, but there was a "leak." Siebens' price rose and the parties decided, at least temporarily, to "walk away" from the deal.

Secrecy was an element of takeovers, and Dome henceforth restricted knowledge of its plans to a tight group who could not even tell their corporate superiors what they were doing. They also began using code-words for takeover targets. Since Bill Siebens was tough, and bald, the code-name for the takeover became "Kojak."

The code-names were, of course, necessary, but they also indicated something else about takeovers. Takeovers were fun, and it made you feel good to be on the inside of big, smart deals. That feeling, and their inevitably increasing isolation, made the acquisition group truly exclusive; Richards' Praetorian Guard. The price they willingly paid was to work almost unbelievably hard, particularly around the closing of deals. The closing of the Siebens deal started on a Friday morning. It ended the following Tuesday night. Within that period,

Wayne McGrath didn't get to bed. Vic Zaleschuk was on holiday when the team decided to make the deal. He was driving around Oregon but nobody knew where. When he eventually reached a hotel in Portland, there was a message waiting from Bill Richards. His secretary had called every hotel and motel in Portland and Richards had had the Highway Patrol looking for him for four days. Zaleschuk called Richards and Dome's president told him to get back right away. There was a plane waiting for him in Vancouver. Zaleschuk went back to Calgary, worked all night, and then was allowed to return the next day to his holiday.

The final signings of the deal were made in Toronto. In the corporate jet on the way back to Calgary, the Dome team looked like zombies. Mike Carten, the young tax-lawyer from Bennett Jones, Dome's principal Calgary legal firm, pulled two bottles of champagne from his case. Half of one was drunk. And that was the anticlimax of all the big deals. At the end, all anybody ever wanted was just to get to bed.

Under the deal finally concluded for Siebens, Canpar, a subsidiary of the CN pension fund, offered $38.50 a share for Siebens, valuing the whole company at $360 million. Canpar then agreed to sell 76% of Siebens' assets to Dome. The day after the deal was consummated, Bill Richards went over to see the Siebens' employees to tell them how much Dome would like them to stay on. Just before Richards began his address, Bill Siebens, who was renowned for his puckish sense of humour, pulled out a little clockwork whale. From its mouth a piece of string emerged that connected it to another smaller fish. He had put a little label on the whale marked "Dome"; the little fish was marked "Siebens." He wound them up and then said: "Look, this is what happened to Siebens." When he let them go the whale bore down and ate the smaller fish. Everybody broke up. The Siebens, father and son, certainly had every reason to be happy. Their share of the proceeds was $160 million. And the other parties also had reason to be pleased. The Bay received $126 million of Dome preferred shares. Canpar had acquired a significant presence in the oil business and Dome had acquired over $200 million worth of assets in a deal that paid for itself in two years. There was only one party to the deal — indispensable but not a participant in any of the negotiations — which was not amused: the Department of Finance. Richards joked to his acquisition team that Dome's next acquisition should be Brink's, so they'd have an armour-plated way of bringing back all that money from Ottawa.

In 1979, Dome took its share in TransCanada PipeLines to 49% and in Dome Mines to 39%. It also concluded another takeover with pension funds. This deal, involving the Canadian properties of Mesa Petroleum of Amarillo, Texas, was much more convoluted than the

Siebens deal and was almost blasted apart by the budget of December, 1979, which sought to close the loopholes used by Dome and Canpar on Siebens. Nevertheless, after intensive negotiations with the government, the deal was allowed a "holiday" from the new rules. The deal involved $100 million of Dome's money and $100 million from a number of pension funds, but since Mesa was also to receive future royalty payments from production on its lands, the total value of the deal was around $600 million. At one stage, Richards tried to get the pension funds of the major Canadian banks to put up the whole $100 million needed on the pension-fund side. They demurred but still put up a sizable chunk. The banks really liked Dome, but they weren't willing to risk their employees' future on it. Yet.

Kaiser: The Chinese Take-Out Takeover

The next acquisition came to Dome in the form of a phone call to Jack Gallagher on January 5, 1980. The call was from Edgar Kaiser, the very private, aristocratic 37-year-old scion of the Kaiser Steel and Aluminum empire in the U.S. Was Dome interested in buying Kaiser Resources, Kaiser's oil and gas company? It was said that Gallagher, increasingly concerned about the pace of expansion, passed the message on somewhat reluctantly to Bill Richards. Richards' team went to work once more.

The corporate cognoscenti recognized Kaiser as an outstanding businessman. He had come to Canada ten years before with his impeccable heritage and his Harvard MBA to sort out the Kaiser empire's troubled B.C. coal operations. He liked Vancouver so much he decided to stay, or at least make the city his home base. From Vancouver, Kaiser expanded his global interests, clocking a million miles a year in his private jet, while he rose through the ranks of the Canadian business elite to become the youngest member on the board of the Toronto-Dominion Bank.

Kaiser Resources was effectively Ashland Oil Canada, which Edgar had purchased in 1978 for $485 million. He had reportedly had problems persuading his board of directors of the wisdom of the purchase. Nevertheless, he had finally convinced them that the oil price increases would make the purchase a good one. Now the international oil market seemed to be proving him right. However, the country was now into another federal election as the result of the Tories' defeat on a motion of non-confidence over their December, 1979, budget. It seemed clear that the Liberals were set to return to power, and Kaiser reasoned that this would almost certainly slow the rate of Canadian

83

oil price increases. He knew that only a large company would be able to buy Kaiser Resources, but that foreign-owned multinationals were out of the question because of the political climate. Hence the call to Gallagher.

The negotiations over Kaiser's value took more than a month because of the two sides' different valuations of the properties involved. In the end, Richards made the decision one night over a Chinese take-out meal in the Dome tower. Whatever the valuations, he wanted the Kaiser properties. So he moved up to the opposition's figure and that night Dome agreed to pay $700 million for Kaiser. Kaiser's group would clear $230 million after tax on the deal.

The financing of the deal was straightforward. Jack just phoned his friends, the chairmen of the Toronto-Dominion, the Canadian Imperial Bank of Commerce and the Bank of Montreal, and the three banks came up with the cash. Everybody at Dome involved in the deal was given a copy of the cheque encased in plastic, a memento of Dome's new and growing corporate clout. Nothing, it seemed, could stop it now.

To the outside world, Dome continued to mean Jack Gallagher. There was no apparent conflict between Gallagher and Richards. Richards' iron fist seemed to fit perfectly into Gallagher's velvet glove, a glove capable of the biggest corporate knock-out punch in Calgary.

Meanwhile, Gallagher claimed he never really sought a high profile, but somehow the myth just continued to grow. Gallagher would board a plane, go up into the first-class section and start donning his sweater and slippers when the chief steward would come up and say: "Gee, Mr. Gallagher, you've had a terrible day, your stock was down one and a half points," having obviously translated that into the $1.5 million loss on Gallagher's holdings; enough to make any grown man cry. But Gallagher would just look up with that glittering smile of his and say: "Yes, but last week it was up $5." Then the steward would go away, convinced that the rich — in particular Jack Gallagher — really *were* different.

However, within Dome there were growing tensions, particularly between Gallagher and Richards. Dome's president was developing a more and more open irritation with his chairman. "Hell," he told a visiting journalist in 1979, "Jack is really useful to us. If we didn't have a Jack Gallagher we'd have to create one. He really doesn't get in the way."

Richards had always liked to present Gallagher with *faits accomplis*. But now it appeared that he was almost deliberately trying to isolate Gallagher, although Gallagher wasn't around a lot of the time anyway. However, Richards still needed Gallagher to bring Dome's board of directors onside. He knew that if he could sell a scheme to Gallagher, Gallagher could in turn sell it to the board.

Meanwhile, the side effects of rapid expansion and the self-confident Dome ethos were now appearing. The toughest parts of the acquisitions often came after the takeover, with problems of absorption and with sorting out new corporate systems and documentation. In addition, staff were being lost to the smaller organizations that were springing up everywhere in Calgary's boom environment. Cost controls were getting out of hand. Sometimes new employees picked up the Dome ethos without the corresponding ability. Dome was developing a reputation for a hard-driving, aggressive style that came straight down from its president.

Meanwhile, Richards sped on like Dome's brand new Class 4 icebreaker *Kigoriak*, a hard-charging executive positively looking for corporate icebergs to ram. Soon he would run up against one of *Titanic*-sinking proportions in the shape of the Liberals' National Energy Program. The iceberg would lose.

7
Dome Canada: The NEP's Billion-Dollar Baby

"Dome Canada had to be as good as gold, otherwise there was no way one of Trudeau's senior cabinet ministers would have appeared to endorse it."

In May, 1979, a highly publicized event in Canada coincided with a slightly less publicized, but arguably much more important occurrence on the world scene. The Tory government of Joe Clark was elected, and the world spot-market price for oil went through the roof. Within ten months, Joe Clark would be gone. Public misunderstanding of the domestic implications of the world oil price upheaval would be a contributing factor. However, the domestic policy implications of world oil price increases would cause massive repercussions for the oil industry long after Clark's departure.

For Richards, these soaring world oil price movements seemed to provide a complete vindication for his aggressive acquisition strategy. The first OPEC crisis of 1973 had shown that the official OPEC price followed the movements of the spot-market price. The intervening period had also made clear that the Canadian price had eventually to follow upwards. Oil and gas prices in Canada seemed destined for a further surge. As those prices increased, so did the value of oil companies. For Richards, now was the time to buy, before the stock market anticipated the future.

In fact, Ottawa's brightest energy brains thought the same way, but with a heavy nationalist twist. The second OPEC crisis was to lead to a revolution in Canadian energy policy analysis. That rethink was to culminate 18 months later in the National Energy Program, one of the most radical policies in Canadian history. The NEP initially appeared to be a disaster for Dome. Within four months of its introduction, Bill Richards had turned it into a billion-dollar bonanza.

The policy's roots lay in work done at the Department of Energy, Mines and Resources (EMR) in 1979 — mostly under the short-lived Conservative government of Joe Clark.

87

When Joe Clark's Tories came to power in May, 1979, Gallagher and Richards lost no time in plugging into the new Ottawa power network. Gallagher would corner any policy advisor he could capture and explain the importance of the Beaufort to Canada's energy future, and how super-depletion was only a little help up front, and was really *very* little when you took into account the huge development costs of the Beaufort. Richards would stroke mandarins and executive assistants, painting pictures of massive corporate plans, and making them feel important. However, Dome found some of the younger bureaucrats difficult to mesmerize, in particular, a radical and increasingly powerful young economist at EMR called Edmund Clark.

Clark was typical of the super-bureaucrats who flourished under the Trudeau regime. He had come straight from academia with a Harvard Ph.D. (his doctoral thesis was entitled "Public Investment and Socialist Development in Tanzania"). He had served first at the Department of Finance and had then caught the attention of the senior mandarins with his work at the Anti-Inflation Board. In the fall of 1978, Marshall "Mickey" Cohen, the EMR deputy minister, had recruited Clark to the department to beef up EMR's policy analysis.

Early in 1979, Cohen was moved to the Department of Industry, Trade and Commerce and was replaced as deputy minister by Ian Stewart. Stewart, like Clark, was a brilliant academic economist. After studying at Queen's, Oxford and Cornell, he had taught at Queen's and Dartmouth, the American ivy league university, before moving to Ottawa. Stewart had worked at EMR before, under Jack Austin at the time of the first OPEC crisis. Then he had been a key member of the team — which included Bill Hopper and Joel Bell, both of whom had subsequently moved to PetroCanada — that had formulated the Liberals' policy response to that crisis. After EMR, Stewart had gone to the Privy Council Office as Pierre Trudeau's senior economic advisor, a position of enormous influence. At EMR in 1979, he and Clark were to agree totally on the nature of — and the solutions to — Canada's energy problems. Their analysis in fact had very little to do with energy *per se*: it concentrated rather on the division of revenues between the Alberta and federal governments, the degree of foreign ownership of the Canadian oil business and the supposedly unfair advantage that large, foreign-controlled companies had under the existing tax system.

Clark and Stewart were highly critical of the complex mish-mash of taxes, royalties and allowances that had emerged from the great clash of 1974 between the Alberta and federal governments.

They believed that the Liberals, in their desire to encourage exploration and petroleum self-sufficiency, had developed a system that

88

was far too generous to the corporate sector, in particular big, foreign-controlled oil. They also believed that Alberta had effectively "won" the petroleum revenue battle. Both these trends were regarded as inherently undesirable. Alberta's multibillion dollar Heritage Fund, into which it deposited a third of its petroleum revenues, and the soaring prices of oil stocks were regarded as the twin symbols of Ottawa's failure to establish an "equitable" system. And when it came to inequities, the policy analysts saw super-depletion — the "Gallagher Amendment" in the "Dome Budget" — as the most glaring.

In their eyes, Dome, for all its pretense of action in the national interest, was still a foreign company since more than 50% of its shares were held abroad. Meanwhile, they made their feelings about super-depletion clear in a secret cabinet document entitled "Outline of a National Energy Strategy" and dated October 15, 1979.

"Super-depletion," the document said, "has been used extensively by the large foreign-owned companies to significantly reduce their frontier drilling costs at the expense of Canadian taxpayers. It is proposed that this tax incentive due to expire March 31, 1980, be modified for the balance of the drilling season and then allowed to expire. The modifications would remove the current abuses ... "

This thinking prevailed in the December, 1979, budget. The super-depletion allowance was reduced from $66^2/_3\%$ of exploratory costs in excess of \$5 million on a well to $6^2/_3\%$. The budget also took swipes at other areas in which Dome was thought to have abused the tax system. Taking aim at the structure of both the Mesa and Siebens deals, Finance Minister John Crosbie declared: "Two types of schemes have recently developed that are resulting in undesirable tax leakage. Some non-residents have found ways of escaping tax on income from sales of resource properties. Measures are proposed in the budget to preclude this possibility. As well, rules are to be introduced to ensure that tax-exempt institutions cannot be used as vehicles to circumvent the income tax rules relating to resource taxation."

The precise form in which frontier exploration would henceforth be stimulated was not specified, but the issue in any case became academic when the Tories went down in Parliament to a vote of no-confidence on the budget, the least popular aspect of which was a proposed 18-cent-a-gallon hike in the excise tax on gasoline. In February, the Liberals were returned to power.

The Grits' Energy Crusade

Gallagher and Richards had no reason to be disappointed with the Liberals' return. After all, it was the Liberals who had given them super-depletion in the first place. However, they did realize that there were policy changes in the wind. Liberal policy making had now been seized by interventionists and economic nationalists, who saw their mandate in the Canadian public's powerful opposition to the Tories' plans to dismantle Petro-Canada. The renewed world oil crisis had stirred up old distrusts about foreign-owned big oil. The polls told the Liberals that now would be the time to move against foreign oil. For once, the thrust of the polls coincided completely with the intellectual analysis of the super-mandarins. The final element in policy momentum was the appointment of Marc Lalonde to the Energy portfolio. Lalonde was an aloof and arrogant technocrat with a huge capacity for work, a forceful personality and a profound streak of self-righteousness. A lawyer, his rise to power had started when he was appointed principal secretary in the Prime Minister's Office in 1968 when his old colleague, Pierre Trudeau, had first been elected. It was during his reign in the PMO that Lalonde gained the reputation of expertise in making things happen, "working the system." In 1972, Lalonde had won the seat for Outremont, Quebec, and had ever since been a key member of Trudeau's innermost group. Like Trudeau, Lalonde had little sympathy for, or understanding of, the corporate world.

Between February and October of 1980 he set to work with his team of super-bureaucrats to "put right" Canada's energy future. Ed Clark remained the intellectual thrust behind energy policy, although he maintained a close affinity with Ian Stewart, who was now moved to the deputy ministership of finance. Mickey Cohen, meanwhile, was moved back to become the senior public servant at EMR.

The year 1980 was to see EMR become *the* department in which to work in Ottawa. The fix of power in bureaucracy is closely related to the importance of the policy being worked upon. That summer, EMR's policy-making group was on a permanent high, working late each night on what they realized was probably the single most important policy initiative with which they would ever be involved. It was, of course, far more than a mere energy policy: it was a macroeconomic thrust that would beneficially restructure the whole of the Canadian oil industry and radically change federal-provincial fiscal relationships.

Not surprisingly, the industry was keen to discover what was in it. Dome executives in particular spent a lot of time that summer in

Ottawa trying to find out what was contained in the new energy policy. Gallagher came and gave both Lalonde and his new executive assistant, lawyer Michael Phelps, the run-down on the Beaufort vision. But the Beaufort vision was wearing a little thin. Lalonde was, of course, impressed with Gallagher, but the Dome chairman would tend to repeat his set speech. Jack would always want to make that additional point at the end of meetings, just to make sure Lalonde was completely sold on the Beaufort. And of course, he would always say, the most important thing was that Lalonde just *had* to come up to the Beaufort. Yes, yes, Lalonde would say, but he couldn't make it in the summer of 1980. He was a very busy man.

Richards would come in separately and bring members of Dome's senior management along. Lalonde found Richards impressive, much more specific and more to the point than Gallagher. He would talk about new megaprojects and Dome's role in them.

And Gallagher and Richards would also work the rest of their network: Tom Axworthy, brother of cabinet minister Lloyd and Jim Coutts' hand-picked replacement as principal secretary in the Prime Minister's Office; Ian Stewart and Sid Rubinoff at Finance; Michael Pitfield in the PCO and a host of others in the departments of Transport and Industry, Trade and Commerce.

Dome managed to pick up the notion that the government was considering some form of grant system to replace the existing system of tax allowances, but as senior Dome personnel gathered around the television in one of the company's meeting rooms on October 28, 1980, to listen to Finance Minister Allan MacEachen deliver his budget, they had no idea what was in store for them.

The NEP Bombshell

The National Energy Program dominated the 1980 budget. It was one of the most far-reaching and revolutionary policies ever to have emerged from a Canadian government. It featured hefty new taxes, expropriation of frontier lands, a discriminatory system of grants based on a company's degree of Canadian ownership, and a firm commitment to nationalize a number of large foreign-controlled oil companies. It was designed to syphon revenue from Alberta, financially hobble foreign-owned companies and greatly extend government intervention. It caused an uproar throughout the entire oil industry, both Canadian and foreign-owned, and drew angry responses both from Washington and Alberta.

The NEP's underlying assumption was that OPEC was firmly in

charge of world oil prices and that these would, therefore, continue to rise. The analysis of the results of that trend dated back to EMR analyses done under the Tories: under the existing pricing and fiscal system, Alberta and the foreign-owned industry would reap most of the benefits. That trend had to be arrested. It was stopped by the introduction of major new taxes, principally the Petroleum and Gas Revenue Tax, and the Natural Gas and Gas Liquids Tax. The "bias" in the system in favour of foreign-owned oil companies — allegedly based on the fact that they had profits against which to set tax allowances and thus had advantages over those having no profits — was to be cured by a system of Petroleum Incentive Payments, or PIP grants.

PIP grants were direct subsidies for exploration and development depending on the degree of the recipients' Canadian ownership and depending on where the recipient companies were operating, with much higher grants for those working on federal rather than Alberta lands.

In addition, the NEP declared that Petro-Canada would be able to "back in" on 25% of all federal lands. Indeed, Petro-Canada, whose senior vice-president, Joel Bell, had been a key consultant on the NEP, was one very clear winner from the whole program. Not only was the company to receive the 25% back-in, but it was also to be the instrument for acquisition of foreign oil companies. To aid it, a uniquely generous new provision, the Canadian Ownership Charge, levied on all gasoline sales, was to be pumped into its coffers.

Dome's executives were horrified by what they heard. Not only would they be badly hit by the new taxes, but since their Canadian ownership level was less than 50%, they received only the lowest level of PIP grant. To cap it all, PetroCan was going to be able to walk into 25% of their enormous frontier acreage.

Don Gardiner, one of Dome's "in-group," who had joined Don Gilley's corporate planning department in 1978 after stints with IBM and in real estate, sat in his office the night of the budget and wrote the initials NEP on a piece of paper. Then he added "-otism." That summed up the oil industry's view perfectly. This was a policy designed to benefit Petro-Canada and its ilk, the favoured children of the intensely interventionist policy-making clique that had formulated the program. Although Dome was categorized in the document as being "Canadian-controlled," the regulations for judging a company's level of Canadian ownership — which were still in the formative stage — clearly excluded it from the most generous of the new grants. Meanwhile Dome's cash flow was going to be murdered by the new taxes. Rapid calculations made the night of the budget suggested that the NEP might cost as much as $100 million annually.

Bill Richards had flown in from London the night of October 28. He appeared as shocked as anybody at the NEP's thrust. In particular, he hated the 25% Petro-Canada back-in. A couple of days later, he would answer the phone to a journalist and tell him he thought the government was "mad" to be "taking over other people's property." His staff almost leaped on him when they heard him making the remark, which, when it was reported, needless to say, did not endear him to the public-spirited brains behind the NEP. Shortly afterwards, Jack Gallagher called Lalonde's office to suggest that Bill had gone off the deep end and was not to be taken too seriously.

"Operation Amoeba"

But despite Richards' outburst, it was not in the nature of Dome's president to brood on such matters, nor to get involved in ideological debate. The important thing was that Dome had half a billion dollars worth of drilling equipment in the Beaufort and a drilling season coming up. Richards' first concern was: how could Dome take advantage of the new system? The answer came to him almost immediately. If grants were available to companies with high levels of Canadian ownership, then Dome would simply create such a company, and funnel all drilling on Dome's lands through it. If the government was doling out money, somehow or other Dome would get to the front of the line.

The following morning, Wayne McGrath, the acquisitions man, Bob Gillanders, head of business development, Don Gilley, Dome's chief corporate planner and Steve Savidant, a young former Imperial Oil engineer and now Richards' assistant, met in Richards' office to plot strategy. They planned to have a preliminary prospectus for the new company out by mid-December. A task force was appointed to work on it. The task force was made up of all Richards' young lions, the group that had formed an *esprit de corps* while working on new projects and takeovers in the previous two years. It included McGrath, Savidant, Gardiner, Vic Zaleschuk, Ed Brown, a lawyer, and Mike Granden, another young engineer and Harvard MBA who had joined Don Gilley's group in early 1979 and now suddenly found himself exalted into Dome's first circle of power. They were all in their thirties, all good family men, all very smart, all personable, regular guys whom Richards had taken and moulded into an unparalleled corporate fighting force.

Their task was to create a new company from scratch that would be controlled by Dome but would have a large Canadian shareholding.

93

The Canadian shareholders would be attracted through a new equity sale. The equity sale would be the largest in Canadian history. It would mean a bonanza of unprecedented proportions for Canada's investment dealers. Not surprisingly, perhaps, the same investment advisors were enormously bullish on the prospects of the new company.

The lead investment house chosen for the new deal was Toronto-based Pitfield Mackay Ross. Pitfield, which was headed by Ward Pitfield, elder brother of Michael, Clerk of the Privy Council, had not been particularly successful in attracting Dome business previously. However, the company had reportedly been working on Jack Gallagher throughout 1980 and Gallagher had eventually sent a note to Dome's corporate finance department suggesting they use Pitfield for their next deal. Within nine days of the NEP, Peter Breyfogle, Dome's chief financial officer, had flown to Toronto for meetings with key personnel in Pitfield's corporate finance department. A few days later, Ward Pitfield flew out to Calgary to meet with Bill Richards.

Richards had picked on Dome Canada's share price, $10, within 24 hours of the NEP, but Pitfield was needed to assess just how many shares the market would take and whether the issue should feature any "bells and whistles," additional features to increase its attractiveness to shareholders.

The Pitfield team suggested that the deal should offer warrants to buy additional Dome Canada shares as part of the package. They also pointed out that there might be legal constraints barring institutional investors — like insurance companies and pension funds — from investing in a company with no earnings record. As a result of this latter point, Dome reorganized one of its own subsidiaries as the investment vehicle and renamed it Dome Canada. To provide further earnings and also pay for its own 48% of the new company, Dome would inject half of its 47% interest in TransCanada PipeLines. It would make up the difference by paying cash for the remainder of its Dome Canada shares. The transfer of TCPL shares in no way decreased Dome Petroleum's control of the pipeline giant because Dome Canada would be completely under the control of Dome Petroleum.

To round out the new company's financial structure, Dome Petroleum arranged for $225 million of a $400 million loan it was negotiating with the Japan National Oil Company — to promote Beaufort exploration — to be lent directly to Dome Canada. Dome executives flew to Tokyo to explain to the somewhat bemused Japanese investors that this deal was even better than their original one because the new company to which they were lending money would also receive huge government grants for Beaufort exploration.

By mid-December, Dome's plan for the creation of Dome Canada, code-named "Operation Amoeba," was conceptually complete. There remained one interested party that had to be informed of the developments: the Liberal government. When Richards went to Ottawa and revealed his plan to EMR, the initial reaction was disbelief. EMR had worked day and night on the NEP for six months. Now, within six weeks, Bill Richards had a plan that seemed to dance rings around it. At first, they were convinced that there must have been a budget leak. But Richards assured them, if they hadn't realized it already, that Dome was a company that tended to be quick off the mark. The second reaction was one of scarcely disguised resentment at the transparency of Dome's scheme to utilize the legislation in order to drill on Dome's own lands, and thus increase the value of Dome Petroleum. There had been concern within EMR about a "leakage" of benefits under the NEP, that is, that the benefits of government grants might go to foreign-owned landholders. Dome's plan wasn't leakage; it was a straight flow-through of benefits. Moreover, the projected size of Dome Canada meant that the flow-through might turn out to be a flood. Once again, it seemed, Dome Petroleum was raiding the treasury.

Lalonde's Imprimatur

Nevertheless, there was one key political element in Dome's favour. The Liberals had expected adverse reaction to the NEP, but they were shocked by the outright condemnation and outrage from the industry, Alberta and Washington. Public opinion still appeared firmly in favour of the move, but public opinion didn't drill any oilwells. Moreover, even the public was bound to notice sooner or later that the most vituperative condemnations of the NEP were coming from the very Canadian companies it claimed to be helping. Dome Canada, at least, indicated a positive response to NEP.

Dome's plan, however, caused great consternation among the bureaucrats, who clearly saw that Dome Canada might be used only to serve Dome's own ends. An intense, and often heated, period of negotiation started between EMR and Dome officials. For EMR, the principal negotiators were Ed Clark and Digby Hunt. Hunt was a public servant of the old school. He had started out in private industry and come to Ottawa in the early 1960s to work on federal land regulations. He had remained in the energy sector, and became a senior mandarin in EMR in the early 1970s. However, when Clark had come to EMR, Hunt had found himself shunted to one side, particularly after Stewart became deputy minister. His practical knowledge was not greatly prized in an EMR where heavy emphasis was placed on macroeconomic theory. Hunt had had no part in the creation of the NEP, but after the policy was announced, he was put in charge of PIP payments. This meant that he and Clark found themselves arguing shoulder to shoulder on the government side.

The bureaucrats were not only concerned with the leakage of benefits to Dome but also that Dome Canada, which was ultimately little more than a puppet of Dome Petroleum, might be allowed to drill only on unattractive Dome Petroleum lands, with the attractive prospects left for Dome. They reportedly drove a much harder bargain than that originally proposed by Richards, but the final agreement still looked uniquely favourable to Dome.

Under this agreement, Dome Canada was to earn up to 50% of lands surrounding wells on Dome Petroleum lands in return for undertaking all the expenses. Subsequent development costs were to be shared between the two companies. However, Dome Canada was excluded from earning any interest in lands near existing discoveries or conventional production acreage lands, and Dome Petroleum also charged Dome Canada fees for managing and administering its activities. In return, Dome Petroleum, because of the size of the agreement, had to commit itself to becoming more than 50% Canadian-owned. The biggest potential hurdle to a successful share sale for Dome Canada was the fact that the NEP legislation — on which the PIP grants depended — had not been passed. Dome thus asked Energy Minister Marc Lalonde to put in writing the fact that Dome Canada would be eligible for the grants, so that a letter from him might be appended to the Dome Canada prospectus. That letter, written under Lalonde's name and dated January 29, 1981, declared that he would "exercise the discretion" he expected the legislation to provide in order to modify the PIP legislation in favour of the Dome Petroleum-Dome Canada agreement.

The elements of the Dome Canada package now seemed to be tied up. There were widespread rumours that Dome was working on a scheme to take advantage of the NEP and on January 27, two days before Lalonde's letter was officially sent to Dome, Dome shares rose $5.25 to $83.50 in anticipation of such a scheme.

Meanwhile virtually the whole Canadian brokerage industry was now involved in what seemed certain to be Canada's largest ever equity sale. Pitfield brought five other groups into the management group for the Dome Canada issue: Wood Gundy, Dominion Securities, McLeod Young Weir, Nesbitt Thomson Securities and Richardson Securities, and recruited another 80 investment firms either to share in the underwriting liability or merely sell the stock.

By the beginning of February Marc Lalonde was in such need of support for the NEP that he decided he would fly out to Calgary to appear on the same platform as Jack Gallagher at the announcement of Dome Canada's formation. The appearance of the aloof energy minister with Smilin' Jack seemed clearly to indicate that Dome really was the Liberal government's "chosen instrument." The appearance also set the seal on the attractiveness of Dome Canada to investors. Dome Canada had to be as good as gold, otherwise there was no way one of Trudeau's senior cabinet ministers would have appeared to endorse it.

An almost mad scramble to acquire Dome Canada shares began. Friends and relatives of Dome employees pestered them to see if they could help them get their allotment. Meanwhile, the most frantic scramble for Dome Canada shares was going on inside Dome itself. It wasn't that the stock was touted within the company; it was just the smell of success. The three-day, cross-country road show put on by Dome and its investment advisors at the end of February to promote the share sale was hardly necessary. Everyone was clamouring for the stock.

When Dome Canada's share offering closed on March 19, the 52% of its shares offered to the public had been fully subscribed, bringing in $434 million to Dome Canada and over $25 million in underwriting commissions to the investment dealers. Pitfield raked in a total of $4.5 million; Wood Gundy $2.8 million, and McLeod Young Weir and Nesbitt Thomson $1.8 million each.

Once the Japanese loan and Dome Petroleum's subscription of cash and TCPL shares had been taken into account, Dome Canada became a company with a total capitalization of over $1 billion, most of which was in cash. Not only had it been conceived and created within the astonishingly short period of less than five months, it had turned the apparent disaster of the NEP to Dome's advantage.

After Dome Canada's formation, Bill Richards travelled to New York to explain the new company's formation to an investment community that was highly confused not only about the financial intricacies of the deal, but also about its political overtones and implications. Bill Richards left them in no doubt that Dome Petroleum was the real winner from the situation, although he also pointed out that there was no doubt in his mind that when he returned the following year, Dome Canada shares would have doubled. That was not to prove the case.

8
HBOG:
A Foot in the Swamp

"These were, however, in Richards' mind 'little deals,'
just a few hundred million dollars, mere corporate
appetizers for a company with Dome's ambitions.
Richards felt it was time for a really big deal."

By the spring of 1981, Dome towered like a colossus over the Canadian oil industry. Its response to the National Energy Program — the creation of Dome Canada — was considered brilliant, a display of corporate lateral thinking that turned an apparent disaster into yet another massive source of funds for the company's limitless ambitions. For employees, investors, the banks and the government, Dome was becoming less a company than a cult. It could do no wrong.

Sixty thousand investors had lined up for stock in Dome Canada. Equally astonishing, shares to the value of some $39 million had been bought by Dome's own employees, and not principally by its executives. Some of Dome's employees earning $30,000 a year had literally mortgaged their houses to buy $100,000-worth of Dome Canada shares. Their faith in Dome Pete stock, too, knew no bounds. One employee who raised a second mortgage to buy shares in Dome Petroleum was asked by a friend in the investment community if he shouldn't consider a "put" option on Dome Pete shares and thus, for a relatively small cost, cover himself against a fall in their price. The Dome employee looked aghast. "Dome shares won't be going down," he said definitively. And besides, the very notion was disloyal. Among the rank and file, dedication to Gallagher and Richards was now approaching apotheosis. A month before the Dome Canada deal had closed, Bill Richards had signed a $400 million loan with the Japan National Oil Company on uniquely generous terms. On February 24, 1981, Dome had reported a further surge in earnings and cash flow for the previous year. Revenue had surpassed $1 billion for the first time; cash flow was reported to have risen to $430.7 million versus $316.6 in 1979, while post-tax earnings had surged 53% to $266.2 million. The share-price continued to soar, and on April 10, the company announced a further five-for-one stock split. The shareholders would be given five shares in exchange for each one they held; and if the new shares would be only around a fifth of the price of the old shares, everybody knew that was merely a temporary state of affairs. The purpose of the stock split was to bring share prices away from the $100 level down to a more "normal" range. From which, of course, they would rise again.

What could Dome do for its next trick? For Bill Richards, there was only one answer: another acquisition. Like the super-bureaucrats who framed the NEP, Richards was now more than ever convinced of the perpetual nature of energy inflation, and he was not alone in seeing world oil prices soaring towards $100 a barrel within the decade — with Canadian prices inevitably following in their wake.

The Iran-Iraq war in late 1980, and the supremacy of OPEC's hawks, seemed clearly to vindicate Richards' belief that it was cheaper to acquire established petroleum reserves than to go out and explore for them. Other companies, in Richards' eyes, were now as cheap as they would ever be. Indeed, as well as dreaming up Dome Canada, Richards' other immediate reaction to the NEP had been to call in Wayne McGrath, now well established as the acquisitions specialist, and tell him to draw up a list of likely targets. If the government wanted Canadianization, he'd give it to them.

To the public, Dome was still primarily Jack Gallagher's company, but Dome's continued expansion had moved control of the corporation further and further towards Richards and his corporate court. Jack Gallagher was still head of Dome, still both chairman and chief executive, but he now knew less and less about what was going on within the company. Gallagher had always essentially been at home in a smaller company, where he could keep an eye on what everybody was doing, and know and develop his staff personally. Dome had now grown far too large for that approach and Gallagher had in any case effectively ceded leadership of Dome to Richards' enthusiasm and ideas. In practical terms, the heart of the company had now become Bill's office. Project groups would troop in one after the other for brainstorming sessions so that the whole Dome universe was contained effectively in only one place, Bill Richards' head.

Gallagher at times felt isolated and would perhaps float an idea of his own outside Richards' group, but this would sometimes annoy Dome's president. Gallagher had always been concerned with cost savings. A frugal man with a modest lifestyle himself, he had always impressed on Dome's staff the need to "conserve the pennies." He'd note that Richards was taking five staff with him to Toronto for a meeting and he'd ask if Richards couldn't do with one. Richards would have to restrain himself. Here he was off to a negotiation worth perhaps hundreds of millions of dollars and Jack's prime concern seemed to be saving on a few air fares. If one of the staff was organizing a working lunch for between a dozen and 20 people, and ordered 20 lunches, then Gallagher would fret about the potential waste of food. It was an approach that had seemed appropriate in a smaller company, but in one the size of Dome it was regarded as picayune or penny-pinching.

Such an approach seemed particularly inappropriate now, for Dome was on the verge of one of the largest takeovers in world corporate history.

Two new code-words were to appear in Dome's corporate cipher book, that list of names given to takeover targets: "Australia" for the U.S. company, Conoco, (whose original name was Continental Oil) and "Swampy," for Hudson's Bay Oil & Gas (known after its initials as "aitch-bog"). But the term "Swampy" was to acquire a greater and more ominous significance as the lengthy and elaborate takeover proceeded. Hudson's Bay Oil & Gas did indeed become the financial swamp in which Dome ultimately bogged down.

A Corporate Cadillac

In April, 1980, six months before the announcement of the NEP, the chairmanship of Hudson's Bay Oil & Gas had been taken over by Gerry Maier, a tough, former Saskatchewan farm boy who had worked in the mines before starting out on the long route up the corporate ladder. Maier was justifiably proud to be the first Canadian chairman and chief executive of one of the largest and soundest companies in the Alberta oilpatch. From his new office in the 42-storey HBOG Tower on Calgary's Seventh Avenue, he surveyed a rock-solid corporate empire of huge landholdings and high quality oil and gas production. HBOG was the country's third largest producer of natural gas, and its ninth largest producer of oil and natural gas liquids, as well as having extensive mining, pipeline and gas processing interests. The company explored in ten countries and already had significant production from discoveries in Indonesia. The year Maier became chairman, HBOG had revenues of $605 million and earnings of $145 million. With virtually no long-term debt, the company had been described as a "banker's dream." Ironically, it was to become an unwilling player in what would turn out to be a banker's nightmare.

A little over a year after becoming chairman, Gerry Maier was to see his corporate world fall apart. HBOG's bank, the Canadian Imperial Bank of Commerce — which had done all the company's business for 55 years — suddenly ditched it in order to lead the financing for Dome's takeover assault upon it, while HBOG's major shareholder, Conoco, deserted it in a desperate scramble to save its own corporate hide.

In the end, Maier was left to fight a lonely battle for the minority shareholders and HBOG employees as the Dome whirlwind swept through his company, slicing it up, selling it off, and creating a diaspora of HBOG executives that was a boon to the rest of the industry but marked the effective death of one of Canada's "Cadillac" oil companies.

Dome's assault was in turn to open a corporate Pandora's box, leading to the ultimate takeover of HBOG's U.S. majority shareholder, Conoco, by chemical giant, Du Pont, in the world's largest acquisition, and to the financial faltering of Dome itself, which within a year of its first move on HBOG was threatening to become the world's largest bankruptcy.

HBOG was the fruit of a 1926 agreement, based on the Hudson's Bay Company's massive Canadian landholdings, between the Bay and American interests, with the U.S. majority shareholding winding up in the hands of Rockefeller offshoot, Conoco (see Appendix A).

HBOG was a prize by any standards. Over the years it had acquired a reputation in the Canadian oilpatch for steady, somewhat conservative management and "good corporate citizenship" (for a number of years, it was Calgary's top corporate contributor to the United Way fund). There had always been a good relationship between its two dominant shareholders, Conoco (with 52.9% of its shares) and the Bay (with 10.1%).

Of its thirteen board members, five were from Conoco, three were affiliated with the Bay, three were HBOG management, and two were independent. Conoco was never considered to play the "heavy" on the HBOG board, and, during the 1970s, it placed increased emphasis on the Canadian company's autonomy. Carl Jones became the first Canadian president in 1970. He was succeeded by another American, Stan Olson, but in 1980, Maier became the first Canadian to become not only chief executive but also chairman of the board. Another Canadian, Dick Haskeyne, was appointed president.

Maier and Haskeyne formed a widely recognized team at HBOG in the latter half of the 1970s. Maier had joined the company in the early 1950s as a drilling and consulting engineer straight out of the University of Alberta. He caught the eye of Conoco management and, in the mid-1960s, was invited to work in Conoco's Australian subsidiary. He returned to HBOG in 1967, but in 1973 was taken once again by HBOG's U.S. parent and in 1974–75 headed its U.K. production company, Conoco North Sea Inc.

Haskeyne, too, had graduated from the University of Alberta —

with a bachelor of commerce degree — and had then articled as a chartered accountant in Calgary before joining HBOG in 1960. He rose to be vice-president of finance and, in 1973, left to join the ill-fated Arctic Gas Consortium that planned to build a natural gas pipeline from Prudhoe Bay in Alaska via the Mackenzie Valley.

In 1975, however, both Maier and Haskeyne were lured back to HBOG with promises of top management positions. Maier had held misgivings about returning to Canada following the much-publicized and damaging post-OPEC dispute between the federal and Alberta governments. He was also giving up a promising career at Conoco. Nevertheless, he believed that he could make HBOG a Canadian-based international resource company. Maier's technical and operating skills, and international experience, and Haskeyne's financial expertise, were considered a formidable combination. Both men were respected and liked throughout the industry. Moreover, HBOG's independence promised to increase further after the accession to the Conoco chairmanship of Ralph Bailey. An affable and outgoing technical man who had risen to the top of Conoco via its Consolidated Coal subsidiary, Bailey was a firm believer in delegating responsibility.

Pushy Neighbours

When Maier assumed the chairmanship of HBOG, he had no inkling that control of HBOG might change hands, or that Dome Petroleum, his nextdoor neighbour on Seventh Avenue, might be the instrument of HBOG's destruction.

Although most of the working oil industry had misgivings about Dome's uncompromising style, Maier had had more direct experience of Dome's *modus operandi* than most. He hadn't liked what he'd seen. The experience had resulted from Dome's takeover, in 1978, of Siebens Oil & Gas, which had five years previously taken over the management of the Bay's mineral rights — on which HBOG in turn held the leasing rights. That meant that HBOG drilled the land, and the Bay got part of the income. The extent of the income was obviously related to the amount of drilling, so the Bay obviously wanted HBOG to be active. Their deal with Siebens had been made partly to force HBOG into a greater level of exploration and development activity. When Dome had taken over Siebens, they had also assumed the role of "prodding" HBOG into action. For HBOG, the experience had not been a pleasant one.

HBOG had an obvious tendency to put exploration of Bay lands on the back burner. After all, they held leasing rights until 1999. HBOG was not necessarily happy in 1973 when Siebens started prodding them, but they recognized that Bill Siebens, if a tough businessman, was at least fair. That, however, was not their experience with Dome. Siebens always tried to make HBOG work hard. But Dome, from the first, seemed to be trying to drive them to the wall, squeezing every last drop out of a deal. Dome always seemed to have a battery of lawyers in the background looking for loopholes. They always appeared to be trying to pull a fast one, delivering a batch of drilling demands on a Friday night, pushing, pushing, pushing.

When he took the chairmanship of HBOG, Maier had no intention of dealing with Dome more than was absolutely necessary. But in Ottawa's corridors of power the National Energy Program was taking shape, and under that program, HBOG was damned. The NEP, with its statistical notions of ownership and control, had no facility for taking into account the realities of HBOG's situation: of its *de facto* independence, its achievements, its Canadian management. HBOG was simply stamped, like a carcass, "foreign controlled," and thus left hanging as a prime target for predators. Through its discriminatory grant system, the NEP clearly declared any company with a significant foreign holding to be a second-class corporate citizen.

Nev heless, there was no immediate panic at HBOG when the NEP emerged. The 25% back-in on all companies' federal lands was not overly problematic for the company, since its frontier landholdings were relatively small. Meanwhile, its size and value provided protection from all but the very largest acquisitors. Most important, however, Maier and Haskeyne believed that Conoco would not sell them out. The two had met with Conoco executives before and after Christmas, 1980, to discuss ways in which Conoco's stake might be reduced. However, unknown to Maier and Haskeyne, HBOG, at the instigation of Conoco's Wall Street investment bankers, Morgan Stanley, was already on the block *before* the NEP was announced.

For most HBOG executives, Morgan Stanley was to assume the role of financial villain, a cold-hearted money-merchant whose sole interest was in doing a deal — any deal — for the highest price. In particular, Maier and Haskeyne blamed one of Morgan Stanley's managing directors, Robert Greenhill, for selling them down the river. Greenhill, a brash and aggressive financial wizard, had a forceful style that reflected the arrogance of his whole company. Morgan Stanley was an offshoot of the great banking family of J.P. Morgan, one of the greatest of America's "robber barons." The company would never appear on a newspaper "tombstone" — newspaper advertisements that list the underwriters or lenders in any major financing — unless its name was at the top. It made its money from underwriting and dealing in securities, but it also made huge amounts of money from takeovers, the fees for which were based on the size of the target. Men like Greenhill roamed the corporate world like financial *agents provacateurs*, trying to encourage aggressive acquisitions from which they reaped millions in fees. The bigger the fight the better.

In the fall of 1981, Greenhill approached former Liberal energy minister Donald Macdonald, a partner in the establishment Toronto law firm of McCarthy & McCarthy. Greenhill wanted Macdonald to act as an intermediary in a possible takeover by Petro-Canada — which Macdonald had brought into existence — of Conoco's stake in HBOG. Macdonald spoke to Bill Hopper, PetroCan's chairman, and, as a result, a number of meetings were held between Hopper and Joel Bell for PetroCan and Greenhill and a back-up team from Morgan Stanley. Hopper and Bell valued HBOG at around $4 billion, the price Dome eventually paid for it, but Greenhill said that Conoco wanted more. Their asking price was a mind-boggling $7 billion. Greenhill suggested that Hopper meet with Bailey, but PetroCan's chairman said he didn't want to do so unless an agreement was likely. One of Hopper's principal concerns was ensuring that PetroCan could get hold of HBOG's minority shares, particularly the 10.1% held by the Bay. However, Greenhill assured him that if Conoco sold out, then Ken Thomson of the Bay would sell too. Their other concern was HBOG's overseas properties, whose takeover they thought might be politically sensitive. Greenhill assured them that Conoco would buy back the properties for $500 million. Greenhill also told Hopper that Conoco was prepared to take Maier and Haskeyne onto its own staff if — as seemed likely — the two men were reluctant to stay on after an acquisition by PetroCan.

The discussion carried on for some weeks after the NEP was introduced, but although Greenhill lowered the price, the two sides were still more than $500 million apart when the talks disintegrated in November.

In the eyes of HBOG management, the fact that Petro-Canada was even considered as a suitor amounted to a betrayal.

The Battle Plan: Tax Magic

In February, 1981, after the formation of Dome Canada had been negotiated with the federal government, Richards and his executive assistant, Steve Savidant, took a "dog-and-pony show" to Toronto, New York, Boston and Montreal. In each of these cities Richards explained to the faithful what a great deal Dome Canada was for Dome Petroleum; how the offering would soon mean that Dome would have $400 million of federal government money injected into exploration on its lands. But during that tour Richards also had acquisitions on his mind, in particular the list of 20 or so companies that his takeover specialists had drawn up for him. Dome already had its corporate eye on a number of companies known to be on the block. It was to bid for Uno-Tex, an American company that would ultimately be bought by Bob Blair's Nova Corporation (as Alberta Gas Trunk Line had now been renamed), and also for Candel, which eventually went to Gus Van Wielingen's Sulpetro. These were, however, in Richards' mind "little deals," just a few hundred million dollars, mere corporate appetizers for a company with Dome's ambitions. Richards felt it was time for a really big deal.

HBOG's financial, operating and asset statistics made Richards salivate. It also fitted in so well with Dome. It paid a high tax rate, and thus could benefit from the large tax write-off Dome had accumulated through its aggressive exploration program. Its landbank was huge, and because of the Siebens acquisitions was in many places adjacent with Dome's. Its production was clean, and its balance sheet was a joy to behold. To most people that balance sheet, with its tiny long-term debt, would have clearly indicated the company's financial prudence. To Richards it indicated underutilization. In fact, both Maier and Haskeyne also thought that HBOG should be more aggressive. But they were to get little chance to put their plans into effect.

Bill Richards was already drawing up his battle plan.

The Conoco stake was obviously crucial to control, but an equally important issue was how Dome could find a way to pay for such a massive acquisition.

In terms of the Conoco stake, Richards and his acquisition team had soon worked out the "tax magic" that would make their deal fly and, typically, allow them effectively to pay more for Conoco's HBOG shares than under a straightforward cash offer. They would buy Conoco shares in the American market and then swap those shares for Conoco's HBOG stake. Such a share swap would be tax-free, as opposed to a cash offer, which would be taxable.

Astonishingly, very little thought was given to what Dome would do after it acquired Conoco's stake — as to whether, and if so, when and how, it would acquire the rest of HBOG, including the 10.1% chunk owned by the Bay. It was typical of Richards' brash self-confidence that it was merely assumed that once the Conoco stake was acquired, the rest of the deal would simply fall into place. Dome would simply borrow the money for the first half of the deal from the banks, and the rest could be worked out later, probably by issuing Dome shares to swap with minority HBOG shareholders. Debt could be reduced by selling off parts of HBOG, such as the Indonesian producing properties, outright. Dome could also sell off percentage shares in HBOG to Dome's "family and friends," companies to whom it was corporately related, like Dome Mines, Dome Canada and Trans-Canada PipeLines, or with which it had exploration agreements, principally Maligne Resources — the oil and gas arm of Dow Chemical Canada. The family and friends were not consulted before Dome made its move on Conoco. It was naturally assumed they would be only too grateful to participate. In the end, those four companies found themselves drawn inexorably into Dome's financial quagmire, paying huge amounts of money to get a piece of Dome's increasingly frantic action.

The way in which Jack Gallagher learned about the takeover seems almost astonishing. He was wandering around Dome's executive suite looking for Bill Richards when he came upon a meeting. He asked them what they were discussing. They told him they were planning the takeover of HBOG. Gallagher seemed enthusiastic and offered to make a preliminary visit to Conoco chairman, Ralph Bailey, to sound him out on a deal.

When Richards revealed his latest brainchild to the rest of Dome's senior management, the sheer size of the deal prompted some misgivings. Richards pointed out, as ever, that this would enable them to play in the big leagues, shoulder to shoulder with the multinationals — a prospect that always appealed to Gallagher. Indeed, this deal would make them the biggest in Canada, bigger than Imperial Oil, the previously acknowledged lord of Canadian oil. Gallagher would be the chairman of a company that had outstripped Canada's oldest and largest oil giant, a company that had a 70-year start on Dome, that had been a powerful force when Gallagher was born and had a coast-to-cast empire when Dome consisted of just Jack and his secretary. When things turned sour, Gallagher would claim that HBOG hadn't been *his* idea, that he had been against it but felt he shouldn't step in the way of the "younger men." But at the time Gallagher liked the idea of being bigger than Imperial, of passing his old classmate and rival, Jack Armstrong, Imperial's chairman. And all this even before the Beaufort had been brought in.

Perhaps one of the reasons strategy for the second half of the deal wasn't discussed in detail was that Richards knew it would have to involve the issue of Dome shares. That was a prospect that never sat easy with Jack Gallagher. In Gallagher's eyes, Dome shares, however much they soared, were always too low in price, because he knew that the Beaufort gusher would be coming in any day. Until that day, issuing more shares was tantamount to giving the company away.

However, issuing equity for the second half of HBOG was in fact necessary for another reason. Dome could claim, by buying out HBOG's U.S. majority shareholder, that it was "Canadianizing" the company.

The irony was, however, that HBOG's overall Canadian ownership was actually higher than Dome's. The minority shares of HBOG were overwhelmingly in Canadian hands, so if Dome could issue its own shares in exchange for this HBOG minority, then it would be acquiring more Canadian shareholders and increasing the level of its Canadian ownership — a commitment it had made to the federal government as part of the negotiations over Dome Canada. Simply offering Dome Petroleum shares for sale would present further ownership problems since the company was so popular south of the border. Thus the share swap seemed an ideal way to make sure new Dome shares finished up in Canadian hands. However, all these details could be worked out later. This approach proved to be an almost fatal error.

In any case, the immediate prospect — getting hold of Conoco's 52.9% of HBOG — seemed daunting enough. Buying a U.S. company's shares and then swapping them with the company in return for its holdings in a Canadian subsidiary was not a new idea. Calgary multi-millionaire Ron Southern's construction-based empire, Atco, had bought shares of U.S.-based International Utilities and then swapped them to gain control of Canadian Utilities. What was different, however, was the size of the transaction involved.

Jack and Bill and the Giant

Conoco dwarfed *any* Canadian corporation, let alone Dome. With annual revenues in 1980 of U.S.$19 billion and earnings of over U.S. $1 billion, it ranked seventeenth among all U.S. industrial firms in assets, and tenth among U.S. petroleum companies. It employed 41,500 people in more than 20 countries and had not only huge petroleum but also coal and chemical operations. To gauge what such a mammoth corporation might be worth, Richards sent for a report from the investment firm, John S. Herold Inc., whose valuation of oil companies were regarded as the most authoritative available. When Richards and his team saw the valuation of Conoco, they realized that the company's shares looked very cheap. They were trading on the New York Stock Exchange at little more than U.S.$50, but Herold indicated their asset value to be a whopping U.S.$150 or more.

Indeed, as Richards' group brainstormed over Conoco, there was the almost inevitable suggestion that Dome might go for *all* of the U.S. gaint, spin off the U.S. and other overseas assets and wind up with the HBOG stake for almost nothing. Dome always made a point of looking at all alternatives, no matter how audacious, but the prospect of actually taking a run at Conoco reportedly frightened even

Richards. A limited share purchase and swap was thought the best strategy.

Jack Gallagher was due to visit Stamford for a board meeting of U.S. mining giant Texasgulf, of which he was a director, and he phoned Conoco's Bailey, whom he already knew, to suggest he might drop by. At that visit, Gallagher broached a share swap. Bailey revealed that Conoco's board had thought about buying in its own shares because they were considered to be so cheap. Dome's proposal might be one way of achieving that. Gallagher also took along some projections made by the acquisitions team. They indicated that if Dome were to take Conoco's HBOG stake and then sell HBOG's Indonesian producing properties back to the U.S. company, the direct revenue from Indonesia would be greater than HBOG dividends, even if these dividends were escalated at 20% per annum over the coming five years.

Gallagher came away from the meeting with the impression that Bailey was far from opposed to Dome's proposal.

On April 22, Gallagher, accompanied by Richards, visited Bailey again. This time Conoco's chief executive was more reticent. However, he explained to the two men that he'd been advised that he couldn't negotiate; that he could listen but that the Dome executives shouldn't leave any paper behind. Gallagher and Richards thought Bailey's stance was related to the tax-free nature of their proposed share swap, and that Conoco believed the deal might become taxable if it appeared that Bailey had in any way participated in organizing it. Conoco was subsequently to claim that Bailey's silence indicated hostility to the deal. However, as Gallagher and Richards drove back from Stamford to Manhattan to discuss the situation with financial *eminence grise* Mark Millard, they were both convinced that Bailey was amenable to a deal. From Millard's Park Avenue office at Shearson Loeb Rhoades, they began to set in motion the tender offer for Conoco's shares, which would then be swapped for Conoco's stake in HBOG. They called Dome's personable U.S. legal counsel, Bob Helman, at his giant Chicago-based law firm, Mayer, Brown and Platt. Helman had been associated with Dome since the early 1970s when he had helped with right-of-way negotiations for the Cochin pipeline across Illinois, Iowa and Indiana. He had later been highly successful in handling suits against other companies and had worked on Dome's plan to increase its holdings in its own parent, Dome Mines. Following Dome's seizure of control of TransCanada PipeLines, he had started representing that company too.

As soon as Gallagher and Richards told him what they planned, he realized the huge amount of potential legal work involved, not merely in drawing up the offer document, but also in litigation if the offer should run into snags, or if rival suitors should appear. In contested takeovers, the first line of defence is always the law, with defence lawyers seeking to slow down aggressors in the jungles of corporate litigation. In the end, 35 of Mayer, Brown and Platt's 270 or so lawyers were to be involved in Dome's assault on Conoco.

Gallagher and Richards told Helman that they had not yet worked out the details of their offer, but that Wayne McGrath, who was at that moment in Houston, would be in Helman's Chicago office the following morning to start working on the details.

The corporate battle that followed was to be a good deal more contentious than any of them then imagined. It was also to have ramifications beyond anything they could conceive at the time.

Conoco's chairman, Ralph Bailey, was later accused of naivete in his dealings with Dome. He, for one, had certainly not thought through the implications of Dome's proposal. He mentioned Dome's visits neither to Morgan Stanley, his own investment banker, nor to Gerry Maier, for whom Dome's plans obviously had the greatest import. That was just one aspect of Bailey's behaviour that Maier was never able to understand.

Under U.S. Securities and Exchange regulations, only holdings of 5% or more of a public company's shares have to be revealed, so it is normal for an acquisitor company to accumulate shares of its corporate target more cheaply up to that level before it makes a public move at a higher price. Dome had been buying Conoco shares surreptitiously on the NYSE, but the purchases were going very slowly and Richards soon saw that accumulating 5% would take an excessive time.

Soon after Gallagher and Richards had returned to Calgary, they had decided on their offer for Conoco. They would offer U.S.$65 a share for between 14 million and 22 million shares, that is, between 13% and 20% of the company. The cost of that purchase, if successful, would lie between U.S.$910 million and U.S.$1.43 billion. It was an extraordinarily large amount of money, especially considering the fact that it would bring them just over half of their real target, HBOG.

For the Canadian banks, however, the issue wasn't whether they would lend Dome the money. The issue was which of them could lend Dome the most.

9
Dome and the Banks: The Open Vault

"Behind all its global responsibility and impersonal style, banking is still a 'people business.' ... It may be the most personal business of all, for it always depends on the original concept of credit, meaning trust. However complex and mathematical the business has become, it still depends on the assessment of trust by individuals with very human failings."
ANTHONY SAMPSON
THE MONEY LENDERS

The 7,300 branches of Canada's five major chartered banks — the Royal Bank of Canada, the Canadian Imperial Bank of Commerce, the Bank of Montreal, the Bank of Nova Scotia and the Toronto-Dominion Bank — are a national symbol of financial security. Clustered around the major intersections of Canada's cities and towns, they are the bases of five gigantic pyramids of power at the apexes of which stand five of the most powerful men in Canada. In the opening three years of the 1980s, those pyramids were to be rocked by tremors emanating both from home and abroad. At home, four of the five chief executives were to become more deeply and personally involved in the finances of one company than at any time in Canadian history. The reason was that never in Canadian history had the banks so exposed themselves to the fortunes of a single cash-hungry company. The company was Dome Petroleum. For the chief executives involved, it was a uniquely messy and distasteful experience.

The CEOs of Canada's major chartered banks seldom rub shoulders with mere mortals. They live in a rarefied world of deep-carpeted corner offices, limousine back-seats, corporate jets and person-to-person calls or discreet meetings with Canada's corporate elite and its political and mandarin establishments. Their public appearances are, as far as possible, restricted to speeches at gatherings of shareholders or business groups, where they dispense homilies on financial prudence, the evils of inflation and the absence of free lunches.

Being "apart" from normal humanity is, as John Kenneth Galbraith

111

once pointed out, an almost essential part of their image. "A banker need not be popular," he wrote, "indeed a good banker in a healthy capitalist society should probably be much disliked. People do not wish to trust their money to a hail-fellow-well-met but to a misanthrope who can say no."

The banker's ability to say no can, at a personal or corporate level, result in considerable frustration and resentment. However, at the national level it is a quality fondly cherished by a country with a prevailing concern for security.

Canada's big five banks are by far the largest financial institutions in Canada and among the largest banks in the world. They are highly autonomous units. Since, under the Bank Act, nobody is permitted to hold more than 10% of any bank's shares, they have tended to become self-perpetuating bodies whose leadership is selected and groomed within the organization. Of the four chief executives who were to become embroiled with Dome, angry with each other and locked in sometimes acrimonious debate with their banking confreres abroad, only one did not fit into this category, Bill Mulholland, chairman and CEO of the Bank of Montreal. Mulholland, a Harvard MBA born in Albany, New York, had been elected president of the Montreal in 1974 after a five-year stint as president and chief executive of the Churchill Falls (Labrador) Corporation Limited. In that job he had masterminded the construction of the second largest hydro plant in North America, finished in 1974 at a cost of $930 million. Before that he had worked for 17 years with Morgan Stanley, the doyen of New York investment banks. Mulholland was brought to the Montreal to shake it up, and he did just that. Feisty and arrogant, he moved the bank forcefully into international markets and told his staff to be aggressive about going after business at home. Going after business meant lending more money.

Mulholland's counterpart at the CIBC was Russell Harrison. Harrison had been born and raised in Grandview, Manitoba, and educated at the University of Manitoba. He joined the CIBC following military service during World War II in Europe. Thence began a steady advance up the corporate pyramid: assistant manager, Hamilton; assistant manager, Toronto: head of the bank's operations in Quebec and then, by 1969, executive vice-president and chief general manager in CIBC's Toronto head office. Harrison was appointed to the board in 1970, appointed president in 1973 and three years later, ascended the last step to the apex, becoming both chairman and chief executive officer. Harrison's autocratic style caused his subordinates to regard him with a combination of respect and fear. He tended to lose his temper easily, and as Dome's lead banker, his blood pressure would rise frequently in the coming two years.

112

The third, and youngest, of the four banking protagonists was Dick Thomson of the Toronto-Dominion. Thomson, with an establishment background, an engineering degree and a Harvard MBA, had been on the fast track at the T-D from the time he first joined in 1957. After six years learning the ropes in the branches, he was appointed assistant to the president in 1963. He became chief general manager in 1968, a director in 1971, president in 1972, CEO in 1977 and chairman and CEO in 1978. Thomson may have been the most youthful of the four, but he was strictly a man in the traditional banking mould. Thomson certainly encouraged his staff to be aggressive, but he also liked to see his loans well secured, backed up with good, solid assets. He also regarded himself primarily as the custodian of the Toronto-Dominion Bank, not the entire banking system. That attitude was to lead to some harsh criticism from some of his colleagues, in particular Bill Mulholland at the Montreal. Thomson was not inclined to fly off the handle like Harrison and Mulholland. After the Dome affair, however, it was reported that when he had to walk south from Adelaide Street to the T-D Centre on King Street in Toronto, instead of walking through First Canadian Place, home of the Montreal, he would walk around the giant complex.

Finally came Rowland Frazee, a mild-mannered man with a professorial look. Frazee was a native of Halifax and had joined Canada's most prominent bank, the Royal, in 1939 before going off to military service and then, after the war, a degree in commerce at Dalhousie. He rejoined the bank in 1948, ascending through the branches and the supervision of regions to a vice-presidency in Toronto in 1970. In 1972, he became chief general manager and a year later a director. He was appointed president in 1977, and chairman and CEO in 1980.

The Royal had a reputation in the banking community as a "class act." It had also always been the number one oil and gas bank in Canada since the Second World War. It was always the Royal's customers that the other banks were after. Significantly, the Royal's exposure to Dome was considerably less than that of its three corporate colleagues. At no time during subsequent events was Rowland Frazee seen to lose his cool. But then given his smaller exposure, he also had less reason.

These four men — Mulholland, Harrison, Thomson and Frazee — shared between them a combined total of 130 years of banking experience. During their corporate climbs, they had assessed thousands of loans; stared into the eyes of thousands of lenders. They read balance sheets with X-ray eyes. The ratios of financial prudence were burned permanently into the circuits of their brains. Via their branches, they were plugged into every nook and cranny of business activity in the country. But also, via their exalted positions, they were plugged into Ottawa thinking, to which, over the years, they and their predecessors had become acutely sensitive. Their fiercest critics saw that relationship as a conspiracy. But the CEOs themselves regarded being in tune with national priorities as a part of their responsibility, part of being the very best kind of Canadians.

One of the problems for the banks during the latter 1970s and early 1980s was that they were operating in uncharted waters, primarily those through which the waves of OPEC power surged. The other problem — related to the first — was that political sensitivity in the wake of the National Energy Program was to lead the banks to finance the pursuit of a disastrous policy: the buy-out of foreign-owned oil at the top of the market.

There had been a revolution in energy banking as a result of the OPEC crises and rocketing oil prices of the previous decade. Sheik Yamani had come, like Cinderella's godmother, and waved his magic wand across the world of oil. A great deal of the stardust had fallen on the Albertan producers.

Bobby Brown and the Bankers

Before OPEC, petroleum financing had been just another area of commercial business — and not a particularly favoured one. Indeed, Canadian oilmen frequently expressed a certain bitterness about the eastern financial establishment's attitude towards them. They were also bitter because the major banks had always seemed far more willing to lend money to foreign-controlled oil to buy out Canadian companies than lend Canadian companies money to expand. Also, because of different attitudes and better tax treatment for oil and gas investors in the U.S., many Canadian oilmen had found it far easier to raise money south of the border. Dome's origins were a clear example of that.

But bankers were also reluctant to finance oilmen because oilmen tended, by nature, to be gamblers, an activity viewed with utmost distaste in the banking community.

There were examples of bankers developing relationships with individual oilmen, but these tended, if anything, to demonstrate the uneasiness of the fit. The classic example of that uneasy fit was the relationship that developed after the Second World War between Bobby Brown, the flamboyant head of Home Oil, and Neil McKinnon, head of the CIBC.

McKinnon had joined the CIBC at the very base of the pyramid as a boy of 14 and rapidly worked his way up to its pinnacle. In his

114

classic account of McKinnon's ultimate removal from power in *The Canadian Establishment*, Peter Newman noted: "It was his vaulting self-confidence that made Neil McKinnon both the best banker of his generation and the only chairman of a major Canadian bank ever to be removed by his own board of directors."

McKinnon believed he had been given personal power in order to wield it and for many years he chose to support Brown, one of the oilpatch's most colourful characters. Before the Second World War, Brown, a baby-faced charmer, had already entered the oil business with his father in Alberta's Turner Valley. By the time he went to Ottawa to serve as a naval procurement officer, he had also developed the style of high living which was to be his hallmark. He set himself up in the Chateau Laurier and proceeded on a round of lavish entertainment. After the war, he eventually returned to Alberta and presided over a rapid expansion in his company, Federated Petroleums. With McKinnon's help, he acquired properties from Imperial Oil and later — in a typically audacious move — merged with the much larger Home Oil and then wound up in control of it through an intricate pyramid of holding companies.

McKinnon supported Brown in an even more ambitious — and ultimately abortive — attempt to gain control of TransCanada PipeLines, but then, in his greatest gamble of all, Bobby Brown broke the rules. When Prudhoe Bay had been discovered, Brown had embarked on a scheme so ambitious it bordered on megalomania: it was an attempt to gain control of the field's discoverer, U.S. giant Atlantic Richfield, through the buying of shares in the market. Brown also committed large amounts of money to earn interests in Prudhoe Bay lands. However, in searching for ever more money to pursue his dream, he turned to another bank, borrowing $12 million from the Bank of Nova Scotia. The stately piles of the Commerce and the Nova Scotia sat facing each other across King Street in Toronto, but for a major customer to walk across the street from one to the other was an almost unforgivable sin.

Lying in an intensive care unit in a Calgary hospital after a heart attack, Brown received a letter from the head office of the Commerce in Toronto. The letter requested that, within a month, by August 20, 1970, Brown should present to the Commerce a mutually agreeable plan showing how he intended to repay the $9.4 million outstanding in his personal account. The letter, it was reported, struck Brown "like a dagger in his heart." When he attempted to call McKinnon in Toronto, he was told that the CIBC's chairman was away on holiday and nobody knew where. Everything seemed to hinge on the drilling of a well at Prudhoe Bay, the results of which would come in before the bank's deadline for repayment proposals.

115

On August 7, the final testing was to take place. Brown took the calls from his sickbed, with his key staff around him. At 10 P.M., Brown was told the well had struck "pure drinking water." The result forced Brown to sell control of Home Oil, and finally negotiate a sale with Toronto-based gas utility Consumers' Gas.

In the end there was a rapprochement with Neil McKinnon, and the Commerce lent Brown $9 million to help pay off his debt with the Nova Scotia, but Brown had given the banking community some scares and the banking community didn't like scares. The $9 million was only lent after Brown's remaining Home stake — worth $13 million at prevailing market prices — had been pledged as collateral.

Eight months after he lost control of Home, Brown died. Three years later, McKinnon himself was removed from the CIBC after a boardroom coup.

Jack Gallagher could not have been more different to Brown, an alcoholic who rejoiced in a $3 million executive jet with gold-plated taps fashioned in the shape of dolphins in the washroom. Dome's chairman, on the other hand, was frugal and a fitness fanatic. Nevertheless, there were also remarkable similarities between the two — or at least between their companies. Both poured money into a "northern vision," both attempted to gain control of TransCanada PipeLines, both had the Commerce as their lead bank and had the Commerce's chairman — McKinnon in the case of Brown, Harrison in the case of Gallagher — as a close associate.

However, Dome's northern vision was primarily funded by the federal government; it succeeded in gaining control of TCPL; and Russell Harrison was forced in the end to *encourage* Dome to deal with the other banks because its financial demands were far too large for his own to handle.

Courting the New Lords of Oil

The principal change, however, was in the prevailing relationship between oil companies and banks. In Brown's time, the relationship he had with McKinnon was the exception rather than the rule. By the beginning of 1981, however, banks were tripping over each other to curry favour with the new lords of Canadian oil. The reasons were threefold: there had been a revolution in the oil business, a revolution in Canadian nationalist politics and finally a revolution in banking. All had their roots in the OPEC crisis.

The OPEC revolution and the rising oil prices had had a dramatic effect on the "bankability" of the oil business. Any entity's attractiveness to bankers depends on its collateral and its income: what does it own? what does it earn? The rising price of oil and gas throughout the 1970s meant that any company's petroleum reserves — the oil and gas it had discovered and which sat "stored" in its natural reservoirs underground — became worth much more. The anticipated further increase in petroleum prices made this value even greater. Meanwhile, projected oil price increases also increased earnings projections. All these factors made bankers more willing to lend money to the oil business. The oil business, meanwhile, was more than eager for money to invest in its own much brighter prospects. New projects, moreover, were of an unprecedented size: multi-billion dollar tar sands plants and other elaborate forms of petroleum extraction, as well as gigantic schemes for exploration in, and transportation from, distant frontier regions.

Also, insofar as the share price of publicly traded companies lagged behind the increase in these values, or failed to take into account future increases in value, oil companies became more attractive takeover targets — a fact of which Bill Richards was by now firmly convinced. Banks provided the financing for these takeovers. This trend had been given a powerful shove by the National Energy Program, which had declared its target of 50% Canadian ownership of the oil business by 1990. But FIRA had earlier put foreign companies effectively out of the running for major acquisitions, which were, in the latter half of the 1970s, carried out almost exclusively by Canadian-controlled companies.

When Petro-Canada had made the biggest — at the time — takeover in Canadian history, the $1.46 billion acquisition of Pacific Petroleums in 1978, Joel Bell, PetroCan's senior vice president of finance, had simply made a call to the Royal in Calgary and said he'd like to borrow "one and a quarter," that is, one and a quarter billion U.S. dollars.

When Bob Blair needed a couple of hundred million to buy Husky shares in the market, Ced Ritchie, head of the Scotia, and Hartland McDougall, chief corporate finance man at the Montreal, had flown out to Calgary over a weekend to arrange the loan.

Meanwhile, OPEC had also accelerated trends that were revolutionizing the supply of banking funds. Suddenly the emphasis of banking changed worldwide. The new watchword was not profits, but asset growth. The name of the game became to get new loans, "new business on the books." The new stars of the Canadian banking order became aggressive young money salesmen, merchants of megabucks. Many of the international loans were organized through banking syndicates lending billions of dollars to developing or Eastern-bloc countries. These deals were doubly attractive. On the one hand, their huge size meant big profits with relatively little administrative effort. On the other, since they were loans to countries, they couldn't go bad. Countries just couldn't default. At least that was the theory.

The same theory applied at home. Large banks have always preferred lending to large companies, because big companies like doing big deals requiring large loans with large profits. Moreover, size in itself has always been considered an indicator of financial soundness. You couldn't have become big without being prudent. The banks liked to trumpet the "special attention" they paid to small business and were keen to stress that more than 90% of all business loans went to small business. However, that 90% figure related to the number of loans, not the volume of lending. Although loans of less than $200,000 might well account for over 90% of the total number of loans, while loans over $5 million accounted for less than 1%, by 1981, $5 million-plus loans were responsible for half the volume of business lending. In the decade up to 1981, although volume through loans of less than $200,000 had increased by a factor of five, that of those above $5 million had increased twelvefold. Moreover, more and more of the big loans were going to Alberta, where companies had the biggest plans and the biggest borrowing requirements.

In October, 1978, Blake Ashforth, vice-president and general manager of the Royal in Alberta, noted that loans, lines of credit and other forms of financial support by all banks to the petroleum products industry had increased from $300 million in 1970 to around $3 billion. But what Ashforth or any of his banking counterparts could never have suspected was that within three years, four of the big five — the Commerce, the T-D, the Montreal and the Royal — would have loans to just one company, Dome Petroleum, for more than $4 billion.

When talking about such exposure, even $4 billion might seem relatively small set against the four banks' total assets, that is, mainly loans, of $195 billion at the end of 1980. However, banks measure their profits in percentages of 1¢ per $100 of assets, and the important figure to set against exposure is not assets but the banks' capital, the only real cushion to depositors in the event of bad loans. At the end of 1980, the combined capital of all four banks was $6.5 billion. That meant that each $1 of permanent capital supported $30 of loans. Put another way, if just one-thirtieth of loans went sour, then the banks' entire capital could be wiped out. Dome's ultimate exposure meant that if it went under, then it had the potential to carry half of Canada's four major banks' capital with it. But of course, at the beginning of 1981, the thought of Dome Petroleum going under seemed ludicrous. It was the smartest company around. Moreover, its acceptability was clearly signalled not only by its obvious popularity in Ottawa, but also by the appointment, in 1980, of Jack Gallagher to the board of the CIBC.

118

There is no more obvious sign of sanction by Canada's business establishment than a seat on the board of one of the big five banks. "The executive board meetings of the five largest banks," said Peter Newman, "represent the greatest source of non-governmental power in the country. During these deliberations are formed, strengthened, and multiplied the kinships through which the Canadian Establishment protects its existence and swells its authority."

Corporate elite theorists often point to the Canadian banks — the vast agglomerations of power represented by their boards of directors — as *prima facie* evidence of corporate conspiracy. But it is more subtle than that. Bank boards are not conspiracies. They represent very — indeed, the most — exclusive clubs. To be a bank director is to stand in the upper echelon of business power, to have been dubbed a knight in the highest order of Canadian corporate clout. Most important of all, obtaining funds becomes a whole lot easier.

Gallagher, in fact, did not reach, or at least accept, this fondly sought position until 1980, although he had been a member of CIBC's International Advisory Board for several years. But Dome had already been marked as an important source of business. Dick Thomson of the T-D could be lured easily into the Dome Tower if he was in Calgary; Russell Harrison, of course, had Gallagher on his board and was always happy to chat with Dome's chairman. As for Bill Mulholland, Gallagher would sometimes just poke his head out of a board meeting at Dome Mines in Toronto and ask a secretary to call the chairman of the Montreal, who happened to be upstairs in First Canadian Place. Within minutes, Mulholland would have invited Jack up and would be waiting with a beaming smile and an outstretched hand for the Dome chairman.

The CEO's accommodating attitude was the gentlemanly veneer on what had turned out to be a desperate scramble for increasing shares of new oil industry business. The competition both to increase one's percentage of overall petroleum lending and to "steal" the position of lead banker to an oil company from another of the big five had become increasingly fierce. It had also led to a situation where traditional credit measures and ratios were ignored in the rush to obtain new business. Debt-to-equity ratios, for example, were allowed to grow far above traditionally prudent standards. This ratio, measuring the proportion of debt commitments versus the firm's risk capital, or equity, is a critical measure of a firm's ability to withstand a downturn. Generally, the higher the relative level of debt, with correspondingly high levels of interest payments, the greater the vulnerability to a downturn. These ratios were allowed to grow out of line because the idea of an oil industry downturn was almost inconceivable. Petroleum price inflation was projected to buoy the industry for at least the coming decade. To keep up appearances and pay lip service to traditional measures of prudence, the banks increasingly gave their clients advice on how to get around their own lending rules, especially how to finance "off the balance sheet." When banks looked at their customers' loan requirements, they included the interest payments on existing debts almost as a matter of course. That meant they were effectively lending companies money to pay interest, an activity that would have caused bankers to shudder not many years before — and was to cause them to shudder not many months afterwards.

Opening the Vaults to Dome

A banker's status depends very much on the size of the loans he or she handles. The Albertan head offices of the major banks were now handing out the biggest loans in the country. Approval still came ultimately from the East, but each of the banks very conspicuously beefed up its Calgary operations. In mid-1979, the Montreal had moved its chairman, Fred McNeil, to Calgary, although the significance of the move was a little more cosmetic than real, since McNeil was close to retiring on his ranch near Calgary. Nevertheless, the Montreal also announced that it would be building a $150 million office complex in Calgary, featuring a 57-storey tower that would be the largest in the West. The tower would sit directly across Seventh Avenue from the Dome Tower, which already had the T-D's head office in Alberta underneath it, the Scotia's head office beside it, the Royal's headquarters behind it and the Commerce's just a block away. The banks even seemed to be paying architectural court to their new favourite.

At the same time, new foreign banks — thanks to the change in the 1980 Bank Act which allowed them to open up branches in Canada — were arriving every month in Calgary looking for business. However, they were having considerable trouble finding it. Some Canadian bankers declared it almost immoral for a Canadian company to borrow from a foreign bank. The foreign banks, meanwhile, were astonished by the gay abandon with which their Canadian counterparts appeared to shovel money out of their vaults.

The foreign bankers, particularly those from the U.S., were the emissaries of some of the biggest banks in the world and not given to being loan-shy, but they were astonished by the volumes of money being lent to individual companies by Canada's big five. The U.S. had strict federal laws about how much could be lent to any company, so large loans in the U.S. were characterized by widespread syndication — that is, assembling banking consortia to share the loan, and

120

the risk. The name of the game in Canada, they discovered to their surprise, seemed to be to take as much of a large loan as possible, indeed preferably all of it.

The New York bankers with their red suspenders and their large 8 A.M. cigars would go around "marketing" the financial executives of the oil companies, trying to discover if there was any vague hope that the companies might do them the favour of borrowing some money from them. But companies like Dome said no thanks, they had lots of money already. Perhaps, however, they might get around to them eventually. Bill Richards came out publicly and said that Dome only went to foreign banks for "small change."

Indeed, Bill Richards almost made a point of saying things that horrified the bankers. For all senior bankers, inflation is declared to be financial enemy number one. But Richards would sit over lunch with them and tell them how energy inflation was going to go on forever and *what a great thing it was*, since it was going to make Dome so big and rich. They may have had to swallow and even perhaps wince a little, but the problem was that they agreed with him. While decrying rising prices on the one hand, they were, on the other, making loans in the energy industry on the assumption that petro-leum-price inflation would be maintained. If it wasn't, they were all in trouble.

From a traditional banker's point of view, Dome was hardly a model of financial conservatism. Indeed, one constant about its financial approach was that it had always sought to stretch itself to the limit. For most of its history it had spent each year approximately 2.5 times its cash flow, that is, two and a half times as much as it actually had available to spend from its own operations. That was a highly unusual ratio for a company that hadn't issued any new shares in 25 years. Apart from highly innovative sources of capital such as drilling funds, and a well-secured loan of $150 million from the giant Prudential Insurance Company, most of that money came from the banks. And after the acquisition phase began, it came in increasingly enormous amounts.

The purchase of TransCanada PipeLines shares in 1978 and 1979 had been paid for by an issue of floating rate term-preferred shares to the CIBC. The Siebens financing had effectively been arranged at a meeting between Richards, Gallagher and Thomson of the T-D. The $700 million for the Kaiser acquisition was raised through phone calls from Gallagher to Thomson, Harrison and Mulholland. Of course, such enormous loans involved a great deal more than a telephone conversation between members of the chosen few and their bankers. There were vast amounts of documentation to go through as well as the arrangement of appropriate security, but this was left to lesser mortals at the bank and Dome. The important thing was that Gallagher had a direct line to the top.

The Kaiser deal was a good example of the banks' jealousy of business. The Royal, the largest of the banks and generally acknowledged as the most sophisticated in terms of oil and gas, had done very little business with Dome before, although Dome's chief financial officer, Peter Breyfogle, had set up a $200 million line of credit with it. Dome decided it would "let the Royal in" for $100 million of the Kaiser deal. But the other three banks reportedly wouldn't allow it. They wanted the whole $700 million for themselves, so the Royal was excluded.

In 1980, Dome's long-term debt doubled to $2.6 billion. But even that massive figure in no way reflected the company's ambitions. Its financial staff projected its requirements would soon surpass the permanent capital of all the Canadian banks if its schemes were brought to fruition. And that *excluded* acquisitions.

Dome's immediate need was for U.S.$1.5 billion to buy the Conoco shares it intended to swap for Conoco's stake in HBOG. There was never any doubt that the company would obtain the funds, despite the fact the money would represent the largest corporate loan in Canadian history.

Now that "Canadianizing" takeovers in the oil business had been given the blessing of the federal government through the National Energy Program, it was difficult to imagine how such an eminently attractive — and nationally responsible — deal could come unstuck. One of Gallagher's first calls was to Dick Thomson of the T-D. Gallagher later told associates that Thomson's initial reaction was that his own bank, the Commerce and the Montreal could manage the loan between the three of them. The Royal wouldn't be needed. However, the Royal was eventually permitted a piece of the action. Gallagher put through calls to the other banks' senior executives. Then Breyfogle, who was at a conference of institutional investors in Toronto, got a call from Calgary asking him to contact the Commerce's main oil and gas banker, Frank Duncanson, who was also at the conference, and start sorting out the details. Breyfogle and Duncanson closeted themselves in Toronto and Breyfogle touched base with other senior bank executives before returning to Calgary to speak to the local bank officers.

It takes a highly qualified banker a week to clear a $50,000 mortgage. It took the banks about the same time to agree on the desirability and terms of the U.S.$1.5 billion loan to Dome Energy, a Dome subsidiary. The loan was due on January 31, 1983, but Dome had an option to extend its term to ten years. The rate was negotiated at $^3/_8$ of 1% over LIBOR (the London Interbank Offered Rate) the reference point for such loans. On May 5, when the tender offer for the Conoco shares was made, the LIBOR rate was $19^3/_{16}\%$. That meant that if the full loan was drawn down, annual interest payments (assuming rates stayed at that level) would amount to $350 million. However, all Dome could be sure of from HBOG was dividends of about $13 million. Getting its corporate hands on HBOG's entire cash flow was therefore crucial, otherwise the bank loan had the potential to suck Dome's coffers dry, however buoyant the price of, or market for, petroleum. This unpleasant prospect was, however, given only the slightest consideration.

The Dome Energy loan brought the lending to Dome of three of the big five — the T-D, the Montreal and the Commerce — to more than $1 billion each, by far the largest loans they had made to a single corporate customer. Only a handful of banks throughout the world had ever loaned a single company more than $1 billion. To have three banks *each* with over $1 billion to one customer was unprecedented. As for the Royal, Dome Energy represented its first major loan to Dome. It was generally perceived that the Royal had always had reservations about lending money to Dome. Ironically, it was now to come in for the biggest, and worst, loan of all.

10
Dome and Conoco: The Giant Killers

*" ... Bailey, Conoco's chairman, had shown a re-
luctance to take seriously an assault by such a piddling company as Dome Petroleum. He simply
couldn't believe that his shareholders, 'didn't love
him more than sixty-five dollars' worth,' as a source
close to him said. On May 27, he found out that
was far from the case."*

Early on the morning of Tuesday, May 5, 1981, Jack Gallagher
phoned Ralph Bailey and told him that Dome planned to make a cash
offer for Conoco shares public the following day. Bailey was shocked
but non-committal. Bailey called a stunned Gerry Maier in Calgary to
tell him that HBOG was Dome's ultimate target, and then spoke to
Conoco's lawyers and investment bankers, in particular, Morgan Stanley's Bob Greenhill. Greenhill in turn was astonished to learn that
Bailey had already had two meetings with Gallagher. Greenhill was
well aware that to have done anything but slam the door in Gallagher's
face was effectively to encourage him. Bailey had thus already made
a large tactical error. However, the other, and far more frightening
potential of the Dome tender offer was that if it was successful, it
would be obvious that Conoco was vulnerable to a takeover. If someone could buy 14 million or 22 million of its shares in the market,
then why not the whole lot? Later the same day Greenhill called Jack
Gallagher in Calgary and said Conoco would do a deal, but only if
Dome called off its tender offer. Gallagher declined.

After stock markets had closed for the day on May 5, at 5:15 P.M.
Mountain Standard Time, Dome issued a news release revealing its
plans. The public battle had begun.

Dome's announcement spurred frantic trading on North American
stock markets. The following day, May 6, Conoco topped the NYSE's
"most active" list, surging U.S.\$6.62 to U.S.\$56.50, while HBOG was
the leading trader both on the American and Toronto stock exchanges.
By May 7, HBOG had jumped \$9, or 40%, to \$31.75 in just a week.
Dome, meanwhile, soared over \$100, thus emphasizing the need for

that five-for-one stock split, which was dutifully approved at Dome's annual meeting on May 8.

The investment communities both north and south of the border were mesmerized at what appeared to be yet another brilliant move by Dome. In Ottawa there was more than a quiet satisfaction that Dome was not merely "Canadianizing," but apparently running rings around a far larger U.S. oil giant in the process.

Dome's tender offer was to close at midnight, New York time, on June 3, but for Conoco, the critical date was May 27, when those who offered shares to Dome lost their right of withdrawal. Conoco's investment bankers and its battery of lawyers thus had three weeks to spike Dome's guns. Greenhill was dispatched to Canada to find "white knights," the investment community's term for companies preferable as suitors to the takeover target. Teams from three prominent U.S. law firms, Skadden, Arps, Slate, Meagher & Flom; Dewey, Ballantine, Bushby, Palmer & Wood; and Davis Polk & Wardwell then set to Conoco's legal defence.

They chose the Oklahoma federal court as the battleground for the first skirmish. Suit was filed on May 11, and for the next two weeks, armies of lawyers beavered away interrogating executives at pre-trial discoveries, taking depositions and reviewing all relevant documents. Conoco's lawyers had argued that there were errors of detail in Dome's offer; that contrary to Dome's claims, the deal was likely to be taxable; and that the money borrowed by Dome to purchase the Conoco shares far exceeded the legal limits set out in U.S. federal banking legislation.

Meanwhile, in the public domain, battle was joined in an exchange of press releases and open letters between the two companies. The day the suit was filed, Dome issued a press release declaring itself to be "surprised and disappointed" at Conoco's adverse reaction. It noted that its tender offer was 30% above the market price of Conoco shares when the offer was made; reiterated that it had no intention of moving for control of Conoco; stressed that the share swap had been suggested in order to optimize the value of the offer to Conoco shareholders; and said it believed that the transaction was also "beneficial to Hudson [sic] Bay Oil & Gas in that Canadianization of this major oil and gas company will maximize the value of its assets and its contribution to oil self-sufficiency for Canada and North America."

The following day, May 12, a letter went to Conoco shareholders under Bailey's name declaring that the offer price was "grossly inadequate, since it represents a potential for control." Bailey portrayed Dome as attempting to force Conoco to sell its HBOG stake "at a price which is grossly inadequate," and on the basis of "highly questionable ... alleged tax benefits."

The letter also dragged the National Energy Program into the fray, pointing out that the NEP both depressed the value of Canadian oil assets owned by U.S. citizens and encouraged Canadian companies to acquire them. "The unfairness of such action raises serious questions not only for Conoco stockholders but also for the national interest of the United States. We believe it is imperative that our government consider what action should be taken so that U.S. citizens are not victimized by Canada depressing the value of their assets and then discriminating in favour of its nationals acquiring those assets at depressed values."

Gallagher, meanwhile, had requested a meeting with Bailey. However, Bailey's advisors, wary of the gaffes he had already made, were keeping him under wraps. The day after Bailey's letter to shareholders, a letter under Gallagher's name was sent by telex to Bailey seeking "to clarify what we consider to be a misunderstanding by you of our position." The letter strongly refuted the notion of "hostility" on Dome's part and stressed that Dome merely wished to negotiate for Conoco's HBOG stake. The sting in the letter's tail was the statement that even if Conoco sold its HBOG stake, that "would not necessarily lead to the withdrawal of our tender offer." Thus the threat of a total Conoco takeover was revived.

A reply the next day from Bailey reiterated the tax risks of Dome's proposed deal and said that Conoco would prefer a cash transaction. It also noted the implied threat of Gallagher's letter, suggesting that the notion that Dome would not necessarily withdraw its tender offer even if the HBOG stake was sold "raises serious questions as to the true motivation of your actions."

Meanwhile, however, Conoco's day in court approached. On May 22, the Friday before the Memorial Day weekend in the U.S., Dome presented itself in full force for the court hearing, bringing its entire executive suite down from Calgary for the day. But the company presented just one witness, Jack Gallagher. He was brilliant. Having been thoroughly coached for several days by Dome's legal team, he climbed on the stand at 7.30 A.M. to face Wall Street's most devious brains, and proceeded to wipe the floor with them. By three the same afternoon, Oklahoma federal judge Lee West had succumbed both to Dome's superior legal arguments and Jack Gallagher's charm. On May 26, Conoco's case was thrown out of court.

The Naked Giant

Throughout the three-week period between Dome's announcement and the effective close of its tender offer for Conoco shares, Bailey, Conoco's chairman, had shown a reluctance to take seriously an assault by such a piddling little company as Dome Petroleum. He simply couldn't believe that his shareholders "didn't love him more than sixty-five dollars' worth," as a source close to him said.

On May 27, he found out that was far from the case.

Bob Greenhill, meanwhile, had been trekking across Canada talking to potential white knights. However, the size and complexity of the deal, plus the required speed of action, made the emergence of such a figure of corporate chivalry unlikely. Morgan Stanley knew long before the date of the tender offer that Dome was going to get at least double the shares it sought offered to it. On May 27, 53 million shares, representing over half of Conoco's outstanding equity, were offered to Dome. Dome took the 22 million shares it wanted, accepting an appropriate proportion of each block offered, but for Conoco, those extra 31 million shares offered to Dome spelled disaster. They indicated Conoco was up for grabs. Indeed, Conoco's defence team was at one time concerned that Dome might be tempted to take up all 53% of shares offered. However, they realized that Dome was relatively small, and also that the Canadian company would have had to amend its tender offer document in order to take everything offered. What terrified them, however, was that a larger and wealthier company might come along and offer Dome a hefty premium for its stake and then snap up the other shares offered. And indeed in corporate lairs far larger than Dome's, the smell of blood was stirring the acquisitive instinct.

Gerry Maier and Dick Haskeyne had obviously not been idle throughout the three-week period between the announcement and effective close of the tender offer. They had, however, been largely helpless. Gerry Maier had called Bob Blair, the head of Nova Corp., to see if there might be a "fit" between HBOG and Nova subsidiary, Husky. However, a fit could not be found, and Blair pulled out of the contention after a couple of weeks. Maier also talked to the group of Canadian co-operatives that was being encouraged by the federal government to get into the energy business. Maier went with representatives of the group to Ottawa to visit Deputy Energy Minister Mickey Cohen and other EMR officials, but Maier felt the bureaucrats seemed eager for Dome to pull off its coup, and another potential white knight disappeared.

A few days after the announcement of its tender offer, Jack Gallagher had called Gerry Maier to explain what Dome was doing and to express the wish that HBOG would welcome Dome as the new majority shareholder. Maier was cool. He said that if Dome took Conoco's place then new nominations for board seats would of course be considered, but he would stay only if Dome adopted the same essentially hands-off attitude as Conoco.

Maier was deeply disappointed in Ralph Bailey and his disappointment increased throughout the takeover as the Conoco chairman remained completely inaccessible. However, HBOG's management received another severe blow when they got hold of a copy of Dome's loan agreement with the banks and discovered that CIBC was effectively the lead bank for the loan. It seemed like a betrayal because CIBC had been HBOG's single bank since 1926. Dick Haskeyne called local Commerce oil chief, Frank Duncanson, into his office and gave him a royal dressing down. Maier was to speak on the phone the next day with Commerce head, Russell Harrison. By the time Maier got through to Harrison, CIBC's chairman knew that HBOG's executives were fuming, and without a trace of apology, he leapt to the attack. Maier wasn't even given a chance to exchange pleasantries before Harrison started yelling that HBOG had no reason to be mad; CIBC wouldn't dream of revealing proprietary information in the case of a takeover. But of course Maier wasn't concerned with whether CIBC had revealed anything to Dome or not. That wasn't the point. It was just that after being the company's sole bankers for 55 years, he felt that CIBC owed HBOG a little more. Harrison seemed concerned that Maier not be allowed to treat him as cavalierly as Haskeyne had treated Duncanson. After all, he was a bank chairman and nobody gets angry with bank chairmen.

Following the success of Dome's tender offer, Conoco's defence team realized how vulnerable they were. They now had two priorities: to do a deal with Dome on the HBOG shares as quickly as possible; then find a friendly suitor who might take the free-floating block of Conoco shares hanging over the market as a means of fighting off predators. Greenhill called Richards in Calgary and suggested he come down to Stamford the weekend of May 30–31 to discuss the swap.

Smoke, Mirrors and $2 Billion

Richards set off in the Dome jet from Calgary with Steve Savidant and Wayne McGrath, stopping off in Chicago to pick up U.S. counsel Helman. When the four men rolled up in their limousine before the

Conoco headquarters in Stamford, they were unaware that watching them through the copper-tinted one-way glass of Ralph Bailey's office were not only Bailey and key Conoco executives, but also Charles Bronfman of the Seagram empire. The Bronfmans were just one of the powerful financial groups that had realized the significance of the massive over-offering of Conoco shares to Dome. Shortly after the Dome offer had closed, the Bronfmans had proposed to Bailey that Seagram might take a 35% stake in Conoco as a long-term investment. They certainly knew that the shares were available to them in the market. Bailey and his advisors had seemed receptive to the move. However, unknown to the Bronfmans, Bailey had, after their call, made a lightning overnight trip to visit his old friend Charles Waidelich, president of Oklahoma-based Cities Service, about a defensive merger between the two companies.

The scene being played out at the Conoco headquarters was one of corporate smoke and mirrors. Richards and the Dome team didn't realize that the Bronfmans were negotiating two floors above them. If they had, it would almost certainly have enabled them to drive a harder bargain. Indeed, they could have threatened to sell out to the Bronfmans. But the Bronfmans in turn didn't realize that Bailey, while apparently receptive to their advances, was desperately trying to negotiate an escape.

The Bronfmans were eventually to use that fact as an excuse for taking the gloves off and making an unfriendly offer for Conoco.

For the moment, however, as the Dome limousine rolled up, Conoco's immediate concern was to deal as quickly as possible with the squat, pugnacious little Dome president, a man who effectively carried 22 million of their shares in his pocket. They had to do a deal on their stake in HBOG and get their own shares back as soon as possible. Meanwhile, they had to keep smiling at the Bronfmans, because if the Bronfmans realized what they were trying to negotiate with Cities Service, they might well go straight to Richards and offer him a big profit for releasing his Conoco stake.

Richards and the Dome team were unwittingly kept virtually under guard in a conference room on the first floor, while the Bronfmans were negotiating in the third floor boardroom. Security men were posted to prevent stray lawyers or investment bankers from either side bumping into each other. Bailey, eager to make the Dome team think nothing else was happening at Stamford, told them that they were making him miss a golf game. However, most of the negotiations for the Conoco side were done by investment banker Greenhill and Joe Flom, a diminutive, pipe-smoking lawyer and master of the maze of legalities surrounding mergers and acquisitions.

In order to drive a harder and quicker bargain, Conoco's main negotiating tactic was to suggest to Richards and his crew that Conoco didn't *have* to swap its stake in HBOG. That would leave Dome sitting there with that big block of Conoco shares that didn't give them control, but which was costing them an arm and a leg in financing charges. Greenhill and Flom painted a picture of a potentially long, hard pull for Dome. The two sides would come together, then break, then come together again. Richards had a number of lengthy conversations over the phone with Gallagher back in Calgary. The Dome side hadn't even expected to do a deal that day, but after three hours one was struck. Moreover, it seemed like an expensive one. Dome agreed to exchange its 22 million Conoco shares plus U.S.$245 million for Conoco's HBOG stake. The total price was thus U.S.$1.675 billion, or just over Can$2 billion.

A number of explanations have been offered for the apparently high price that Dome paid: that Richards — believing that every petroleum asset was as cheap now as it would ever be — didn't believe that it *was* a high price; or that Gallagher wanted to get a deal through as quickly as possible to show that he was a man of his word and was really only interested in acquiring HBOG and not Conoco. But it also seems likely that Greenhill and Flom did manage, to some degree, to put the wind up the Dome team by painting a picture of Dome being left "hanging out" with 22 million Conoco shares, while interest charges gobbled up Dome's cash flow. Whatever the case, Richards effectively left Stamford that night with 53% of HBOG in his pocket.

The Sting in the Tail

On Monday, June 1, the announcement of the swap was made and paeans of praise to Dome's brilliance sounded throughout the Canadian press. One group, however, was less than ecstatic about Dome's victory — HBOG. Bailey called Maier early on the Monday morning to let him know that the controlling block had changed hands. Even though Gerry Maier had been expecting the call, the news still hurt. Later that morning, Maier got another call. An unfamiliar voice said: "Congratulations. You're now Canadian." Then the voice said: "Oh, hello Gerry, this is Jack." It was Jack Gallagher, welcoming Maier to what Gallagher liked to call "the Dome family." Gallagher's initial comment was not well received. "Thank you," replied Maier stiffly, "but I have to confess that I've always operated HBOG with my Canadian national hat on, and I've never thought of it any other way."

Gallagher invited Maier to lunch that day at the Calgary Country Club. Richards, who was obviously cock-a-hoop about having HBOG in his pocket, called Dick Haskeyne from the Dome jet over Manitoba, and invited him also. The meeting was strained. Whether or not Gallagher and Richards expected Maier and Haskeyne to express delight at Dome's new controlling position, it does seem likely that the Dome executives would have liked to engage at once in some "joint programs" that would enable Dome to get its hands on HBOG cash by selling HBOG assets.

Maier and Haskeyne, however, were extremely cool to such notions. Gallagher and Richards started talking about joint management meetings. Jack Gallagher thought they ought to get together every morning. Maier told him that such a situation would create terrible conflicts of interest. He didn't want to be unco-operative, Maier said, but he had the remainder of the shareholders to think of. He couldn't start directing expenditure according to Dome's wishes. That would create management and morale problems.

If Dome's management had held any thoughts about directing HBOG's activities with 53% of its equity, the meeting shattered these illusions. Maier was adamant about protecting the minority shareholders. If Dome wanted control, then it would have to buy them out. It was buying these shareholders out that was to drive Dome to the brink.

The largest remaining minority shareholder was the Hudson's Bay Company — known affectionately as the Fur Traders after their distant origins as merchants of beaver pelts — controlled now by Ken Thomson's International Thomson Organization. But Dome had already made a tactical error in dealing with the Fur Traders that was to cost them dearly. Even before the tender offer for Conoco had been announced, Bill Richards had received a call from Toronto investment dealer, Ivan de Souza, who was acting as an intermediary for Ken Thomson's right-hand man, Toronto lawyer John Tory. De Souza said the Bay was willing to offer its 10.1% of HBOG and had a figure of $40 to $45 a share in mind. Richards, believing he was in the driving seat, made what Tory and Thomson considered a derisively low offer, of around $27 a share. The offer seemed deliberately insulting because Dome itself was talking a range of value for HBOG of between $40 and $60. However, if it wanted all of HBOG, Dome needed to be sure of 90% of the shares to force the remainder to sell out. Since the Fur Traders held 10.1%, they had the potential to stop Dome. Richards would subsequently regret his light treatment of the key minority block. The Fur Traders would ultimately have Dome's hide.

As for Conoco, Dome's tender offer had been like a carcass dropped in shark-infested waters. Soon the predators were all around. Over the next two months, the public was to see the world's largest acquisition fight featuring phalanxes of lawyers and investment bankers battling with complex financial offers and even more complex legal injunctions. Having made their "friendly" offer, the Bronfmans, once rejected, claimed that Bailey had negotiated in bad faith because he was talking behind their backs about a merger with Cities Service's Waidelich. Such a merger was about to be announced when a tender offer for Conoco shares from Seagram blasted it out of the water. That, however, was only the start of the fun. Within weeks, two of the Seven Sisters, Texaco and Mobil, would enter the fray for Conoco, Ralph Bailey would approach giant chemical conglomerate Du Pont to become Conoco's white knight, and Du Pont would eventually become Conoco's owner for a massive U.S.$7.6 billion, the biggest takeover in the world. Perhaps strangest of all, the Bronfmans would wind up with 35% of Conoco and then swap it for 20% of Du Pont.

And it had all started, ironically, because Bill Richards had wanted to make his offer for Conoco's stake in HBOG as attractive to Conoco as possible. In fact, the deal emerged as the corporate kiss of death. And not just for Conoco.

The day after the official announcement of Dome's acquisition of Conoco's stake in HBOG, Richards gave a typically upbeat address to the Toronto Society of Financial Analysts, in which he boasted about Dome's speed of response to the National Energy Program. "Dome directly and through its associated companies," he said "has a broad and diverse asset base in the Canadian petroleum business."

The figures did sound impressive. Dome's production of oil and gas liquids was running at 75,000 barrels a day, while that of HBOG was running at 78,000 barrels. Natural gas production was 358 million cubic feet a day for Dome and 388 million cubic feet a day for HBOG. "The combmined total," said Richards, " ... makes the Dome group the second largest producer of oil and gas in Canada." Moreover, he stated, the combined exploratory acreage of Dome and HBOG was, by a wide margin, the largest in Canada.

There was, however, a problem. HBOG's production and land-holdings were irrelevant to Dome as long as Dome had no access to the revenue from them. Dome might include HBOG's assets on its balance sheet and include a proportion of its earnings in its profit and loss account, but these were phantom figures. Dome's long-term debt, however, was not. At the end of 1980, it had been a hefty $2.6 billion. By June 30, 1981, it was a potentially crippling $5.3 billion.

11
Bogging Down

"For Jack Gallagher, however, the Dome share price was the gauge of the public's psychic concurrence in his Beaufort dream, and Gallagher didn't believe in diluting that dream."

In the great corporate tragedy of Dome, an unlikely Cassandra was played by Peter Breyfogle. Breyfogle was something of an oddity within the Dome executive suite. A graduate of Cambridge and a Harvard MBA, he had spent 20 years with Massey-Ferguson, Canada's multinational farm equipment company, and had at one time seemed destined to take over the presidency from Albert Thornbrough, the establishment czar at Massey who showed such apparent reluctance to release the reins of power. However, when he was just one rung from the top, as head of Massey Europe, Breyfogle had a stormy run-in with Thornbrough that led to his departure.

Breyfogle was every inch an eastern establishment figure. His father had been the head of Citibank's office in London, the dean of American bankers in the world's leading banking centre, and Breyfogle himself had developed an autocratic — and sometimes overbearing — style that was perhaps aggravated by his frustrations at Dome.

A tall, slightly stooping figure with a high, domed forehead and sharp, aristocratic features, he spoke with a slight speech impediment which had a trace of the effete about it. But there was nothing effete about his management style or the way he dealt with bankers or the investment community. Any of Breyfogle's subordinates who made errors — and many who made no errors at all — were treated to dressings down that made them want the floor to open up and swallow them. Bankers and investment dealers who came to Breyfogle's door offering cash or ideas were frequently treated like lower forms of life. This did little for Breyfogle's popularity, but ultimately — and to the final detriment of the company — it damaged his credibility within Dome. Breyfogle was one of the few within Dome who saw the dangers of not moving quickly after the second half of Hudson's Bay Oil & Gas and thus gaining access to HBOG's cash flow.

From the first, Breyfogle must have realized he was getting into a quite unusual corporate set-up. He had his initial interview with Jack

Gallagher for the job of chief financial officer of Dome in August, 1978. Gallagher explained that he was trying to phase himself out of the day-to-day business of the company, devote himself to broad strategy and government relations and give more responsibility to Richards, who was already performing many of the functions of the chief executive. Gallagher, it seemed, wanted to go half-way to being non-executive chairman. He therefore told Breyfogle that he would be reporting to Richards, who couldn't meet him at the moment because he was so busy. This seemed most unusual to Breyfogle. Eventually, Breyfogle got half an hour with Richards and two days later the purchase of the Canadian Pacific stake in TransCanada PipeLines was announced. Breyfogle asked for another meeting with Richards and this time he was squeezed in for a quick visit while Richards was visiting Toronto — ostensibly for a board meeting. In fact, Richards was just putting the finishing touches to the Siebens acquisition!

Breyfogle was thus joining the company just as the great acquisition boom was beginning. In fact, the position that Breyfogle was assuming had, until that time, been held by Richards, a fact that may have lessened Richards' enthusiasm for the new financial officer. However, Richards was prepared to go along with Breyfogle's appointment because he knew that it would keep Gallagher happy, a priority for Richards. Also, Dome was entering a period when its outside financing needs were to rise dramatically. Some of the Dome people believed that Gallagher hoped Breyfogle might be a brake on Richards since he himself always had great difficulty in saying no to his expansive president.

But if that *was* a part of Gallagher's purpose, it could hardly be said to have been achieved. Breyfogle was to help raise a great deal of money in the three and a half years he was at Dome, but like everybody else, he found himself sucked along in Bill Richards' enormous corporate wake. Richards didn't expect, or permit, others to make key decisions, and Breyfogle also suffered the frustrations of being part of an organization where all roads led to the president — usually by short cuts. In the end, Breyfogle was to consider himself lucky that he at least sat in an office next door to Richards, so that he could grab any of his own staff members he saw emerging and try to find out what was going on!

But if Breyfogle was to have problems with Richards' management style, in terms of Dome's financial needs, he saw Jack Gallagher as the problem. Breyfogle had first suggested that Dome needed to issue more equity in mid-1979, but Gallagher didn't like the idea. It wasn't greed on Gallagher's part, it was just that he felt he had a responsibility not to dilute the shares. After all, there was all that oil in the Beaufort that wasn't reflected — in Jack's opinion — in the price of Dome's shares. When Dome Petroleum had increased its stake in Dome Mines in 1979, it had — because of the two companies' corporately incestuous relationship — reduced its own outstanding shares by 2%. Breyfogle asked Gallagher if he could just issue that amount of shares. Surely that couldn't be considered dilution. Oh yes it could, said Jack.

For Breyfogle, trained in conventional financial analysis, the obvious attraction of a common share issue was that it was "free" financing until a dividend was paid. Of course, it meant that earnings per share declined relatively, but it eased the heavy burden of debt interest cost. For Gallagher, however, the Dome share price was the gauge of the public's psychic concurrence in his Beaufort dream, and Gallagher didn't believe in diluting that dream.

Breyfogle had an additional problem. Bill Richards' dream of aggressive acquisition was gathering momentum. After the acquisition of the first half of HBOG, Breyfogle realized for the first time that the conjunction of two such expensive dreams could turn into a financial nightmare.

The Fatal Delay

At an executive committee meeting after Conoco's HBOG stake had been acquired, Breyfogle recommended that Dome move at once to acquire the minority shares of HBOG with convertible preferred shares of Dome. These would initially carry a dividend but, once converted, would strengthen Dome's equity position. Breyfogle believed there were pressing reasons for moving at once. The Dome stock price, at between $23 and $24 after the five-for-one stock split, was close to an all-time high. The second quarter results, however, were not particularly good, while there was also going to be a change in Dome's accounting methods which might raise the old bugaboo of accusations that Dome "played with numbers." A quick move, said Breyfogle, would pre-empt any attempts to hold up Dome "for ransom" over the minority shares — which was feared if the Bay turned unfriendly. Also, as long as a takeover of the minority shares was regarded as inevitable, the value of HBOG would increase and that of Dome would decrease.

A further compelling reason to move quickly on the HBOG minority was that total control would enable Dome to reduce its debt by selling off some of HBOG's assets. Breyfogle was greatly concerned about Dome's ongoing financeability in the face of further increases in interest rates and growing evidence of an oil glut. Interest payments were already greater than Dome's cash flow, a surefire recipe for disaster, and yet such considerations were brushed aside. The factor that prevailed was Gallagher's reluctance to issue equity before the year's Beaufort results were in. Whatever the financial realities, financial projections still *looked* rosy. And after all, this might finally be the year that the Beaufort gushed forth.

The meeting turned down Breyfogle's recommendations and afterwards Gallagher came up to Breyfogle, and, smiling as always, put his arm around him. "I know you don't agree," he said, "but this is the right way. Let's look at the whole thing again in a couple of weeks."

Thus began an expensive period of delay. And perhaps one of the amazing features of the exercise was that there was little or no pressure from the banks on Dome to move quickly on the second half of HBOG. Dome had pulled it off before. They would pull it off again.

Breyfogle and Richards visited Toronto in mid-July to meet with bankers and, if necessary, explain Dome's procrastination. But the bankers didn't seem to mind. Representatives of the Montreal, T-D and Royal met together with Richards and Breyfogle. The Commerce's Harrison asked for a separate meeting, but his only concern seemed to be that Richards might ask for more money. When Richards didn't, he seemed perfectly happy. Within Dome, Breyfogle's increasing sense of urgency was blunted by the powers from above. By the last week of July, Breyfogle had worked himself into a bout of pneumonia that was to lay him low for six weeks.

Breyfogle's concerns were increasingly shared by the rest of Dome's financial staff. These included Doug Martin, a tireless financial whizz kid brought in from Dome's U.S. operations to work on Richards' grandiose megaprojects; Vic Zaleschuk, the quiet, methodical controller who had become a key member of Richards' acquisition team; and George Watson, the former executive of the Canadian Imperial Bank of Commerce brought in to replace Don Gardiner when Gardiner had moved to be Gallagher's executive assistant. All three now shared a growing conviction that Dome was heading into financial trouble.

Gallagher and Richards, however, remained almost impervious to such concerns. Astonishingly, they allowed HBOG in July, 1981, to borrow $350 million to purchase Cyprus Anvil Mining Corp., which operated an open-pit lead-zinc-silver mine at Faro in the Yukon. The company was 63%-owned by Los Angeles-based Cyprus Mines Corp., but the U.S. parent had been taken over by Standard Oil of Indiana and FIRA refused to let ownership of the Canadian subsidiary change too. Refusing transfer of ownership was one of FIRA's methods of forcing Canadianization of such subsidiaries. Maier had in fact negotiated with Cyprus Mines several years previously about acquiring Cyprus Anvil. The mine formed part of a long-term plan hatched by

Maier and Haskeyne to build a full-scale integrated mining operation. Now suddenly, Maier found that Cyprus Anvil was available. He decided to bid for it.

But in the back of his mind, Maier might have had another reason for going for Cyprus Anvil: to force Dome into clarifying its intentions. If Gallagher and Richards really planned to go for the HBOG minority, then Maier believed they would obviously be reluctant to allow HBOG to acquire further debt, which in turn would increase Dome's own massive debt-load. However, Gallagher and Richards showed not the slightest reluctance in allowing HBOG to borrow $350 million to go for Cyprus. In fact, they suggested, why not "sweeten the pot" and pay a little more for Cyprus to make sure they got it. After all, as Richards knew, everything was as cheap now as it would ever be.

Others, however, were aghast at the acquisition. In fact, Dome Mines, with which Dome had such long and lasting ties, had itself looked at Cyprus Anvil and decided it was worth only half of what HBOG — and, thus, effectively Dome — was paying for it.

From the banks' point of view, the most significant aspect of the deal was that the whole $350 million loan was being taken by the Bank of Nova Scotia. It was not offered to the CIBC because — in the eyes of Maier and Haskeyne — Commerce had broken its trust, whatever the rules might say. Ironically, one of the very few ways of getting back at the Commerce was *not* to borrow large amounts of money from it. Russell Harrison was now being well and truly ditched.

What was more, the Scotia made sure that it had lots of good, solid collateral tied down in the shape of HBOG assets. If it ever came to a crunch, then it would be better secured than the others of the big five.

In the event, the acquisition was to prove disastrous. Cyprus was effectively acquired in August, 1981. On June 4, 1982, because of a combination of depressed metal markets and high operating costs, it was closed down. By then, Cyprus belonged to Dome. And Cyprus, for good measure, had $135 million of debt.

When the purchase was made, however, the storm clouds had hardly begun to gather. Euphoria still bore Gallagher and Richards along. Moreover, Cyprus was just a "little deal." They had bigger deals to negotiate, in particular with the Bay.

The Fur Traders Get Mad

The Bay was extremely wary of Dome. There was a certain residual feeling that Dome had got the better of the Fur Traders in the 1978 Siebens acquisition, although the Bay had emerged with $126 million

139

of Dome preferred shares tax-free. Now relations with Dome had got off on the wrong foot because of Richards' attempt to squeeze John Tory. Things hadn't improved when George Richardson, former Governor of the Bay, doyen of the investment community and director of both HBOG and the Canadian Imperial Bank of Commerce, had concluded that there were material discrepancies between what Gallagher was telling him and what the Dome chairman was telling John Tory. It looked like Gallagher was trying to pull a fast one. Dome was aware that the Bay was short of money, but the Bay was aware that Dome was *very* short of money. Meanwhile, if the minority shareholders' side needed another champion, they had one in Gerry Maier. If Dome was going to get control of his company, then he was going to make them pay for it.

Within Dome, meanwhile, Richards and Gallagher had finally become convinced that action was necessary. In the first week of August, HBOG shares rose by $6.62 to $42.75 in anticipation that Dome was about to buy out the Bay and the other minority shareholders. Following the share-price surge, Richards, on Friday, August 7, called Maier and asked for a trading halt on HBOG shares. The following Tuesday, August 11, Dome issued a press release announcing it planned to offer one $50 preferred share — which would be convertible into Dome shares — for each outstanding minority HBOG share. "The dividend and conversion rates and other features of these shares," said the release, "will be set within the next few weeks." But of course, it was those terms that were to be the rub. Moreover, there had been a two-month delay since Breyfogle had first suggested a similar deal, and things were beginning to turn sour. Interest rates were still up, and petroleum markets were turning down.

At Dome, projections both for the company and for HBOG were still looking relatively rosy. Dome's figures, however, were way off beam. Dome's ten-year financial projections tended, in any case, to be as much marketing tools as forecasts, and thus always leaned towards the optimistic. In addition, HBOG's internal forecasts, which had always been considered conservative, were now looking optimistic as well.

On Friday, August 14, three days after its public announcement, at a regular HBOG board meeting, Dome outlined its broad plan to HBOG's other directors. It was decided that in order to come to a fair price, there should be independent appraisals of both Dome and HBOG. Specifically, an "independent committee" of HBOG directors would report back to the board on the plan's fairness. This group consisted of Ian Barclay, chairman of British Columbia Forest Products, George Blumenauer, chairman of Otis Elevator Co., Walter Light, president of Northern Telecom, George Richardson and Peter Wood, the Bay's executive vice-president. It was decided that Maier and Haskeyne would be excluded from the committee. Nevertheless, Maier was determined that he play a role in stiffening the independent committee in its negotiations with Dome. In particular, he was concerned that Dome might try to negotiate a deal with the Bay that would be better for the Bay than for the other minority shareholders.

Maier had long had misgivings about Dome's operating methods but by now he was increasingly doubtful as to whether its corporate left hand knew what the right was doing. Gallagher had annoyed Maier by usually turning up late for HBOG board meetings. When Maier asked where Gallagher was, Richards would say: "I don't know. I haven't spoken to him." It seemed extraordinary to Maier that a company's president would have no idea of the whereabouts of its chief executive when they had an important meeting to attend.

After Dome had announced it was going for the minority, Maier, still believing that Gallagher was in charge, had suggested an alternative to him at lunch at the Calgary Country Club. Why, asked Maier, did they not split HBOG up into two companies, with Dome taking 53% and leaving the remaining 47% intact? That would mean that Dome, without further expenditure, would be able to gain access to both assets and cash flow. After several weeks' delay, Jack Gallagher said that he found the idea interesting but that he really felt they should go for total control. Maier was never sure if his suggestion had even been passed on.

As the finance houses did their evaluations in September and October, the feeling of urgency grew within Dome. Richards and Gallagher, however, still did not seem to feel there was a major problem. But Dome was being increasingly boxed into a corner, paying more than $300 million a year in interest payments for 53% of HBOG and getting virtually nothing in return. Dome's shares were dropping in price, and with them, the possibility of an equity financing. Perhaps more important, the independent directors of HBOG, stiffened by Gerry Maier, were saying that they didn't want to finish up with shares of Dome Petroleum anyway. They wanted cash, or something just as good.

The independent committee wanted the services of HBOG's main investment banker, Dominion Securities, but Maier and Haskeyne insisted on keeping Dominion's services for themselves, to carry out what they believed to be their own managerial and directorial responsibilities. The independent committee retained Burns Fry. Dome meanwhile retained Nesbitt Thomson to provide an evaluation of Dome and, separately, Nesbitt, Pitfield Mackay Ross, Wood Gundy, and McLeod Young Weir to provide a "joint opinion" on the fairness of the securities offered to HBOG minority shareholders.

Burns Fry's tasks were to determine a fair value for HBOG shares, to determine what price Dome had paid Conoco for its HBOG shares and to decide whether Dome's offer to the minority was "fair." Burns Fry's conclusions were that HBOG shares were worth between $54.65 and $63 on September 31, 1981, and that Dome had paid $54 a share to Conoco for its HBOG shares.

The critical elements of the discussion now, however, were in what form Dome would make its payments and from where it would get the money.

The Bay also wanted a tax-free deal, and so Dome's financial wizards came up with the idea of retractable preferred shares, where the shares would be redeemed for cash rather than Dome shares at a later date. But how, questioned Maier and the independent directors, could they be sure the money would be there? They wanted it tied down in an escrow account where they knew Dome couldn't get its hands on it.

The Bankers' Rude Awakening

Not till August and September, 1981, was there any sense of alarm in the banking community. But once it had appeared, it began to evolve into the emotion most feared by all bankers — panic. Alarm was exacerbated by developments on the political front.

One major uncertainty throughout 1981 had been the future course of Canadian oil and gas prices. New prices had been dictated under the NEP, but the federal side well understood that these were only a negotiating stance. Alberta had to agree to any new pricing and tax structure. The knights of Peter Lougheed's provincial round table had been so incensed by the NEP that it took almost six months before the two sides started negotiating. However, following tough meetings throughout the summer, the provincial and federal negotiators finally closeted themselves for six days at the end of August in a Montreal hotel.

They emerged amid an orgy of self-congratulation and, on September 1 in Ottawa, Pierre Trudeau and Peter Lougheed signed an enormously complex new pricing and taxation agreement. After the adverse effects of the previous year's NEP, the industry didn't believe that an even more onerous agreement was possible. It was. At the beginning of August, Richards had been showing capital spending estimates to the banks of $1.7 billion for the following year. They seemed optimistic under any circumstances. Under the September agreement they became a fantasy. Featuring yet higher taxes and a totally unrealistic picture of the future course of world — and hence Canadian — petroleum prices, the pricing agreement hit not only cash flows but also the value of all the security Dome had pledged for its loans.

However, more pressing than the problem of security was whether Dome had sufficient cash flow to meet its interest and repayment schedules. To do so, it had to gain the remainder of the HBOG shares as quickly as possible. The deal being negotiated with HBOG's independent committee, the Bay and Gerry Maier, however, required further loans, but the Canadian banks were now drawing in their skirts and saying they would provide no more.

A significant factor in the changed attitude was the sudden concern of William Kennett, Ottawa's Inspector-General of Banks, about the bankers' exposure to Dome. He was alarmed to discover that in one case, that of the Toronto-Dominion, loans to Dome totalled around 75% of the bank's net capital. Kennett had a quiet word with the bank chairmen and told them that no loan should exceed 50% of their bank's capital. He noted that it should be a rare occurrence for any loan to go that high, indeed, any loan exceeding 20% of their net capital should receive his special attention. Finally, he asked them to make sure that their assets-to-capital ratio didn't exceed 30 to 1. The banks weren't used to having their knuckles rapped, either publicly or privately. The pressure applied to them soon found itself transferred to Dome.

It seems more than coincidental that suddenly the T-D — the bank with the highest exposure to Dome — began to take the hardest line with its former star lender. Ted McDowell, the T-D's vice-chairman, passed the word to Dome's financial executives that his chairman, Dick Thomson, was growing very concerned about Dome's position and that he thought Jack Gallagher should consider selling his HBOG stake. An old banking adage says: "Your first loss is your best loss." That was the case now, said the T-D. Dome should get out while it still could. But getting out was easier said than done.

The potential loss on the sale of Dome's HBOG stake was enormous. Some internal Dome estimates put it as high as 50¢ on the dollar. That meant a loss of $1 billion. It seemed unthinkable. The other key difficulty was who could possibly afford to purchase the HBOG stake, even at firesale prices? The T-D looked around desperately. Only one candidate stood out as having both the financial clout and the political acceptability: Petro-Canada. The T-D told Dome it should consider selling to the state oil company.

For those concerned about the interventionist thrust of the NEP — which amounted to virtually the entire Canadian business community — the T-D's proposals could only appear like a desperate, and almost corporately amoral, attempt to save its own neck. In retrospect,

T-D's "first loss" principle may have had merit. To recommend a sale to PetroCan, however, was something else. Indeed, the recommendation was more than ironic because Thomson had been as great an opponent of PetroCan as he had been a supporter of Dome. A couple of years previously, at a private meeting, Thomson had had a heated clash with the national oil company's chairman, Bill Hopper, over Dome. Hopper had, as usual, expressed severe reservations about the Beaufort's potential. Thomson had turned on him angrily and accused him of having "no vision."

Not many months before, a Dome executive had asked a banker from the T-D what the upper limit on Dome's borrowing with the bank was. "Don't worry," the banker had replied, "we *like* Dome. We like your deals." When pressed, the banker admitted that anything much more than $1 billion *might* just be pressing it. "But don't," he hastened to add, "mention that to Jack Gallagher."

Now loans to Dome were over $1 billion, and the pressure certainly was on. Dick Thomson had perhaps been the most enthusiastic of Jack Gallagher's supporters. In many ways, the younger Thomson was reminiscent of Gallagher. He had a similar, disarming smile, a similar low-key approach, and, if you closed your eyes, he even sounded just like Gallagher. His voice had the same "Manitoba Calm." But with his bank's heftiest corporate loan at risk, Thomson's calm appeared to leave him.

Meanwhile, the banks' rapidly changing attitude was just one — if ultimately the biggest — of Dome's problems.

12
Another Budget,
Another (Two) Billion

"Fifteen minutes before he was due to go into the House to announce the change in legislation, MacEachen, accompanied by a taut Ian Stewart, met with Richards and Wood. MacEachen showed them the statement he was about to make. The proposed share exchange would be permitted to proceed tax free. 'Is that all right?' he asked. And before he turned to go into the House he said, without a trace of a smile: 'You people sure know how to put pressure on a guy.' They thanked him and headed back to Calgary."

In the final quarter of 1981, the crises at Dome came thick and fast. They had to negotiate a deal over the HBOG minority; they had to finance that deal under increasingly difficult conditions; and they had to find a way around a surprise federal budget that threatened to blast the HBOG deal — and Dome itself — out of the water. From being the darling of the financial community and the chosen instrument of the government, Dome suddenly found itself the focus of immense hostility. The spell had been broken. The Bay and Gerry Maier seemed determined to nail Dome to the wall on HBOG; the Canadian banks began screaming for their money; and the federal government seemed determined to make sure the company could not pull any more tricks on the tax system.

The final, critical, negotiations over control of HBOG took place at Toronto's King Edward Hotel between October 24 and November 5, 1981. There, the teams from Dome, the Hudson's Bay Company, the investment banks, the lawyers, HBOG's independent committee and — not so quietly in the background — Gerry Maier met to hammer out the final terms of the agreement. Dome was trying to split the Bay away from the other minority shareholders, but Gerry Maier and the independent committee were having none of it. At one time, Dome's investment dealer, Pitfield Mackay Ross, tried to lay a take it or leave it deal on Dominion Securities, who were still acting for the HBOG management. Dominion told them to go to hell.

All along, Dome had hoped that the Bay would be in worse financial shape than themselves, and thus would accept some form of Dome "paper" rather than cash, but as things went on, Dome's position had deteriorated much more rapidly, while the Bay, whatever its condition, had the Thomson empire's money behind it. September had been frittered away in getting the investment dealer's independent appraisals of Dome and HBOG, and in waiting for the Beaufort. But when the Beaufort results came in, they were disappointing. Richards, with typical Dome hoopla, had sought to dress them up by having the world's leading petroleum consulting firm, Degolyer and MacNaughton of Dallas, Texas, to assess Dome's Beaufort holdings.

"In our opinion," the consulting firm wrote to Dome, "based on the tests that have been made, these discoveries have the potential to be hydrocarbon accumulations with oil in place between 1.8 to 4.5 billion barrels in the Kopanoar structure and 2 to 5 million barrels in the Koakoak structure, of which recoverable efficiencies could range from 15% to 40% under existing engineering and operating techniques."

The figures, at first sight, looked impressive, and their release at least achieved front-page headlines. But in fact they confirmed that, in the worst case, neither field was economic. Taking 15% of the lower reserve figure in each field produced 270 million and 300 million barrels respectively, and Dome itself, which had never been known for its pessimism, had indicated that a field required at least 400 million barrels to be economic.

Investment dealer Nesbitt Thomson, in return for a $400,000 fee plus expenses, produced an appraisal of Dome as being worth — without the 53% of HBOG and its related $2-billion debt — more than $50 a share. Under the final agreement, however, which was effectively for cash, this generous assessment was largely irrelevant.

To accommodate the Bay's financial status, and satisfy demands for a cast-iron guarantee of cash payment, a complex deal was worked out whereby minority shareholders would be issued with retractable preferred shares in a Dome subsidiary, Dome Resources. These interest-bearing shares that would be bought back later by Dome for cash. Dome committed to retract these on December 31, 1984, for $57.50, or at a negotiable price before that date. The final price was forced up by Maier, who said he would "blow the whistle" if the independent committee settled for less. In addition, and as a sweetener, minority shareholders were to receive for each HBOG share one and one-third Dome warrants, enabling them to purchase Dome shares at a price of $23.1125. On August 10, just before Dome had made its announcement about going for the HBOG minority, Dome shares had stood at $22.25. By November 2, just before the deal was signed, they had sunk to $15.25. They were to fall much lower. On December 15, the four investment bankers employed by Dome were to come up with a value of the offer of "approximately" $57.50 a share. That meant the warrants were worth "approximately" nothing.

Nevertheless, the minority's $57.50 was well and truly tied up, since the U.S. $1.8 billion Dome needed to retract the preferred shares was to be deposited in escrow and could only be taken out to pay for the retraction of the preferred shares.

Dome's negotiators knew it was an expensive deal, but they desperately needed it completed. They were borrowing money just to pay interest and their corporate empire was hemorrhaging. HBOG's cash flow would provide a fiscal transfusion, and Dome was hoping to close the deal the first week in December.

However, first the proposal had to be put to an HBOG shareholders' meeting and massive documentation was needed to explain the so-called "Plan of Arrangement." A tome eventually stretching to well over 200 pages had to be sent to each minority shareholder. On November 12, the independent committee met to recommend the plan of arrangement to the entire board, which approved it. That same night, Allan MacEachen tabled his second major budget. Under its provisions the plan of arrangement was destroyed.

A Disastrous Budget

For the executives gathered in the Dome Tower to listen to the November, 1981 budget, its full impact did not at first sink in. Details from Allan MacEachen's Commons speech weren't complete, and budget documents, which were usually available from the Bank of Canada building on Calgary's Sixth Avenue, were several hours late in arriving. Terry Hargreaves, a former CBC journalist who had recently joined Dome's Ottawa staff, read parts of the document over the phone.

Under the budget, the plan of arrangement so tediously negotiated was torn apart. The swap of HBOG shares for Dome preferred shares and warrants became subject to capital gains tax, while the Bay would also have to pay tax on the income from the preferred shares. But the most remarkable aspect of the budget was that it contained no provision for "grandfathering," that is, exempting deals that were already in the works.

When the Dome VPs finally realized the budget's full impact, they felt numb. Some of them had been working night and day, seven days a week, for almost six months on the HBOG deal. A group of

147

them wandered over to the offices of Dome's lawyers, Bennett Jones, and broke out the booze. This was it, they thought. This was the end. No grandfathering could only mean Ottawa had deliberately set out to get them. Paranoia was rampant. By the early morning hours in Bennett Jones' office, it had turned into drunken paranoia.

Many in Dome knew that at the Department of Finance, Dome, which had tied the department's tax system in knots and treated its precious notions of equity like a doormat, was pet hate number one. By not grandfathering Dome's deal with the Bay and forcing the Bay to pay taxes, the department was effectively killing the deal. They had got Dome at last.

But they had not taken into account the power of Bill Richards' perseverance. Doug Martin, who had been a key figure in originating and negotiating the deal with HBOG's minority shareholders, went to bed about 6 A.M., totally deflated after the morose session at Bennett Jones. His world seemed to have gone down the tubes.

At 9 A.M. his phone rang. It was Bill Richards.

"Where the hell *are* you?" asked Richards. Rhetorically.

"I'm in *bed*," Martin snapped back, wondering why anybody should be concerned about turning up for work the day after the world ended.

"There'll be a plane on the runway at 11 o'clock," said Richards. "We're going to Ottawa."

So Martin dragged himself and his hangover to the Dome terminal, where he met up with Richards, Steve Savidant, Mike Carten, a young tax wizard from Bennett Jones, and Colin Kenny, who had been hired from the Prime Minister's Office in 1979. Martin, and others, had wondered about Kenny's function and his usefulness to Dome. In the next week that usefulness became apparent.

Kenny, like Breyfogle, was something of an oddity even within a corporation that thrived on creative eccentricity. A short, dapper figure given to sporting the occasional bow tie, Kenny had served in the Prime Minister's Office as one of Trudeau's palace guards for a decade, joining straight after taking an MBA at Ivy League college Dartmouth shortly after Trudeau first came to power.

He served first under Marc Lalonde, when Lalonde, as principal secretary, was imposing a style of rigid efficiency on the office, and later becamer part of the PMO in-group, particularly after Jim Coutts became principal secretary. Kenny's almost militaristic dedication to Trudeau's schedule and his brusque manner meant that he was not the most popular figure in the Sun King's court. He was given a nickname, Kolonel Klinck, after the prison camp commandant in the old TV comedy series "Hogan's Heroes."

After the Liberals' electoral loss in 1979, Kenny joined Dome as manager of regulatory planning. Typically, he received a call on the

148

Sunday before he was due to start work telling him he would be going to Washington for a hearing the following day. "How many shirts?" he asked. "About seven," he was told. Thus began Colin Kenny's initiation into the company that never slept.

However, Kenny was Dome's — and in particular Bill Richards' — kind of player. His decade in the PMO had taught him all about membership in a dedicated and exclusive team, and he had novel talents to bring to the company: a comprehensive knowledge of Ottawa's arcane workings; a network of contacts among Ottawa's first circle of power; and a supremely efficient approach. In the wake of the National Energy Program, those attributes drew him into Dome's decision-making elite.

Government relations had to be more than just knowing people at cocktail parties, Kenny told the Dome people. You had to be systematic in keeping files of useful contacts. But most of all you always had to understand the public policy perspective. No use going to Ottawa to tell them *your* troubles; you had to present them with something that "fit their pistol." But first, you had to be able to open the right doors. In the week after the November, 1981 budget, Colin Kenny showed that he had an abundant door-opening talent.

Jack Gallagher did not go to Ottawa. Indeed, a deliberate decision had been taken to keep Gallagher away from the capital. Richards and company were frightened that he might just start in on a Beaufort panegyric when time — and the attention of key ministers and bureaucrats — was at a premium. And they didn't want to bring up anything that might remind the Department of Finance about super-depletion. That might not fit their pistol at all.

In Ottawa, the group was joined by the tall and very British figure of Peter Wood, the Bay's executive vice-president. For most of the next week, Richards and Wood were to form an odd, but eventually effective, lobbying team in the nation's capital. They visited everyone who would listen to their case, entered every door that Colin Kenny could open. Richards would tell anyone he could buttonhole that the deal was *terribly* important to the future of Dome — and hence of course Canada; Wood would explain how *terrible* the budget was for HBOG's minority shareholders.

On Friday night, November 13, the group set up a command post in the Inn of the Provinces, and Colin Kenny went to work plugging into his network. The first meeting with Finance officials was not auspicious. A young but senior official of the department actually said: "We've got you at last" at the beginning of the meeting. Nobody was sure if he was joking or not. There was, it seemed, some ground for paranoia.

149

Lalonde Bats for Dome

One of the group's first calls — and perhaps its most important — was on Marc Lalonde, still minister of energy and still, fortunately for Dome, the most powerful minister in Trudeau's cabinet. His opening words when Richards came to see him — delivered with his most charming and intimidating smile — were: "Hi, Bill. I guess you're here to ask us to bail you out again."

Fortunately for Dome, Lalonde remained very much on their side. Dome had been one of the very few companies that had made a positive response to his National Energy Program, so Lalonde inevitably still favoured it. He had also hitched his own star to that of Dome through his public support of Dome Canada. To a significant degree, if Dome went under it would drag down with it Lalonde's shaky credibility.

Allan MacEachen, by contrast, proved, at first, totally inaccessible. MacEachen at the best of times had trouble dealing with the flesh-and-blood business world, and he was predictably reluctant to give an audience to a group that wanted to turn his budget upside down. Any major change in a budget so soon after its announcement was an indictment of the minister ultimately responsible for its drafting, no matter how much in the thrall of his super-bureaucrats he had been. In the end, therefore, Dome's fate came down to a straight fight between Marc Lalonde and Allan MacEachen.

But if Allan MacEachen didn't want to stand up to them and defend the budget, there was still one enormously powerful figure who did, Deputy Minister of Finance Ian Stewart. For years, Stewart had fought for a fundamental view that he believed to be in the best interests of Canada. He had never basically seen eye to eye with the business community, which regarded him as brilliant but misguided, a typical academic Trudeaucrat. In fact — although Michael Pitfield had always had a higher profile — Stewart was considered by many to be *the* archetypal academic Trudeaucrat. Now, he and his like-minded mandarins had introduced what they believed to be a revolutionary but necessary budget, and suddenly the whole world was descending on them with selfish requests for exemptions and grandfatherings.

Stewart now saw himself as Horatio at the bridge, trying to hold back the enemy. But he also took the attacks against the budget personally. For that reason, his meeting with Richards was likely to be fiery. In fact, it turned out to be explosive.

Before the meeting with the finance deputy minister, Richards asked Mike Carten, the lawyer, who was dredging up all his constitutional knowledge in the Dome cause, whether he was allowed to tell Stewart exactly what he thought of his budget. Carten thought it highly inadvisable, but Richards, whose personal status was damaged because of the budget's provisions relating to land development and corporate perks, couldn't contain himself.

After the initial pleasantries, Richards told Stewart in so many words that he considered his budget a pile of *crap*! Stewart's dedicated financial officials bristled. Stewart hit the roof. Here he was, a true public servant who slaved 15-hour days for the public good, a model of selflessness, being dressed down by the president of a company that was the classic example of the private sector's selfish amorality. He wasn't going to take it. The Dome team recoiled. Stewart seemed to some of them to be on the point of losing control. Bill Richards' plain speaking was not considered to have advanced the Dome cause. Nevertheless, the team pressed on. Within a week of the budget, they were to have their way.

Realizing it was unwise to be seen to make a minister lose face, the Dome team tried to make all sorts of feeble excuses on MacEachen's behalf, but in the end it was obvious that he had had to bow to Lalonde.

Fifteen minutes before he was due to go into the House to announce the change in legislation, MacEachen, accompanied by a taut Ian Stewart, met with Richards and Wood. MacEachen showed them the statement he was about to make. The proposed share exchange would be permitted to proceed tax free. "Is *that* all right?" he asked. And before he turned to go into the House, he said, without a trace of a smile: "You people sure know how to put pressure on a guy." They thanked him and headed back to Calgary.

The budget hurdle had been removed, but the financing hurdle remained. Dome had to come up with U.S.$1.8 billion to deposit in escrow so that HBOG's minority shareholders could be sure their deal was as good as cash. Dome had to pull off that financing against a background of increasing hostility from the Canadian banks. But as one set of banking doors closed to it, another, even larger, set opened, those of Citibank, one of the largest banks in the world.

Citibank Puts Up the Cash

Founded in New York in 1812, Citibank had enjoyed its first period of spectacular expansion around the turn of the century under James Stillman, a man described as "drab of personality, tight-lipped, cold and passionless." Because of Stillman's friendship with John D. Rockefeller's younger brother, William, Standard Oil's funds were lodged with the bank and it became known as the "Standard Bank." In time, the Chase Manhattan Bank was to become better associated with the Rockefellers, particularly through David Rockefeller, but Citibank's president in the early 1950s, James Stillman Rockefeller, one of the so-called "poor Rockefellers," presided over the beginning of the bank's second rapid expansion and put it, as Anthony Sampson said in *The Money Lenders*, "in the forefront of the American era."

Citibank's head at the beginning of the 1980s was Walter Wriston, a banker who had the possibly dubious distinction of leading Citibank forcefully into the Third World to peddle the huge OPEC funds generated by the quadrupling of the price of oil in 1973–74. Wriston liked to downplay the mystique of banking. "Some people like to dream up a conspiracy," he once said, "but there's less in this than meets the eye." He also said: "I'm just trying to deal with a succession of accidents." His bank's experience with Dome Petroleum was to prove his words frighteningly true.

Throughout the latter part of the 1970s, the foreign banks in Canada, which were tightly controlled, had tried, and failed, to get a piece of the petroleum industry action. In American banking, syndication was the name of the game: gathering various banks under a consortium leader in order to spread the risk of loans. The U.S. bankers looked on in amazement as the big five Canadian banks made enormous loans all by themselves, jealously guarding customers and keeping other bankers at bay. Syndication was not the rule in Canada, it was the exception, and there seemed to be an unspoken pact among the big five that foreigners had to be kept out of the banking market at all costs. In any case, federal legislation was designed to keep the foreign banks small. Citibank had the largest Canadian operation of any of the foreign banks, but its assets were less than a twentieth of the Toronto-Dominion, the smallest of Canada's big five.

While the Canadian banks were at last beginning to realize the potential dangers of their exposure to Dome, Citibank saw its opportunity to break into the big, wonderful world of Canadian energy lending, and, in particular, of its biggest and most wonderful energy borrower, Dome Petroleum. But loans of the size Dome wanted weren't matters for Citibank's tiny Canadian operation; they were matters to be dealt with at head office back in New York on Park Avenue.

When Peter Breyfogle had taunted foreign bankers with the question: "Why should I borrow from you?" they had wrung their hands at their own obvious inadequacy. However, Breyfogle also knew that at some stage he would *have* to go abroad for money. Dome's virtually insatiable appetite for cash had inevitably to test the limits of the whole Canadian banking system. By the fall of 1981, Dome's loan

152

exposure to the Commerce, Montreal, T-D and Royal banks was of sufficient magnitude to threaten that system.

On a trip to the Beaufort Sea in June, 1981, just after the first half of HBOG had been picked up from Conoco, a senior Citibanker had invited himself along. During the *de rigueur* snapshots at midnight under the Arctic sun, he had turned to Breyfogle and said the magic words: "We'd like you to have some money. We think we could probably raise a couple of billion for you."

By September, Breyfogle was more than happy to make the deal. As it happened, Breyfogle through his father, already had good connections at Citibank and knew Gerry Finneran, the senior vice-president eventually responsible for the loan, from his days in London. The other key figure in putting the loan together and syndicating it was Penny Foley, whose brusque attitude to potential syndicate members indicated what it was to be a Citibanker. When Citibank led a syndicate, then other banks were lucky to get a piece of the action.

The lead bank, however, also had an additional burden of responsibility and Citibank had to set out to establish the viability of the loan, firstly in terms of Dome's ability to meet its obligations, and secondly in terms of tying up adequate security in case it could not. It proved to be far more adept at the latter than the former, for within three weeks of Citibank signing its loan with Dome, Dome was on the point of bankruptcy.

When the Canadian banks realized that Dome was no longer going to be able to issue equity for the second half of the HBOG acquisition, they became twitchy. They realized that Dome, if it could, would have to go to foreign banks for the money. That, in itself, made some of them angry, since they had fought so long to keep the commercial invaders off their Calgary turf.

But when they heard the terms of the foreign loan, or rather when they saw the collateral the Citibank group was demanding, they became almost apoplectic.

The Citibank consortium, which eventually comprised 27 banks, was effectively making a production loan against HBOG, that is, repayments were to come out of the revenue generated by HBOG's production. For collateral, Citibank wanted HBOG assets, or more specifically $62\frac{1}{2}\%$ of HBOG's assets, that is, all the assets left after the planned disposition to corporate "family and friends," plus a cash collateral account of U.S.$400 million stocked up with proceeds from those dispositions. For the Canadian banks, this arrangement was doubly offensive. On the one hand, *their* collateral consisted of HBOG shares, but the Citibank deal was effectively removing the assets from *under* the shares and thus removing the shares' collateral value. On

153

the other, the Canadian banks had by now demanded that Dome use the proceeds of planned asset sales to pay down the Dome Energy loan; now they found the first U.S.$400 million from that sale would go into the Citibank loan's cash collateral account.

The Scramble for Security

The Canadian bankers became livid. However, they also realized that unless Dome successfully carried off the second half of the HBOG purchase, it might well sink. And they would be financially damaged too. Nevertheless, now that Dome had effectively changed their collateral, they had the right to seek further security. The problem was that the values of both Dome and HBOG assets were dropping because of sagging oil markets and the impact of the previous September's federal-provincial petroleum pricing and taxation agreement. The Canadian banks then began an unseemly scramble to tie down every Dome asset not pledged to Citibank. They could not only see the writing on the wall for Dome; they wanted the wall as security. The bankers who had just six months before elbowed each other out of the way to lend Dome money were now climbing over each other to make sure they got it back. And quickly. They didn't just want new collateral, they wanted Dome to pay them their money back as soon as possible. Under the original terms of the Canadian bank loan to buy the Conoco shares, the loan was repayable on January 31, 1983, but with an option to extend it for ten years. Now the big four said they wanted their money back sooner. In fact, they wanted it back by September 30, 1982. Richards was told to get the second half of the HBOG deal done and then start selling assets so he could pay them back. The increasingly agitated and panicky bankers decided it was time to inject a little cold, hard reality into the corporate dreams of Gallagher and Richards. There could be no colder douche than the demand that Dome come up with $2 billion in less than a year.

Dome was now faced with a terrible dilemma. If information about the shortening of the Canadian bank term became public, then it was virtually inevitable that the Citibank loan would fall through. If that happened, then Dome could not acquire the remainder of HBOG and sell off its assets, which was, in turn, the only way the company could meet the new term of the Canadian bank loan. In other words, the Canadian banks had taken an action which, if it became public, would almost certainly drive Dome into bankruptcy. Their action was, to quote one American banker "a little like shooting themselves in the foot."

154

Discussions of the shortening of the loan had taken place in November, and the move had been agreed to by Richards by the end of the year, but the Dome president was making speeches in January of 1982 complete with charts of Dome's debt position that gave no indication of the shortening of the Canadian bank loan.

Richards subsequently explained to the author that the changing of the term was not considered "critical" at the time. However, he said: "One would have to concede [that] we didn't have an appreciation of the extent to which conditions had altered the values of oil and gas properties ... I can only say that in the light of the plans we had at the time we didn't view that as being terribly adverse or as a difficulty. It had been our plan to sell off assets to reduce that debt within the framework of the term anyway."

Only Bill Richards' unshakable optimism and self-confidence could lend such a statement even a trace of credibility. But perhaps more astonishing was Jack Gallagher's subsequent claim that he had not known about the discussions over the change in the terms of the loan. The breakdown in communications within Dome appeared to be reaching crisis proportions. Richards had for several years pursued a policy of keeping the full range of his megaschemes from Gallagher until they were well advanced. He told his staff not to let Gallagher know about plans. Richards' staff would, in turn, be terrified if they should be confronted by Gallagher and asked questions, because they never knew how much *he* already knew. Bill Richards still believed he could — like the greatest of corporate Houdinis — escape from Dome's difficulties. After all, he said, Dome's problems were really merely a temporary shortage of cash flow. The company still had assets coming out of its corporate ears. All it needed, after all, was money. That was where Dome's "family and friends" came in.

13
"Family and Friends"

"The essential point is not that Dome is paying more than HBOG is worth ... it is paying more than the consolidated unit can afford and still be able to continue on-going businesses such as exist today. For the new unit to be able to meet its on-going obligations it will have to sell off routinely the very assets today's on-going business requires."

DR. VERNE ATTRILL
TO THE NEW YORK SOCIETY
OF FINANCIAL ANALYSTS.
JANUARY 25, 1982

The resource empire of Dome and its "family," Dome Canada, TransCanada PipeLines and Dome Mines, spanned the length and breadth of Canada. It ranged over the petroleum lands of the western provinces, out into the murky depths of the Beaufort, down into the country's most productive gold mines and through the thousands of miles of steel pipe that linked Alberta natural gas and gas liquids to their eastern Canadian and U.S. markets. More important, it stretched deep into the vaults of every major Canadian bank. A disposition of some of HBOG's assets to "family and friends" now became a critical part of Dome's financial survival.

Dome had always thrived on OPM, Other People's Money. Originally, it had been financed from the endowment funds of the Ivy League universities and an original group of equity investors. During the massive expansion of the previous six years the money had come from the Canadian taxpayer, the drilling funds and, most important, the banks. The Citibank consortium was now offering to complete the HBOG takeover with the biggest chunk of OPM ever lent to an entity other than a government. But in order to meet the terms of the $2.1 billion loan, Dome needed U.S.$400 million in cash to deposit in a "cash collateral account." Also, unknown to Citibank, the Canadian bankers were demanding repayment of their loan, specifically, $2 billion, by September 30, 1982.

There was only one way of raising the U.S.$400 million for the cash collateral account and the money for the Canadian banks: through a sale of assets. Suddenly the three members of the Dome family and the "friend," Dow Chemical Canada, became critically important in easing the financial burden of the HBOG acquisition. Under previous agreements, each of them had options on taking parts of Dome's acquisitions. That they should do so now became crucial for Dome, and the banks.

In fact, the very same banks now demanding their money would finance a hefty share of the family's purchase — although in some cases with extreme reluctance. Nevertheless, they realized that merely by transferring HBOG assets — and the loans to buy them — away from Dome, they were spreading the risk and thus increasing their own security.

Amid the family and friends, however, there was growing disquiet.

Dome Petroleum now controlled 48% of Dome Canada, 49% of TCPL and 39% of Dome Mines. Each company therefore had large outside shareholdings whose interests had to be protected. The role of protector is meant to fall to all the directors of each company; however, in the case of overlapping directorships, conflicts inevitably arise. The burden of shareholder protection then falls particularly heavily on the "independent" directors. Both Gallagher and Richards were on the boards of all three family companies. They were persuasive and forceful and, at least originally, had had little trouble in selling pieces of their dream — at a handsome profit — to their corporate relatives.

Corporate control is a tenuous concept. It by no means depends directly on the degree of equity ownership, although 100% ownership almost invariably goes with 100% control. When equity ownership of any company is widespread, then a small percentage of overall share-ownership may carry a disproportionately large amount of corporate clout — so long as, so the theory goes, that clout is exercised prudently. The Bache-Michel interests, for example, had been a dominant force on the Dome Mines board for over 60 years, although they held just 2% of Dome Mines' shares. Through that interest, Clifford Michel had held his dominant position on the Dome Pete board. However, his departure in 1975 meant the end of the Michel family interests on Dome Pete's board, at least for the moment.

When Clifford Michel had left the board, he had wanted his son-in-law, Alan McFarland, another investment banker, to take his place. However, the move had been blocked in the Dome boardroom. The Michel family interests believed the blockage had come from John Loeb, another of Dome's founder-investors and a former partner of Michel. The problem was that Loeb — described by a fellow Wall

Streeter as "one of the toughest sons-of-bitches in the valley" — had fallen out with Michel several years before about the direction of Loeb, Rhoades. As a result, Michel had left the company. The inevitable rift which had developed between the two old friends was thought to have kept Alan McFarland off the Dome Pete board.

McFarland's failure to win a board seat indicated a more than subtle change in the power relationship between Dome Petroleum and Dome Mines. Within the following couple of years, that relationship would shift completely.

Dancing Closer with the "Miners"

The "Miners" had been Dome Petroleum's parents; then, after 1976, Dome Pete had bought up 39% of Mines' shares and effectively adopted its own progenitor. This move had been partially in response to the Foreign Investment Review Agency, but it had also been, for Jack Gallagher, a move to protect his corporate flank. Since Dome Mines owned 25% of Dome Pete, anyone taking over Dome Mines would also control Dome Petroleum. Now the two companies were linked by seven overlapping directorships: those of Gallagher and Richards, of Major-General Bruce Matthews and Malcolm "Mac" Taschereau — respectively Dome Mines' chairman and president — and of three lawyers, Rene Amyot from Quebec, Maclean "Mac" Jones from Calgary and Fraser Fell from Toronto. Gallagher, Richards and Jones were from the "Pete" side, while Matthews, Taschereau, Fell and Amyot came from the "Miners" board.

Bruce Matthews was a pillar of the Canadian establishment. His father had been a lieutenant-governor of Ontario, and he had commanded the Second Canadian Division during World War II before going into the family's investment business. Now Matthews was close to retirement, but he had been at the pinnacle of Canadian corporate power. He had been an executive vice-president of the mighty Argus Corporation, whose holdings extended from food stores, through mining, broadcasting, paper and the trust business to control of Massey-Ferguson, of which he had, at one time, been chairman. Through Argus, Matthews had sat on the boards of Dominion Stores, Hollinger Mines and Domtar. He had been a director of Dome Mines since 1947 and a board member of Dome Petroleum since 1954.

Mac Taschereau was a very different man from Matthews. A mining man by background and by nature, he did not aspire to establishment status. As president and CEO of Dome Mines he automatically became a board member of Dome Petroleum. Taschereau was plain-spoken,

159

and had little to do with the world of high finance until he became president of Dome Mines and a Dome Pete board member. The more he saw and learned of the ways of high finance, the less he liked it.

Through their Dome Pete holdings, the Miners had always been involved in the oil business. However, once Gallagher and Richards came onto the Dome Mines board, it was almost inevitable that they would become more involved. Matthews and Taschereau were to find themselves in an increasingly uncomfortable position.

Until Dome Pete had bought into Dome Mines in 1976, there had been an almost paternalistic relationship between the two companies. Dome Mines was a stable and somewhat staid concern which looked to its offshoot Dome Petroleum for its corporate "kicks." However, soaring gold prices in the latter half of the 1970s caused an enormous increase in Dome Mines' revenue and earnings. Related to worldwide uncertainties surrounding petroleum, the average price of gold had increased sixfold between 1976 and 1980. Moreover, Dome Petroleum's earnings too had soared, boosting those of Dome Mines. Dome Mines' share of Dome Pete's earnings increased from $12.8 million in 1976 to $62.8 million in 1980. Meanwhile, Dome Pete's share of the earnings of Dome Mines increased over the same period from $3.6 million to $29.6 million. If incestuous, the relationship certainly seemed a fruitful one. For the Miners, 1980 was a red-letter year as the price of gold, and corporate earnings, reached an all-time peak. The original mine at South Porcupine, Ontario, and the mines of Campbell Red Lake at Balmertown, Ontario, and of Sigma at Val d'Or, Quebec, produced 329,086 fine ounces of gold — or just over 10 tons of the precious metal — from almost 1.5 million tons of laboriously mined and milled ore. That was one fifth of a glittering ounce for each dirty ton. But the average price of gold in 1980, $720.50 an ounce, almost double that of the previous year, made the exercise highly profitable.

The capacity of the Red Lake Mine had recently been expanded by 30%. Now it was decided to increase the mill capacity at South Porcupine by 50%, to 3,000 tons a day, and to upgrade other facilities at a total cost of $92 million. An agreement had also been reached in 1980 with Amoco Canada Petroleum Ltd. for Dome Mines and Campbell Red Lake each to take 25% of a new gold mine at Detour Lake in Northern Ontario. The open pit mine would begin operations in October, 1983, with a capacity of 2,200 tons a day. There were plans to expand it to 4,400 tons by 1987. The total cost of the Detour Lake program was estimated at $146 million. Business was booming.

However, there were also signs of instability in the market. While the price of oil began a hefty increase in 1980 following the Iranian revolution, the price of gold showed dramatic fluctuations. It opened 1980 at U.S.$559 and in three weeks had soared to an all-time high of U.S.$850. From there it slumped to U.S.$474 in March before rising again gradually through the summer to U.S.$720.50. It closed the year at U.S.$589.50.

Dome Mines' net income in 1980 was a record $126.5 million, up 42% from 1979. However, said Richards and Gallagher, look at all the taxes Dome Mines was paying — $106 million in 1980. Dome Petroleum, they said, could offer a way to shelter some of those taxes and also help the Dome Mines group get more directly involved in the most booming business of all, oil and gas. Why didn't Dome Mines take a piece of their petroleum action?

So it was decided that Campbell Red Lake Mines and Sigma Mines, which were, respectively, 57% and 66% owned by Dome Mines, would together commit a hefty $141 million to the oil and gas business. As of July 1, 1980, Campbell and Sigma acquired 5% — respectively, 4% and 1% — of certain of Dome's producing properties and wells in progress, principally those acquired through the acquisitions of Siebens and Mesa, for $42 million. The two companies were also committed to spending $100 million in 1980 and 1981 on a Dome Petroleum-directed exploration program on Dome's non-producing western land in order to earn, again, a total of 5% of those lands. Campbell and Sigma were also committed to contributing their share of future exploration and development costs on the properties. The two companies also had the right to participate to the same extent, that is, 4% and 1%, in "future acquisitions of producing or exploratory lands by Dome Petroleum in the area of mutual interest."

Dome Petroleum was making a healthy profit on the lands it sold. It was to have $100 million of exploration on its wildcat lands. Sigma and Campbell had to pay Dome Petroleum royalty and management fees. If they failed to provide their future share of exploration or production costs, they would be subject to a penalty. If they refused to participate in an acquisition they effectively lost the right to participate in future acquisitions. It appeared an enormously attractive deal, primarily for Dome Petroleum.

Deeper into Dome's Pit

Within five months of the deal being signed, the National Energy Program, with its punishing new taxes, had taken the glow off the oil business. Nevertheless, the creation of Dome Canada served to boost further the euphoria attached to the Dome team. In fact, Dome Mines decided, with the help of a little persuasion from Gallagher and Richards, that they should increase their stake in Dome Petroleum.

Gallagher told the Dome Mines board that Dome Petroleum would probably issue equity in connection with the takeover of the second half of HBOG. If it did so, then the Miners' stake would be diluted. It was important not to let it drop below 20%, at which level Dome Mines could "equity account" for Dome Petroleum's earnings, that is, include a proportion of Dome's earnings in its own. Dome Mines should buy now, said Gallagher, while prices are cheap. He pointed out that there were really only two times in the year when Dome stock could most profitably be bought, either before the Beaufort season got underway, or after the results were in. In recent years, Dome stock had always risen ahead of drilling disclosures. He also told the board he had evidence that other groups were building positions in Dome Pete stock. Finally he suggested that there was a basic imbalance in Dome Mines owning only 25% of Dome Pete while Pete held almost 40% of Dome Mines. Not everyone agreed with Gallagher. More than one director suspected that Gallagher's main motive was to make sure the price of Dome Pete shares was maintained.

Nevertheless, stock market enthusiasm continued to surround Dome Petroleum, and the Dome Mines board decided to go along with the purchase. A total of $74.3 million was spent on 3 million shares of Dome Petroleum. The price was close to their all-time high. The additional Dome Pete shares did nothing for cash earnings, since the company paid no dividend. Moreover, it wasn't as if the Miners had cash to spare. In fact, Dome Mines had to borrow the money for the purchase. The group had had no significant debt before, a clear reflection of their conservative attitudes. Now $74.3 million was borrowed under a $125 million revolving line of credit with the T-D. Campbell and Sigma too each acquired $10 million of long-term debt. Meanwhile, even as the share purchase was made, the gold market was declining as gold prices moved into a downward trend.

In Dome Mines' annual report for 1981, the directors' statement to shareholders revealed the acquisition of Dome Pete shares as a "long-term investment," noting that: "Over the years Dome Mines' percentage interest has been diluted ... " In fact, the statement made little sense. Dome Petroleum had, since 1955, issued equity only in connection with employee incentive plans. Indeed, Dome Mines had almost exactly the same percentage of Dome Petroleum's shares in 1981 — before it bought the additional 3 million shares — as it had when Dome had been created in 1950.

The $74 million increased Dome's stake in Dome Petroleum by exactly 1.2%. The Miners' shareholders may have had particular cause for concern about the purchase because, later the same year, their own dividend would be cut, from 22.5¢ to 15.75¢ per share.

Meanwhile the issue of Dome Mines' participation in the HBOG takeover had now come up. The Dome Mines' board decided that a firmer line was needed with Dome Petroleum. They declared that Campbell and Sigma would not be participating in the acquisition. However, Gallagher had a much bolder proposal for Dome Mines. He wanted them to take the bulk of Cyprus Anvil off Dome's hands. The rumoured price was $250 million. But Dome Mines had already made a much lower valuation of Cyprus' assets. The Miners certainly had no intention of effectively paying as much as Dome had paid for them, particularly with the mining industry suffering almost as badly as oil and gas. Gallagher was reportedly genuinely disappointed that they refused to agree to the deal.

Nevertheless, the Canadian banks still felt Dome Petroleum was short of the additional security they were demanding for the Dome Energy loan. They were determined to see Dome Mines involved. They declared they would not close the deal without some form of contribution from Dome Mines. Dome Mines was in a bind. Its stake in Dome Petroleum clearly gave it an interest in the successful conclusion of the HBOG takeover, but now some of its directors felt it was being punished for the expansionist sins of Dome Petroleum. In the end, the Dome Mines board agreed to provide a $250 million loan guarantee, in return for which Dome Petroleum would pay them a fee. The Miners now felt themselves unavoidably drawn into Dome Petroleum's ever-deepening financial pit.

To support this and other guarantees, and as collateral for the $125 million line of credit used for the purchase of the 3 million Dome shares, Dome Mines suddenly found that the Toronto-Dominion Bank had a hammer-lock on virtually all of the company's assets. Dome Mines' entire stake in Sigma and Campbell Red Lake had to be pledged, as well as its equity investments in Denison Mines, Noranda Mines and Canada Tungsten Mining Corporation. In addition, the bank demanded Dome's South Porcupine mine and the new project at Detour Lake as security. From being its own company, debt-free and a model of financial conservatism, suddenly Dome Mines could hardly move without the permission of the T-D. They were also now more firmly tethered to their sick relation, Dome Petroleum, than they would ever have wanted. And they were not the only ones.

Dome Mines was deeply ensnared in Dome Petroleum's problems, with virtually all its assets now pledged in the Dome cause. However, the company had successfully avoided putting up any cash, and that was what Dome Petroleum needed most desperately. The two other family members and the friend were the chief prospective source.

Dome Canada: A Tenuous Independence

Dome Canada, for all intents and purposes, had no separate existence from Dome Petroleum. It also had huge volumes of cash and short-term investments, the result of the previous March's share offering. At the close of its first nine months of activity, at the end of December, 1981, that figure stood at $594 million.

As soon as the Dome Canada offering had closed the previous March and the money had come in, Bill Richards, in the words of a former executive, "could hardly wait to spend it." That was exactly what Ottawa had feared. Of course, part of Dome Canada's mandate was acquisition, but few could have imagined that it would have spent most of its liquid assets within a year. Dome Petroleum pointed out that the purchase of HBOG assets gave Dome Canada both reserves and production income. However, by the time the deal was concluded, there was little doubt that it was Dome Petroleum's interests that were taking priority.

Dome Petroleum's management had originally considered that Dome Canada might take 5% of HBOG to provide it with assets and cash flow. However, now Dome Petroleum needed to load as much of HBOG onto Dome Canada as it could.

Dome Canada had three "independent" directors: Fred McNeil, former chairman of the Bank of Montreal and still a director of the bank; Stan Roberts, former president of both the Canada West Foundation and the Canadian Chamber of Commerce; and Norman Martison, a retired executive of the Burmah Oil Company. Although all were undoubtedly honourable men, questions could be raised about the "independence" of two of them. As a former chairman and present director of the Montreal, McNeil could not be unaware of his bank's enormous exposure to Dome. He obviously realized the importance of the sale of HBOG assets to Dome Canada both in completing the overall HBOG purchase and recovering cash for his bank. It was obvious that his interests as a director of the Bank of Montreal did not necessarily coincide — and might well conflict — with his interests as a director of Dome Canada.

Stan Roberts was well-known as a long-time friend, admirer, close associate and sometime worker for Jack Gallagher. Like McNeil, Roberts undoubtedly took his responsibilities to Dome Canada shareholders very seriously. But once again there was at least the perceived

164

potential for conflict. As for Martison, he had had enormous international experience — including a long stint in Australia and time working in the North Sea — but he was basically an exploration and operations rather than a financial man. Moreover, he had known Gallagher a long time and had briefly consulted for him before Dome moved into the Beaufort.

It was in no way surprising, or even reprehensible, that Gallagher should have picked people he knew for the board of Dome Canada. Any other CEO in his position would have done the same. It is a very rare executive who calls for tighter and more objective scrutiny of his own activities. Nevertheless, shareholders of Dome Canada might well have asked why neither the federal government nor the leading investment house for the Dome Canada issue, Pitfield Mackay Ross, pressed for more obviously independent outside directors. The need for such directors became abundantly obvious in the HBOG acquisition, particularly since the management that the independent board members had to rely on for advice about the purchase of the HBOG stake was the same management that was selling it to them. The disposition of HBOG assets was also far more than a simple participation by Dome Canada in a Dome Petroleum acquisition; it was a disposition on which Dome Petroleum's very future depended.

The directors were given financial projections for HBOG and assured it was a good deal. However, they had no independent consultants at their disposal. There was no haggling over the price; no discussion about the size of the HBOG chunk. Nevertheless, they did insist that they received no worse a deal than the theoretically arms-length arrangement being made with Dow Canada — whose wholly owned oil and gas subsidiary, Maligne Resources, was also buying 12.5% of HBOG's assets. The assumption, of course, was that Maligne *was* getting a good deal.

Dow's Helter-Skelter Ride

Dow Canada's involvement was perhaps the strangest of all the tangled components that went towards completing Dome's takeover of HBOG. The National Energy Program had been specifically designed not merely to discourage further U.S. oil investment, but also to squeeze out investors already in Canada. Yet here was a 100% U.S.-owned and controlled company committing $451 million to the purchase of Canadian petroleum properties.

Dow Chemical Company, founded in 1897 and based in Midland, Michigan, is the sixth largest chemical company in the world and

165

second in North America only to Du Pont. In 1981 it ranked twenty-fourth on the *Fortune* 500 list of leading industrial companies. It had 60,000 employees and operated in 77 countries, but it was as American as apple pie. That hardly recommended it to the fiercely nationalist federal government, whose NEP had been designed to discriminate against foreign-owned companies.

Perhaps the answer to the riddle lay in the fact that this was one case where personal ties and commitments carried more value than balance sheets. One man who felt that way about his relationship with Dome was Cliff Mort, a soft-spoken Canadian chemical engineer with a background in chemical marketing and business development. His sense of loyalty was to earn him "early retirement."

Mort had forged close links with Dome, and in particular with Bill Richards, during the two companies' partnership in the long regulatory struggle over the Cochin pipeline and Alberta petrochemical development in the early 1970s. In 1974, Richards proposed a joint exploration agreement to Mort under which Dome and Dow would put up money to explore on Dome's lands, with Dow receiving in return a 25% interest in all non-producing reserves and wildcat lands. Dow would also take 25% of new acquisitions. The essence of the program was that Dow would be involved in all future activities and thus couldn't be "highgraded," that is, have Dome give precedence in exploration to lands in which Dow had no interest. When Mort made the agreement, he had no idea where it would lead.

For the first three years of the joint program, exploration proceeded at a relatively mild pace. But then, in 1977, activity began to heat up. Mort had gained approval from his board in 1977 for a $12-million exploration budget for oil and gas. Coming into the last quarter of the year, it appeared that some of the money would be left over. Then suddenly the news broke that a small company, Canadian Hunter, had discovered a massive natural gas field in northwest Alberta. Furious bidding for lands in the area began. Dome bought aggressively and Dow was willingly dragged along in its wake.

Mort had to return to his board for more money twice before the end of the year. For 1978, he secured an exploration and acquisition budget of $18 million. It was gone by May. Dow spent $35 million on the joint venture that year. In 1979, Dow had spent $90 million by the beginning of December *without* acquisitions.

The president of Dow Chemical through most of the 1970s, Ben Branch, was a great supporter of his Canadian subsidiary's move into oil and gas. He had met and been impressed both by Gallagher and Richards, although he had been a little surprised when Gallagher had pulled out his maps of the Beaufort — mainly because Dow's agreement only applied to onshore lands. However, Branch retired in 1978 and was succeeded by less enthusiastic management. Within three years, Dow was moving out of oil and gas everywhere except in Canada. In Canada, however, oil and gas activities were expanding at an ever greater rate. Dow Canada was an eager partner in Dome's acquisitions of Siebens and Mesa. However, it simply couldn't keep up with Dome's growing ambitions. The problem was that unless it continued to participate, its relationship with Dome could be ruined. The only answer was to bring in a partner to take a share of Dow's existing properties and, more important, of its commitment to future acquisitions.

The ideal opportunity came with Dome's acquisition of the controlling block of TransCanada PipeLines and TCPL's decision — with the fullest encouragement from its new controlling shareholder — to increase its activities in oil and gas. Dow sold half its oil and gas interests to TCPL for $315 million, bringing the chemical company a tidy $90 million pre-tax profit. It also brought TransCanada into a partnership whereby each took 12.5% in Dome's future onshore exploration and acquisition activities, although TCPL decided that it would negotiate separately for future acquisitions. Each took its share of Kaiser Petroleum for $130 million, but then along came HBOG, and a whole different league. A 12.5% stake in HBOG was going to cost each company an amount of money that five years before would by itself have represented the largest sum spent on an acquisition in Canada.

Meanwhile, the NEP had a severely adverse effect on Dow Canada's status *vis-à-vis* Canadian-owned and controlled companies. After Dome had acquired Conoco's 53% of HBOG, Dow was not sure if it would be asked to participate because it was not certain if Dome would be going for 100% control. In the late fall Richards approached Mort. Under the agreement with Dome, Dow had an obligation to participate, subject to satisfactory financing, but down in Midland, Michigan, there was very little enthusiasm for the deal. The parent company was in the process of disposing of its oil and gas properties in the U.S. Moreover, the amount of money involved caused a company even of Dow's size to balk.

Mort was told he'd have to drive a hard bargain with Dome. The critical point, Mort décided, was to get a commitment from Richards that Dome would buy back the properties from Dow if Dow requested it. Over a weekend in November, Mort and his Maligne oil and gas team worked out an agreement in principle with Dome's president. However, the attitude of the banks towards financing oil and gas acquisitions had reversed in a remarkably short space of time, as Mort discovered when he approached the Toronto-Dominion Bank to finance the HBOG deal.

Over the preceeding couple of years, Dow's American parent had been putting pressure on its Canadian operation to take a little more money from Citibank. However, the T-D had kept on saying "No, take a little more from us," and the loans to Maligne had just grown and grown. By the time the HBOG deal came along, Maligne had $130 million from the T-D and about $100 million from all its other bankers. Mort's belief was that under Dow's agreement with the T-D he had enough lending power left with the bank to do the HBOG deal. The T-D told him otherwise. At one meeting in Calgary, Mort got so mad with one of the T-D's senior bankers that he felt like throwing him out of the window.

Mort's scramble to finance the deal went all the way down to the wire, and in the end represented a complex arrangement whereby Maligne would acquire 12.5% of HBOG's onshore oil and gas properties (10% of the company as a whole) for $451 million, to be paid over nine years. There was also the provision that Maligne could sell back to Dome Petroleum $74 million worth of properties a year for the ensuing five years.

For Mort, his association with Dome Petroleum had provided the most exciting years of his business career. He felt a powerful personal obligation to help them through this "tight spot." But within four months, the move had effectively cost him his job.

The final family member to participate in the HBOG deal was TransCanada PipeLines which, through its oil and gas subsidiary, TCPL Resources, took 13% of HBOG's assets for $560 million. The money was provided by the Commerce and the Royal.

The three family members had thus each taken a slightly different bundle of HBOG assets. TCPL took an interest in eveything but HBOG's coal, pipeline and non-resource assets. Maligne took 12.5% of onshore oil and gas. Dome Canada took 12.5% in all HBOG's Canadian oil and gas properties including offshore and the company's stake in the Syncrude tar-sands project.

As a result of the sales, Dome would receive $1.24 billion in cash and marketable securities and an amount receivable (from Maligne) for $259 million. Of the total amount, U.S.$400 million had to go to the Citibank consortium for its cash collateral account, part of its loan package to Dome, while the remainder had to be paid to the Canadian banks. Despite these dispositions, however, Dome would still have to find almost $1.4 billion by the following September 30. But very few people outside Dome Petroleum and the banks were aware of that fact. In particular, the Citibank consortium had no idea of how much the Canadian banks had toughened their stance.

14
No Rabbits Left

"We had been busy pulling rabbits out of the hat throughout this whole thing, and I guess they fig-ured maybe we'd pull another rabbit out. But there were no rabbits left."

BILL RICHARDS

Bill Richards had always been like a corporate circus performer, spinning increasing numbers of plates simultaneously. In the first quarter of 1982, his juggling talents were pushed to their limit. One day he would have to put on a show for Toronto investment analysts, the next for members of the Citibank consortium in New York. Often he would give several performances in a day, distracting the skittish members of Dome's family and friends in the morning before giving an afternoon matinée in front of the toughest audience of all, the Canadian banks.

Richards' packed schedule for the first three months of 1982 read like this:
- Gain HBOG minority shareholder approval for Dome's offer.
- Gain agreement in principle from Dome's family and friends to purchase their respective chunks of HBOG's assets while also help-ing some of them with financing.
- Finalize the $2.1 billion Citibank loan.
- Complete the asset sale to Dome's family and friends and repay almost $1 billion of the Canadian bank loan.
- Avoid bankruptcy at the end of March.

Assuming the company survived the first quarter, and the ensuing six months, it faced the Herculean task of paying off the remainder of the Canadian bank loan at the end of September. Escapology had to be added to Richards' juggling skills.

In the meantime, Richards also had to practise a little sleight of hand. If Citibank was to discover that the Canadian banks were plan-ning to shorten the term of their loan to Dome, then the Citibank deal would fall through. Later Richards would claim that he wasn't trying to hide anything because he believed Dome would be able to raise further money to pay off the Canadian banks once the Citibank deal was closed; thus closing the deal was his priority. Paying off the rest

169

of the Canadian banks' loan was a trick for a later performance. Nevertheless, at the time, he had to convince the Canadian bankers that he was devoting a great deal of thought to further asset sales.

The problem of Dome's internal management also had to be dealt with by Richards during the first three months of 1982. Jack Gallagher had decided he should do more to help Dome out of its difficulties. The result was like having two performers on the same stage with a screen separating them. Neither was quite sure what the other was doing, and the audience wasn't sure which one it should be watching.

Gallagher subsequently claimed — which many people found astonishing — that he knew nothing about the proposed shortening of the Canadian banks' loan. However, he certainly did know about the Canadian banks' anger over the whole issue. Bill Mulholland had learned about the Citibank loan by reading about it in the newspaper. He was livid. When the Bank of Montreal's annual cross-country outlook conference visited Calgary in January, 1982, Mulholland and Gallagher had a three-hour lunch in the Petroleum Club at which the Montreal's chairman could hardly contain himself. Dome had initiated the deal with Citibank without consulting its Canadian bankers. Gallagher told Mulholland that the company had thought the Montreal had so much Dome commitment already that it wouldn't want any more. Mulholland fumed. Surely that was his decision, he said, not Dome's.

What infuriated Mulholland was the conflict that Dome's actions had caused between the Canadian banks and the Citibank group. Dome was pledging assets to the Citibank group that the Canadian banks had financed. But Mulholland, and his fellow Canadian bankers, knew that they had to go along with the terms of the Citibank loan, because if the HBOG deal wasn't completed, then they were *really* in trouble. Once it was completed, however, Mulholland wanted assets sold and his bank's money paid back. "Either you sell off assets and pay us back," Mulholland told Gallagher, "or we'll sell them off for you."

When Gallagher reported the conversation to Richards, Dome's president was agitated. Mulholland's attitude wasn't going to make the fight for Dome's corporate life any easier. But Richards seemed to understand much better than Gallagher how desperate the situation was. Even as Dome was performing, the stage was collapsing.

The OPEC price of between U.S.$36 and U.S.$40 reached at the end of 1980 was economically unsustainable. It depressed demand and exacerbated economic recession. In 1981, OPEC production was forced down by 16.4%. As Dome fought to keep up financial appearances in the first quarter of 1982, even oil from Saudi Arabia — the

170

most conspicuous dove of the oil producers — was being sold on the spot market for less than the official price.

The National Energy Program had boldly stated that world oil was, and would continue to be, ruled by politics rather than economics, and thus that the world price would continue to soar. The September 1981, federal-provincial agreement had been based on the same assumptions, although the disarray in OPEC was by then obvious. All over the globe, the dramatically different petroleum market outlook was having a profound effect on the relationships between producers and consumers and on the attractiveness of oil investment.

During the bitter dispute between the federal and Alberta governments in 1981, Alberta had attempted to pressure Ottawa by cutting back producction. The move had backfired. Additional exports had been contracted for and Albertan oil remained shut in. Dome claimed that it was losing 25,000 barrels a day of production due to the cutbacks. Meanwhile, the interest payments on the $2 billion borrowed for the first half of HBOG was swallowing cash flow. Dome — primarily under Bill Richards' influence — had been swept along by the NEP syndrome. Richards had not only believed in acquisition as one route to corporate glory, he also believed that as large a share as possible of enormously expensive petroleum megaprojects, such as tar sands plants, which he saw as the wave of the future, should be grabbed. Now that wave, too, was crashing around Dome's ears.

Canada was already a global leader in synthetic oil extraction from tar sands, with the world's only two commercial plants, Syncrude and Suncor (Great Canadian Oil Sands), operating in Alberta's Athabasca tar sands. When the NEP had been written, the only potential problem foreseen by Ottawa was the windfall profits that might accrue to the projects' private sector sponsors.

Dome had originally taken a 4% stake in the giant Alsands project — led by Shell Canada — that planned to extract 140,000 barrels of synthetic oil daily from the Athabasca tar sands at a capital cost of over $13 billion. Before Dome drew a bead on it, HBOG had also committed itself to taking 8% of the plant, so Dome was now a potential participant in 12% of Alsands, a share that would cost in the region of $1.5 billion to finance. Fortunately for Dome, the project crumbled in February, 1982. If Dome had been the only company to withdraw, then attention would have been drawn to its mounting financial problems. However, two of the soundest companies involved, Amoco and Chevron, were the first to pull out. Dome's subsequent withdrawal merely appeared to be part of the project's overall disintegration in the face of slumping world oil prices. Shortly afterwards, despite panicky concessions from both the federal and Alberta

171

governments, the project collapsed. However, Alsands was merely a side show, one of the smallest of Dome's problems.

Typically, Bill Richards' public face wasn't merely brave, it was self-confidently brazen. In January, while speaking to an oil and gas seminar in Calgary, he said Dome had been subject to "misconceptions" and had been "surrounded by swirling and usually false rumours." His sense of humour unshaken, he said: "There have been some people who have been so narrow-minded as to suggest that perhaps we have a high debt." Richards told his audience to remember that the company's underlying value was $20 billion, an estimate of mind-numbing audacity. The company's cash flow, he declared, was $1 billion. After the HBOG deal closed, he noted, and the asset sale to the company's family and friends had been completed, Dome's debt would be down to $4.6 billion. By the end of the year, he continued, Dome's objective was to have the debt down to $3.8 billion. All the figures were flights of financial fancy. Dome's year-end debt would in fact be twice that figure.

Maier Bows Out

Of all those involved in the purchase of the HBOG minority shares, the only group who could be unreservedly happy was the HBOG minority shareholders. Once the Citibank loan had been finalized, their $57.50 a share would be safely tied up in convertible shares that were as good as cash.

On January 13, 1982, the tension-charged special HBOG shareholders' meeting was held at the Calgary Convention Centre. For Gerry Maier, HBOG's chief executive, it was to be a poignant meeting indeed. It was here that he would lose control of his company. Maier had held a team concept of HBOG. He had tried to instill an *esprit de corps* within the HBOG tower. That he had succeeded showed clearly on this particular day. The meeting was packed solid with HBOG workers who were also shareholders. In many ways, although he had lost his company, Maier had won most of his personal objectives in his dealings with Dome. In particular, he had made sure that all the minority shareholders got a good deal. An acquisitor almost always pays more for the controlling block of a takeover target; however, in this case, thanks to Maier, Dome had been forced to pay more for the minority.

Now Maier was the only one of the top three HBOG executives left. Senior Vice-President Ken Burgis had retired in October, and Dick Haskeyne had quit to move over to Home Oil as president. Maier, too, had resigned at the end of December, but was staying on to see the deal finalized. He would only resign as a director when all the documentation on the Citibank loan was signed on March 10.

Gerry Maier had felt that he should chair this final HBOG shareholders' meeting, but the Dome lawyers had taken even that away from him. Bill Richards was in the chair.

Everybody at the meeting seemed edgy, except Smilin' Jack. Gallagher, like Richards, had taken to making little jokes about Dome's debt position, in particular, he had a favourite old joke that he'd used many times. Smiling, he now stood and told the assembly how Dome had started out 30 years before with $250,000 of equity and $7.5 million of debt, and that what had happened in the last 60 days proved that the company wanted to maintain that ratio. To the Dome financial people present it was no longer such a funny story. Peter Breyfogle cringed. Aftewards he would beg Gallagher: "*Please* don't tell that joke any more."

Otherwise, the meeting held few humorous moments. A young shareholder got up to disagree with the valuations of the two companies. George Richardson was asked to respond for the HBOG committee of independent directors. Uncharacteristically, he put the young man down. Even Bill Richards was nervous and sounded defensive, as he went on at great length about what a wonderful deal the HBOG purchase was for Canada.

Finally, Maier said he'd like to speak. Sitting there listening to Bill Richards wax lyrical about Dome Petroleum and Dome Canada had made him a little angry. It just emphasized the whole one-sidedness of the affair. From the very first, it had been Dome, Dome, Dome. Nobody in the press or Ottawa or in the Canadian public outside the oil business seemed to consider HBOG and its employees. So Maier got up and pointed out that it had been HBOG employees and shareholders who had made the company the very desirable property that it was.

And then the vote was taken, and, as anticipated, it was overwhelmingly in favour of the Plan of Arrangement.

Dome had cleared another hurdle. But many remained.

International Dreams

When it came to additional asset sales to repay the banks, HBOG's international properties were the most attractive candidates. Jack Gallagher, despite his earlier experiences as a globe-trotting geologist with Standard Oil, had always declared himself opposed to Dome's

173

involvement in overseas exploration. He always explained that the company had more than enough to do in Canada, particularly in the Beaufort. Nevertheless, when the Conoco stake in HBOG had been acquired, and the various vice-presidents of HBOG had given presentations on the company's activities, Gallagher had been particularly interested in the presentation of David Powell, the British-born and British-educated former Burmah Oil employee now in charge of HBOG's overseas operations.

Gallagher was interested in HBOG's exploration philosophy and its attitude to political risks. Weren't the risks in Indonesia, where HBOG had its most promising properties, high? Powell explained that a company had to look at how quickly any project would pay out and then relate this to the potential speed of political destabilization in a country. On that basis, said Powell, Indonesia was not that risky. For Gallagher, this was an intriguing concept. He reiterated that he thought Dome had enough to do in Canada, but noted to HBOG's overseas exploration staff that if Dome *was* to go international, then he would want a good spread of geological, geographical and political risks. Gallagher's interest had obviously been aroused.

Dome's chairman decided to look at HBOG's overseas properties, and at the end of January he took off on a three-week tour. The first stop was HBOG's Perth office. Gallagher met with government officials and was impressed both with HBOG's Australian operations and its relationship with the authorities. From Perth, Gallagher flew to Indonesia, where HBOG had enjoyed enormous exploration successes in the preceding couple of years and was already producing around 11,000 barrels of oil a day. Dome's chairman was received with respect by officials of Pertamina, the Indonesian state oil company, and was guest of honour at a dinner for a number of leading figures in the oil industry. In both Australia and Jakarta, where he was invited to speak, he related his hopes for the Beaufort.

Gallagher was enormously impressed by the whole Indonesian set-up, from the attitude of the government right down to the recreation facilities. While visiting HBOG's offshore operations in Java and Sumatra, he was flown by helicopter onto one of the company's recreation islands. There he swam in the warm tropical waters, reflecting, perhaps, that this whole area might be a highly desirable addition to the Dome empire. Before he left Indonesia, Gallagher, it seems, had decided that Dome should do everything possible to hang onto HBOG's overseas operations. He also realized that Dome needed cash, so somewhere in the exotic surroundings of the Far East, he formed the kernel of an idea: Dome would put its U.S. properties and the international properties of HBOG into a "pot" and form a new company, Dome International. Dome Petroleum would operate the company and retain 20% ownership, while the remaining 80% would be sold for $800 million. After he left Singapore, Gallagher travelled on to Hong Kong to discuss the idea with associates there. His plan was to sell shares of Dome International primarily to Japanese, European and Hong Kong investors. But while Gallagher was dreaming up this scheme, Wayne McGrath, at Richards' instructions, was in Japan trying to sell the very same properties outright. While McGrath was in Tokyo, he received phone calls and telexes from Gallagher summoning him to Hong Kong. There, Gallagher briefed him on his plan and McGrath was dispatched back to Tokyo to pitch a completely different deal to the Japanese. Gallagher, Powell and McGrath also visited Europe to test the waters for Dome International.

Richards was reportedly furious with Gallagher for pitching Dome International out of the blue. Meanwhile, there was little enthusiasm for the scheme among potential purchasers, many of whom were interested in buying the international properties outright, but had little desire to take shares in a global hotchpotch of properties with Dome Petroleum as operator.

In any case, although the concept of Dome International was imaginative, to organize such a scheme would have taken considerable time, and Dome just didn't have time.

The Citibank consortium had little interest in Dome's confused efforts to raise money on HBOG's overseas properties. Their loan was to be secured on the production, and production potential of HBOG's Canadian properties. Nevertheless, their lack of knowledge about Dome's mounting cash-flow crisis seemed astonishing.

They were about to lend $2.1 billion to a company on the brink.

Three-Ring Circus

The closing of the HBOG second half was one of the largest and most complex financial transactions in corporate history. Takeover closings are usually marked by large teams of professionals — principally bankers and lawyers — working through last-minute financial or legal problems, but Dome's closing was like a three-ring circus. On March 10, 1982, three floors of New York law firm Shearman & Sterling were taken up by Dome and the other parties to its multiple agreements. Meanwhile the 33rd floor of the Dome Tower back in Calgary was also packed solid with lawyers and signatories to the numerous documents. The Citibank loan, the acquisition of the remainder of HBOG and the sale to corporate family and friends had to be concluded simultaneously. However, Canadian bankers were also signing a document at Shearman & Sterling that the Citibank group knew nothing about: it was the official shortening of Dome's loan.

Citibank took a full-page announcement, or "tombstone," to celebrate the largest petroleum production loan ever. No ads were placed by the Canadian banks about their shortened loan. The fact that neither Dome nor any of the Canadian banks felt obliged to reveal the shortening to the Citibank consortium would be the cause of enormous friction. In the event, however, massive problems would crop up for Dome long before the Canadian bank loan became due.

After the closing of the deal, Richards held a barbecue at his ranch outside Calgary. It was a strange celebration. Anybody there from Dome's inner circle realized the company was fast approaching a financial crisis. In any case, some of the bankers were forced to stay away because unpleasant events were unfolding elsewhere in the oil community. Frank Duncanson, CIBC's chief oil banker in Calgary, couldn't come because another company to which the Commerce had lent a great deal of money, Turbo Resources, had that day declared itself in financial trouble. The floodgates were beginning to open.

Around Calgary, many other companies were in deep trouble and Dome's suppliers were fighting for their lives *because* of Dome. But that wasn't the only reason for the lack of sympathy around town. Many of the multinational oil companies could scarcely conceal their delight at Dome's problems.

Richards had always pooh-poohed the big oil companies' professional managers, claiming that they were puppets, and that they didn't have shareholders "biting at their ass" the way he did. He left them in no doubt that he thought he was a whole lot smarter than they were. He called Imperial "Imperious Oil," and asserted that the country's biggest multinational was so frightened of being "taken" by Dome that it wouldn't deal with it.

The foreign-owned companies had been enraged by the National Energy Program. But they had also watched in amazement while Dome, *another* foreign-owned company — but one that happened to be in bed with Ottawa — had taken the federal government to the cleaners via Dome Canada. Moreover, the federal government had applauded Dome for doing so.

Richards had always berated the big oil companies for their caution and lack of ideas. But now the fruits of caution were apparent. Suddenly the nationalist stars of Canadian oil discovered why the debt levels of the big, foreign-owned companies were so low. It was called prudence.

In the executive suites, the sly digs about Dome and its management began to make the rounds:

176

"Shame Jack Gallagher wasn't as good at finding oil as he was at finding money."

"Perhaps if Imperial had offered him a better job he would never have left."

And then the Dome jokes started to circulate:

"Bill Richards goes into Jack Gallagher's office and he says: 'Jack, I've got some good news and some bad news.'"

"Well," says Jack, "first tell me the good news."

"And so Bill says: 'Imperial Oil is for sale for just $8 billion.'"

"Oh," says Jack, "that sounds pretty cheap. What's the bad news?"

"They want $50 down."

There was another joke that Bill Richards was calling for cash-flow forecasts every *15 minutes*. But that "joke" was close to the truth.

One of the enormous problems for any large company in a cash crunch is simply to slow down spending. Corporations have momentum from their ongoing operations and it takes time to slow the outflow of funds. Val Eshleman, the Dome executive who had run the U.S. operations, had been called in several months before to try to cut overhead and production expenses. Richards' $1.7 billion capital budget for 1982 had been slashed. Payments to creditors had been slowed to the point where some of Dome's suppliers were being forced out of business. The Dome switchboard was getting more and more calls from desperate service companies who needed to be paid to survive themselves. But nobody except certain Canadian bankers and those at the heart of the company knew what desperate straits the company was really in.

Bill Richards was asking for cash-flow forecasts so often because he wasn't sure Dome could survive the end of the month. Since it was the end of the year's first quarter, a number of interest, principal and other payments came due. If Dome's income and lines of credit weren't sufficient to meet those payments, then the company would go into default.

Peter Breyfogle, as the chief financial officer, had become virtually a nervous wreck in his attempts to cajole the banks into lending Dome more money. But apart from a couple of relatively small loans from European institutions, the financial cupboard was bare.

"Peter's Prefs"

Breyfogle's last shot — described somewhat disparagingly within the company as "Peter's Prefs" — was a suggestion that Dome should try to persuade HBOG minority shareholders to swap the retractable preferred shares they were due to receive under the plan of arrangement for convertible preferred shares of Dome Petroleum. This would enable Dome to get its hands on the escrow account in which the funds for retraction were held. Breyfogle believed that as much as $300 million might be raised in this way. However, the deal was never thought plausible within Dome and when investment banker Wood Gundy gave it the thumbs down, the deal effectively died. One last attempted dip into the Eurodollar market also faltered when Morgan Stanley refused to act for Dome.

Breyfogle's abrasive manner had never made him popular within Dome. When pneumonia had kept him out of action for six weeks the previous summer, other financial executives within Dome had lost no time in expressing their misgivings about him to Bill Richards. Jack Gallagher, who was particularly concerned about the treatment of Dome employees, had also become unhappy about Breyfogle's management style. In March, Breyfogle was fired.

Dome's chief financial officer may have had an unfortunate manner. Nevertheless, he had tried — to the detriment of his health — to press Gallagher and Richards to issue equity quickly to pay for the second half of HBOG. If they had done so, Dome would not now have been in such terrible straits.

Less than two weeks after one of the world's largest and supposedly most sophisticated banks led a syndicate to lend Dome $2.1 billion, Dome was on the point of bankruptcy. It simply couldn't meet its end-of-month payments. The cream of Calgary's bankers were called to a meeting. They were told that Dome needed $100 million to survive. The bankers sat in silence and then left. The silence lasted for a week. Dome wasn't sure if the bankers were taking them seriously. And even within Dome, the realization of potential default took time to sink in. The company had specialized in living close to the edge. Bill Richards later said: "We had been busy pulling rabbits out of the hat throughout this whole thing, and I guess they figured maybe we'd pull another rabbit out. But there were no rabbits left."

On March, 29, there was another major meeting with Dome's Canadian bankers in Calgary. The meeting went on late into the night. At one stage in the discussions, Frank Duncanson of the Commerce suggested to Steve Savidant that the Dome team should go down to Toronto to speak to senior bank officials in person.

Colin Kenny had gone home that evening at about 10 P.M. At 11:30, after he had gone to bed, he received a call from Savidant telling him that the Dome travelling road show was once more taking off. Savidant told Kenny the plane would be leaving at 12:30 A.M. The fact that Kenny was one of the most important links with Ottawa's corridors of power was not without its significance. In a little more than

24 hours, the Ottawa network would be Dome's only apparent hope of survival.

Meanwhile, Jack Gallagher was still in London trying to enthuse investors over the concept of Dome International. There he received a call from Don Gardiner, who had in the past year skillfully managed to combine acting as Gallagher's executive assistant along with working as a key member of Dome's financial team under Richards. Gardiner advised Gallagher that Dome's situation was now serious and that he should fly to Toronto to meet the rest of the Dome team and join in the negotiations with the banks.

The Dome plane eventually took off from Calgary for Toronto at 3 A.M. on the morning of March 30. The men from Dome checked once more into the King Edward Hotel to grab a couple of hours sleep before confronting the big day which they knew lay in front of them.

As soon as the banks' executive offices opened, the Dome men started doing the rounds, calling all the senior executives for an audience. Some agreed to see them, some did not. After each expedition, the members of the team would regroup in Richards' suite. The reports were not good. They continued to make calls to the bankers' homes late into the evening, but the reception remained icy.

Already, back in the Dome Tower in Calgary, a certain pre-execution serenity had settled over those who knew how serious the situation was. In Toronto, where the rules were made and the referees lived, it seemed the game was finally over. Dome would go under the next day. There would be no great hoopla. A cheque would be presented — probably, the Dome team had worked out, in a Vancouver branch — and it would bounce. Then Dome would technically be in default.

It seemed astonishing to the Dome executives that the banks might be prepared to jeopardize their huge loans to Dome, but then the banks weren't perhaps revealing their whole battle plan. One bank executive then suggested something that Dome must already have had in mind. "Why don't you," he said, "speak to Ottawa?"

15
The Armageddon File

"Cohen was duly called and, for the next few hours, phones rang and lights went on in the homes of Ottawa's most powerful men."

Shortly after midnight on the morning of March 31, 1982, Marc Lalonde's executive assistant, Mike Phelps, was woken by a telephone call from Colin Kenny. The former Liberal government insider gave the current Liberal government insider a message that jolted him out of his drowsiness: Dome Petroleum was on the point of bankruptcy.

Kenny was phoning from Bill Richards' suite in the King Eddy, which on the previous day had been the base for a fruitless search for $100 million, the amount of money Dome needed to survive. The whole Dome team had spent the day phoning around and traipsing to and from the bank towers of their major borrowers, all situated within a couple of blocks of the hotel. All the bankers had said no.

At least one of the bankers had shocked the men from Dome by suggesting that the government was now their only hope, and they had sat in Richards' room for a couple of hours throwing together a desperate strategy. They needed either money from the government or, more likely, the government to apply pressure to the banks to make them part with the money. To persuade Ottawa to take either course of action Dome would have to make a powerful case showing that the company's failure would be economically disastrous. They would scarcely have to remind the Liberals of the political embarrassment that would ensue from the collapse of their "chosen instrument."

Colin Kenny had pointed out to his colleagues that they couldn't wait until morning to deliver their message. Not only was time running out, but all the most influential men in Ottawa had busy schedules and would be difficult to reach once the workday started. Kenny should know. He had spent a decade working with the schedule of the most powerful politician of all, Pierre Trudeau. The only place they could be sure of reaching them, said Kenny, was in their beds. He set to work to draw up a list. Mike Phelps' name was close to the top. Phelps, a lawyer in his mid-30s, had joined Lalonde in the spring of 1980, as the NEP was in its formative stages. He had assumed

181

enormous power under his strong-willed and arrogant political master, and had quickly become one of EMR's ruling quadrumvirate of power. Most mornings, he and his minister would meet with Mickey Cohen, EMR's deputy minister and Ed Clark, the number two mandarin in the department and the whizz-kid economist credited — and later blamed — for much of the thrust of the NEP. Through much of 1980, these four had plotted the shape and reach of the NEP. During 1981 they had spent most of their time arguing strategy and tactics in the critical price and revenue-sharing negotiations with Alberta. They were to spend most of 1982 coping with disaster.

The four had occasionally joked about Dome overextending itself, but they had never seriously considered that possibility. They all lived in Ottawa's cosy world of financial security, where budgetary control was considered long and earnestly as a semi-academic branch of political science.

In Ottawa, you could spend yourself into a mild but confidential rap on the knuckles, or, at worst, a mention in the Auditor General's report. You could never spend yourself into bankruptcy. Somehow, Dome had come to be considered part of the same cosy system. As a chosen instrument, how could it get into *real* financial trouble? The four men had relatively little to do with the commercial world — although they had, with the NEP, attempted to revolutionize one important part of it. Their knowledge of banking was acquired primarily at the academic and personal level. Phelps was the first of them to be awoken, literally, to the stark reality that there really were limits to financing, even for chosen instruments.

Phelps, considered a "friend" of Dome, was a popular figure both with the oil industry and his provincial counterparts in Alberta. He felt a special affinity with Dome because Bill Richards — who had taken care to court him — was another former Manitoba lawyer. Phelps had taken, and been encouraged to take, a keen interest in Dome's activities, and had been duly impressed by Gallagher's charm and the Beaufort vision. He had participated in the political side of Dome Canada's creation and had persuaded his minister to attend its Calgary launching. He had been phoned 48 hours ahead of Dome's announcement of its tender offer for the Conoco shares, the tender offer that was to spark the battle for control of HBOG. For Dome, he was a critical part of the Ottawa network.

Now he might be *the* critical part of that network, for he was guardian to the gate of the only man they knew with enough power and information to help them, Marc Lalonde. Lalonde had already exerted his enormous power within the cabinet to have Dome's Plan of Arrangement with HBOG's minority shareholders grandfathered after the disastrous 1981 budget. He had very publicily supported the creation of Dome Canada. He had done his tour of the Beaufort. Now Dome wanted him to exercise his power in an area where it was less certain, with the Canadian banks. Kenny wanted Phelps to speak to Lalonde and put the minister in touch with Bill Richards. Dome needed Lalonde, he said, to use some "moral suasion" to persuade the banks to cough up some more money. An hour or so later, Richards spoke to Lalonde. The Dome group had made some rapid calculations about the implications of their bankruptcy in terms of jobs lost, suppliers put in financial jeopardy, and the possible default of other members of the "family." This rough picture would later be worked up into a comprehensive economic disaster scenario called the "Armaggedon File."

Lalonde sat silently in the dead of the Ottawa night as Richards reeled off the possible consequences of a Dome default. There were at least 10,000 jobs at stake; thousands of small companies would be dragged under if Dome sunk; Dome Canada could become responsible for the immediate repayment of the $400 million loan from the Japanese through a cross-default provision in the loan agreement; Dome Mines would have to put up its $250 million loan guarantee.

Lalonde was deeply shocked. "You'd better call Mickey," he said.

Cohen was duly called and, for the next few hours, phones rang and lights went on in the homes of Ottawa's most powerful men. Ian Stewart, deputy minister of finance and another key figure in the formulation of the National Energy Program, was woken, as was Michael Pitfield, Clerk of the Privy Council and mandarin overlord of the Trudeaucracy. To each, Bill Richards repeated his sobering message. Unless they did something, Dome could go under the next day.

A couple of hours before dawn, Colin Kenny and John Beddome, effectively Dome's number three executive after Gallagher and Richards, returned to Beddome's room to put calls through to Alberta's tough and taciturn energy minister, Merv Leitch, Tom Wood, his powerful assistant, and Barry Mellon, the province's outspoken senior energy bureaucrat.

Dome's relations with Albertan politicians and officials had never been as close as those with the federal government. The company's fate was of obvious concern in Edmonton because of its pervasive presence in the province. However, Alberta's government had been intensely angry with Dome when it had appeared to respond positively to the National Energy Program through the creation of Dome Canada. That ensured a cool attitude on Alberta's part towards helping the company out. But Dome was desperate.

183

Dome Canada: Desperate Measures

By now, Dome had not merely committed every asset it owned to the banks and exhausted its own lines of credit, it had also cajoled its corporate family and friends into stretching their financial resources to the limit. Within the family, there was now only one acquiescent source of funds left, Dome Canada, the Richards-inspired and government-blessed response to the National Energy Program. Dome Canada's liquid resources had, in fact, all been used up in the purchase of its HBOG stake. However, the company had no debt — apart from the Japanese loan of $225 million, whose repayment was many years down the road — so it still had considerable borrowing power. Dome Petroleum simply had to find a way of "accessing" that borrowing power. In other words, it had to find something else to sell Dome Canada, and for which Dome Canada could borrow the money. Given Dome's financial condition, it was going to be difficult to make any such arrangement look other than financial pillage.

The management of Dome Petroleum and the management of Dome Canada — who happened to be the same people — decided that what Dome Canada needed to buy from Dome Petroleum, with borrowed money, was a big chunk of its Beaufort drilling fleet. This proposal placed an enormously heavy burden on the outside directors, who only had Dome Petroleum staff to rely on for valuation of the deal. Nevertheless, Fred McNeil, the former chairman of the Bank of Montreal, reportedly raised hell behind closed doors about what Dome was doing, and at least ensured that the terms of the deal were favourable to Dome Canada. But the point was, what did Dome Canada *want* with half an Arctic drilling fleet?

Under the deal eventually hammered out — effectively between McNeil and Dome Petroleum management — Dome Canada would buy 46.5% of the Canmar fleet and its shore-based facilities for $200 million. However, one major problem with the sale was that Citibank held a negative pledge on the fleet as part of the security for its HBOG loan. No part of the fleet could be sold without Citibank's approval. And there was an even larger problem: the Canadian banks were simply refusing to lend Dome Canada the money for the purchase. Dome badly needed Ottawa to help persuade the banks to make the loan.

When Lalonde called the bank chairmen on the morning of March 31, he was extremely careful not to suggest that they do anything on a non-commercial basis. He was also keen to avoid possible accusations of having applied pressure to them. However, he asked them to take a long, cool look at the situation. Eventually, the banks agreed to go ahead with the loan to Dome Canada, but they demanded certain conditions. In particular, two banks wanted a change of Dome management. Bill Mulholland of the Montreal felt most strongly about this. He met with Rowland Frazee to talk about a successor to Gallagher. The name they came up with was Bob Bandeen, head of Canadian National Railway. Bandeen had announced the previous January that he intended to leave CN. Now Mulholland and Frazee visited him to suggest that he might become the banks' representative on the Dome board with a view to becoming chairman and CEO. Bandeen already knew Gallagher quite well and travelled out to Calgary for preliminary talks with him. During the two days he was there, Gallagher never let him out of his sight. However, Dome's chairman realized he had to appease the bankers, so he suggested that he would make Bandeen vice-chairman with the promise of the chief executive position somewhere down the road. This wasn't good enough for Bandeen and the negotiations eventually fell apart.

The other condition imposed by the banks in return for the $100 million loan to Dome Canada was that Dome would be subject to bank surveillance. By April 6 Dome Canada had been advanced the money, which was immediately transferred to Dome Petroleum as a "deposit," a deposit that was, according to Dome Canada's annual report a year later, "made with the offer in order to secure favourable terms." No announcement of the decision was made at the time. On July 15 the deal fell through because, according to Dome Canada, long-term financing had not been arranged. The reason it had not been arranged went back to the fact that Canmar was already pledged as collateral to Citibank.

As a *quid pro quo* for allowing the sale of part of Canmar, Citibank demanded further collateral. Specifically, they wanted a second lien on Dome's natural gas liquids operations. However, the first lien on those operations was held by the Bank of Montreal, which refused to allow the second lien. But Dome had *also* promised a second lien on the NGL operations to Dome Canada's directors as security for the advance. When Fred McNeil found out through his continuing contacts with the Bank of Montreal that the bank had no intention of permitting the second lien, and that if it was allowed it would go to Citibank rather than Dome Canada, he was furious. Nevertheless, by now the $100 million had been handed over. However, it was the Bank of Montreal's stance that eventually stopped the deal from going through. The $100 million, meanwhile, was kept by Dome Petroleum in return for interest payments and a fee.

Bill Richards subsequent justification for the deal was that Dome

Canada had a keen interest in Dome Petroleum not going under, primarily because of a cross-default provision in the $400 million Japanese loan signed at the beginning of 1981. Although $175 million of the loan went to Dome Petroleum and $225 million went to Dome Canada, each company became liable for the whole loan if the other company went into default. Nevertheless, the Dome Canada-Canmar deal ranked, in the words of someone intimate with the arrangement, "about minus ten on the smell test." Eighteen months later, Dome Petroleum still had Dome Canada's $100 million.

About 60,000 investors, most of them small ones, had been enticed into Dome Canada, at least partly because the company appeared to have the clear blessing of the federal government. First Dome Canada had been used in Dome Petroleum's purchase of HBOG. Now it had been virtually pillaged in Dome's increasingly desperate attempts to survive.

Whose Problem?

The government meanwhile realized that it had a full-fledged crisis on its hands. Indeed, Dome was potentially the largest corporate crisis any Canadian government had ever had to face. In economic terms, it wasn't so much the volume of jobs involved, although that was important, but the exposure of the four banks. Part of the four banks' loan to Dome had been repaid through the disposal of HBOG assets to corporate family and friends, but they still had over $3 billion outstanding to the company.

The attitudes of the four banks involved in the Dome situation varied greatly. Harrison of the Commerce and Thomson of the T-D were eager for the government to help the banks out. Mulholland of the Montreal and Frazee of the Royal were against asking for government assistance. Mulholland is even reported to have suggested to Lalonde at a private meeting that the government *not* put any money into Dome. The argument of Harrison and Thomson was that, in lending huge volumes of money to Dome, they had been merely following national priorities, supporting the Ottawa-blessed chosen instrument. Dome, they claimed, was the "flagship of the government." Now it was the government's responsibility to bail it out. To a degree, that posture was a brave facade. Nevertheless, the government did realize that the collapse of Dome would be acutely embarrassing, since it would further confirm that the National Energy Program had been an unmitigated disaster. For both sides, however, the first priority was to discover the extent of the problem.

186

Early in April, a team from Dome, headed by Bill Richards, flew to Ottawa to spell out the difficulties. There, in the boardroom at the Department of Finance at Place Bell Canada, they met with Ian Stewart and Mickey Cohen, still the two most powerful deputy ministers in the mandarin establishment. Stewart had with him Mark Daniels, a rising star within Finance who had been involved with the Massey Ferguson bailout, while Cohen had with him Ed Clark, previously the whizz kid of the entire public service. Now Clark's star was, at least temporarily, falling. Stewart, who had continuing problems with the ramifications of the disastrous November, 1981 budget, would play little part in the Dome negotiations. Mickey Cohen, in Ottawa's terminology, "took the file," assisted by Ed Clark until Clark went off in the summer for a year's sabbatical in France. Daniels emerged as Finance's "main man" during the negotiations.

Cohen, despite the fact that he had been the senior bureaucrat responsible for the NEP, somehow managed to avoid the enormous flak attached to its collapse. He was still well regarded in the business community and would earn further respect for the way he dealt with the negotiations on the Dome bailout. Later in the summer, after a cabinet reshuffle, he would follow Marc Lalonde to the Department of Finance to become deputy minister there. He would take the Dome file with him. During the bailout negotiations, he would privately remark to colleagues how astonishing he found the pettiness of the Canadian banks.

Daniels' performance earned him respect as well. At that first meeting with the Dome executives, Daniels remarked that they might perceive Dome's problems as huge, however, they should see the *rest* of the problems the government had.

Most of the talking for Dome at the first meeting was done by Doug Martin. Martin had worked twelve-hour days and seven-day weeks for the past year since returning to Calgary from Dome's U.S. operation. In that year, he had seen Dome go from the pinnacle of corporate acclaim to the morass of impending bankruptcy. Like many of his colleagues, he was becoming somewhat jaded by the struggle.

It took several hours to describe the nature of Dome's loan agreements and their cross-default provisions. Then Dome's projected cash flow was laid out. Finally, the "Armageddon File," which had now been beefed up by Don Gilley's economists into an economic horror scenario, was presented. One feature immediately agreed upon by both sides was that there would be no public discussion of the negotiations. For six weeks or so, there would be no public knowledge of Dome's plight, although swirling rumours were reflected in a slumping share-price.

187

Over the course of further meetings, Dome laid out various solutions, trying to emphasize that the company could solve its own problems with a little help from the government and banks. Company representatives talked about selling its U.S. and Indonesian assets and even suggested a proposal whereby the government might buy a portion of its Beaufort assets. However, Dome and government valuations of the Beaufort were far apart.

To assess Dome's financial problems independently, the government appointed international management consultants Peat Marwick to go through Dome's books. In April, the Peat Marwick team from Toronto descended on the Dome Tower. For most of the following month, they sat sequestered in requisitioned offices, sending out for details of accounting systems and auditing cash-flow projections. Dome's financial staff waited anxiously to provide whatever the team wanted. Like a group of physicians running the most comprehensive examination of an ailing body, they had to discover both the nature of the disease and the viability of a cure.

In fact, the fundamental nature of Dome's ailment was apparent from the very beginning of the negotiations: the company had financial anemia. It needed two elements to boost its financial lifeblood: first, it needed the terms of its bank loans to be extended; second, the company required a massive injection of equity capital. Survival was impossible without the former, ongoing viability was impossible without the latter. Peat Marwick's principal job was to find out the extent of the needed equity transfusion. The terming of the loan could only come from the banks; the equity would have to come both from the banks and government.

The government was very keen that any cash injection into Dome would be on an equal basis with the banks. It didn't want to be perceived as acting merely to save the banks' bacon. For political as much as economic reasons, it also wanted to ensure that Dome survived as a viable company. Ottawa wanted a permanent solution so that Dome would not be returning for money in a couple of years.

The bankers, meanwhile, were angry with Dome and angry with themselves. One feature of the negotiations on which all the banks agreed was that Dome — and in particular, Gallagher and Richards — should be involved as little as possible. Not all the CEOs agreed on the apportionment of blame between the two men, but they did agree that they *were* to blame. Even now, in corporate *extremis*, both men were *still* trying to drive hard bargains. The fact that they had suggested the sale of the Beaufort assets — which had been developed almost entirely with taxpayers' money — infuriated some senior mandarins. Meanwhile, Richards' asking prices for the company's overseas assets were considered by both Ottawa and the banks to be far

188

too high. It was rumoured that Dome had a chance to dispose of its U.S. operations long before the crisis struck, but that the deal had fallen through because of attempts to squeeze the potential buyers. Such behaviour, annoying at the best of times, was now considered intolerable. As a result, for the coming six months, Dome would effectively be excluded from discussions about its fate.

The initiative on the banks' side was taken by Russell Harrison, chairman of the Commerce. In mid-April, at Harrison's suggestion, he — accompanied by his executive assistant, Bill Neville, a pudgy, hard-driving former journalist and political pro who had been Joe Clark's chief-of-staff during the 1979 Tory government — visited Ottawa to see Lalonde.

Over lunch in Lalonde's Centre Block office — at which Phelps and Cohen were present — a general framework was established. Harrison tried to emphasize the government's responsibility for Dome's condition — noting that both Dome and the banks had merely been acting in response to Ottawa's declared priority: the Canadianization of the oil industry. However, Lalonde left Harrison in no doubt that the banks would be expected to do their "fair share." As a result of the meeting, a committee procedure was set up, with Cohen, Daniels and Clark leading the government side. The banks' team would consist of Don Fullerton, CIBC's vice-chairman and president, Bill Bateman, Montreal's executive vice-president of corporate and government banking, Ted McDowell, T-D's vice-chairman in charge of commercial banking services and Joe Regan, the Royal's executive vice-president for national accounts.

Dick Thomson: Focus of Anger

When Marc Lalonde had phoned the bankers on the morning of March 31, the angriest of the four had been the T-D's Dick Thomson. Over the coming months, however, Thomson was to become the target of the other CEO's anger because of his unwillingness to put any more money into Dome. The focus of the controversy was the $250 million Dome Mines' guarantee, which the T-D had agreed to fund. If Dome Mines was called upon to come up with the money, then the T-D would have to provide it. The guarantee — and the line of credit — were due to expire either when the HBOG-related bank loan was repaid or on December 31, 1982, whichever came sooner. The other bankers believed the T-D was stalling in the hope that the guarantee would run out, thus reducing its exposure. Both Mulholland and Harrison would grow extremely angry at what they considered to be Thomson's uncompromising and unco-operative attitude.

189

At the eleventh hour, Mulholland's anger with the T-D would almost blast apart the agreement on a Dome bailout.

Bad feeling increased markedly during a meeting in Ottawa between the CEOs and the government on St. Jean Baptiste Day (June 24), 1982. The meeting had been called by the government because Dome needed another $100 million to tide it over another short-term cash crisis. However, at the meeting Thomson declared that there was no way in which the T-D proposed to do any more to help Dome out. He said that the T-D was the smallest of the four and that it had already done its fair share, and that no matter what anybody else did, his bank just wasn't going to do any more. He was absolutely opposed to the concept of the banks and the government sharing the burden of an equity injection equally, and he insisted that the Dome Mines guarantee had to go. This stance hardly endeared him to the other bankers.

Meanwhile, the behind-the-scenes wrangling of the Canadian bankers was more than matched by the anger of the Citibank consortium when it found out not only about Dome's financial difficulties but about the shortening of the Canadian bank loan. For Citibank, anger was mixed with embarrassment. It was also mixed with fear. As consortium leader, it held prime responsiblity for the soundness of Dome's $2.1 billion loan. Many of the other Canadian, American, British, French and Japanese banks in the consortium had joined it *because* Citibank was leading it. Citibank feared the possibility that one or more of these banks might seek legal recourse against it, claiming either that it did know, or should have known, about the shortened term of the Canadian loan.

The irony of course was that the Canadian bank loan had been officially shortened in the same New York offices, and at the same time, as the Citibank loan had been signed on March 10. Dome was well aware that if the Citibankers had known of the Canadian bank loan's shortening, there was no way that the deal would have been closed.

Citibank first discovered Dome's plight through the company's filings at the Securities and Exchange Commission (SEC). Requirements for prompt statements about changes in a corporation's financial situation are much more rigorous in the U.S. than in Canada. Form 10Q — a quarterly report demanded for companies whose shares are publicly traded on U.S. stock exchanges — dealing with the first three months of 1982, and dated May 14, stated Dome's situation for all to see.

On page three of the 10Q was a comparison of Dome Petroleum's consolidated balance sheets for March 31, 1982, and December 31, 1981. For the average layperson, the term "balance sheet" implies the dull and arcane world of the chartered accountant. But balance sheets are seldom boring to business people. For any interested observer, this particular balance-sheet comparison was fascinating; for a lender to Dome it was horrifying. Under the liabilities appeared an item with a shock value for the Citibank consortium comparable to finding a dead body in a closet. The figure was for long-term debt due within one year. On December 31, 1981, that figure had been $151 million. For March 31, 1982, it was shown as $2,273 million. The financial statements merely noted that the increase had occurred "as a result of the financing arrangements required to complete the acquisition of the minority shareholders' interest in HBOG together with certain other long-term financing arrangements which became current during the first three months of 1982."

The report also indicated that Dome needed another $100 million (on top of that extracted from Dome Canada) during April and May and a further $600 million by the end of the year. It declared that it planned to raise this money, and take care of a portion of its current debt requirements, through the sale of assets, additional long-term and short-term debt, and possibly the issue of equity. It also revealed that Dome was trying to renegotiate its current debt. The bottom line showed that Dome was obviously in one hell of a mess.

This information came out of the blue to Citibank, which at first had difficulty understanding what it meant. It took a full month for the consortium to discover what had happened. In the words of a member of the Citibank consortium: "You had four [Canadian] banks owed $4 billion, so they decided to drive their borrower to the point of bankruptcy. It didn't make a hell of a lot of sense."

At the end of June there was an acrimonious meeting between Citibank and Dome's executives. However, Bob Helman, Dome's U.S. council, pointed out to the Citibankers that however angry they were, it didn't make much sense to get into a public dispute. Bill Richards told them not to worry: the Canadian bankers would extend their loans; they had to. Dome was worth much more to them alive than dead, so they obviously had a vested interest in putting it back on its feet. In rational terms, that was true. But it didn't make the Citibankers any happier. They felt that the Canadian banks had also pulled a fast one on them. They felt they had been sucked into the situation without knowing Dome's true financial position so that the Canadian bankers' chances of being paid back might improve. Canadian bankers rejected such assertions, declaring high-handedly that either the Citibank *had* known about the loan's shortening, or, if they hadn't, they *should* have known. Both suggestions were considered obnoxious by the Citibankers and their consortium.

However, because Citibank believed it held better security than the

Canadian banks, it did hold the whip hand. Its main collateral consisted of all HBOG's producing properties, but its other security included the Canmar fleet and the hefty cash collateral account. Publicly, of course, the Canadian banks would all claim that they were better secured, but privately they admitted they weren't. Moreover, the Liberal government's policy — which asserted that foreign ownership of the Canadian oil business was inherently harmful to the Canadian economy — meant that if Dome did fall into receivership, then the market for its assets would be restricted to Canadian companies. That would severely limit the price of the assets and mean losses for the Canadian banks.

The Canadian banks now wanted the Citibank consortium to share their financial misery, either giving up some of its collateral or increasing the term of some of its loans — so Dome would be able to pay back the Canadian banks more quickly. A representative of Citibank was invited along to a meeting with the Canadian banks, but he made clear that he had duties and responsibilities to the other members of his bank's syndicate. In other words, when they talked to him, they were talking to 26 banks. The government in particular didn't like that. The Citibankers were not asked to participate again, until, that is, the Canadian bankers would later fly down to tell them "what was expected of them."

16
Summer
of Discontent

"Dome's financial staff now developed the height-
ened sensitivities of a bomb-disposal unit, aware that
the smallest slip might blow them all away."

For all those involved in the Dome affair, the summer of 1982 was a period of confusion and frustration. For the employees in the Dome Tower, it was particularly depressing. While their fate was being decided in the cabinet rooms of Ottawa and the executive suites of Toronto, they saw their fellow staff members fired, or quitting in disgust; they had their salaries cut and their perks removed; they watched the value of their lovingly accumulated Dome stock plummet. What they didn't realize, however, was that the negotiations between the bankers and the government were proving to be just as confusing and frustrating. While Dome's employees had to endure the growing number of "Dome jokes" circulating around the unforgiving oilpatch, the most farcical scenes were being played out in Toronto and Ottawa.
"What's the definition of an optimist?"
"A Dome employee who brings a packed lunch to work."
"What's the definition of a supreme optimist?"
"A Dome employee who buys a 30-day bus pass."
"What's a pessimist?"
"A Dome employee who arrives at work but keeps the engine of his car running."
For the 500 or more staff who lost their jobs in the first six months of 1982, and the hundreds more who were to join the unemployment rolls over the rest of the summer, these jokes weren't funny.
Management, meanwhile, was striving to put on its bravest face. If Gallagher had always been the optimist, then Bill Richards in recent years had become the supreme optimist. That attribute came in particularly useful now. Richards thrived on trench warfare. Like Winston Churchill — to whom he was compared within Dome — right down to the bulldog bearing and fat cigars, Richards rallied the troops and refused to acknowledge the possibility of defeat. But fighting in the trenches wasn't Jack Gallagher's style.

It was as Dome's "public face" that Gallagher remained important. To most shareholders, Dome Petroleum was still synonymous with Smilin' Jack. It was to him that they now looked for an explanation of Dome's stock market decline.

Dome's shares had been falling steadily all year, but when the extent of Dome's financial problems became obvious with the SEC filings in May, they slumped further. On the Toronto Stock Exchange on May 20, Dome's shares fell $1.12 to $6.87, a three-year low and scarcely a quarter of the price of a year before. On the AMEX, Dome traded 2.68 million shares, the third largest in the exchange's history, as U.S. investors unloaded and the stock fell U.S. $1 to U.S. $5.50.

The TSE phoned Dome to ask them to clarify their financial position. In response, Dome issued a statement declaring: "Several months ago the Company announced a program for the disposition of certain non-Canadian oil and gas assets and certain other assets unrelated to the Company's basic business of Canadian oil and gas.

"Pursuant to this program the Company is proceeding with these dispositions, some of which are expected to be completed before year-end."

The company had approximately $1.4 billion in debt due in the latter part of 1982, but the press release treated it almost as a secondary matter. Again, there was no specific announcement as to *why* this $1.4 billion was suddenly coming due.

On June 18, Gallagher, single-handedly, faced the packed share-holders' meeting in the auditorium at Commerce Court in Toronto, appropriately buried beneath the bank towers of its major lender.

The confusion of the meeting was a fair reflection of the confusion at Dome's Calgary headquarters. Gallagher appeared on the podium and consulted with Harry Eisenhauer, Dome's corporate secretary, an old company retainer. A television camera swung round on Gallagher and the famous smile — like some independent entity that reacted to television lights — jerked into life.

The meeting was filled with the usual combination of older Dome shareholders, most of whom still held an unshakable faith in Gallagher, and the representatives of the financial powers, the banks and the investment houses. At 10:00 A.M., Gallagher called the group to order and then noticed for the first time that he didn't have a speech. He called for his assistant as the hall broke once more in a buzz of conversation. Gallagher was handed his speech and the meeting began.

"I have always looked forward to these meetings over 30 years," said Gallagher. "I know things today will be different and more searching."

In fact, things turned out to be scarcely different and certainly far from searching. Directors were proposed and elected without dissent. New by-laws were proposed and passed. Gallagher ran through the events of the previous year and showed slides of the Dome family. Then he ran through the company's financial results: "We'll go through these figures quickly," he said. He pointed out that Dome now had the largest exploration acreage in Canada, and that it was responsible for one-fifth of the country's drilling footage. And then it was time for the inevitable Beaufort slide-show, delivered also at a somewhat more rapid pace than usual. Addressing at last the issue of the share price, he noted that Dome shares had been split 60-for-1 since they had first been issued, which meant that even at their current price of $6, their value compared with their original sale price of $11.22 (U.S. $10) was $360. Unfortunately, there weren't too many people present who'd bought their shares back in 1951. Quite a few had bought them in 1981, at $25.

As for the negotiations with the government and the banks, Gallagher said that the company was expecting a "positive answer within the next few weeks." Somebody suggested that the government was the culprit, but Gallagher, being both tactful and truthful, disagreed. "We are at fault," he said. "We possibly overextended."

In fact, Gallagher was in no doubt that Dome was at fault and that it had overextended itself, but the man he blamed for the move was not even at the meeting. Bill Richards was in the trenches, leading the fight for Dome's survival.

Although bank-government discussions centred on a long-term solution to Dome's problems, and an undoubted financial crunch was looming with the repayment of the Canadian banks' loan on September 30, Dome still had to scramble to survive *until* September 30. It was still possible for Dome to slip into default in that intervening period. Dome's financial staff now developed the heightened sensitivities of a bomb-disposal unit, aware that the smallest slip might blow them all away.

George Watson, the young former banker, was now in charge of the bomb squad. A painstaking procedure for conserving capital was introduced. In the terminology of accountants, payables were slowed down and receivables were accelerated. What that meant was that every cheque was examined three times before it was allowed out the front door while Dome's debtors found themselves constantly harrassed for payment.

In June, Dome had another cash-flow crisis. It desperately needed the payment of the first PIP grants to Dome Canada — which would then be passed on to Dome Petroleum to carry out exploration on Dome Canada's behalf. However, the legislation on which the grants depended had not been passed. (Richards, with typical gall, had

195

suggested to the government that Dome might receive interest on the late PIP payments!) Once again, Dome Petroleum needed Dome Canada to borrow money on its behalf — a $100 million bridging loan until the PIP grant arrived. That had been the prime reason for the government's request that the four bank CEOs come to Ottawa on St. Jean Baptiste Day. There, the government side, led by Lalonde, MacEachen and their deputy ministers asked the bankers to advance more money. The government people knew that the bankers would demand a guarantee for their loan and suggested that the guarantee be provided by Petro-Canada. Considering Dome's previous rivalry with the national oil company, the situation was more than ironic. Joel Bell, PetroCan's chief financial officer, refused to provide the guarantee without an order-in-council instructing him to do so. Mickey Cohen promised the bankers that he would have the guarantee for them in Calgary the next day so they could advance the funds. They agreed to the loan.

Later that day, there was a conference call between Hopper, Richards and other senior Petro-Canada, Dome and bank officials. Hopper announced that he wanted collateral for the loan. Richards seemed annoyed. "You don't need collateral," he said. "Well if that's the case," snapped back Hopper, "then why don't you just get the money from the banks?" There was silence on the wires, and then Richards agreed to pledge some TransCanada shares as security. "And what about a fee?" demanded Hopper, rubbing it into his old foe. Finally, Richards agreed to a $100,000 fee and the following night, as the deal was to be signed in the Calgary offices of Bennett Jones, Hopper made sure he had the $100,000 cheque in his hand before he affixed his name to the dotted line.

A press release was issued on behalf of Dome Canada by Dome Petroleum's public affairs department (Dome Canada had no such staff of its own). The release, dated June 26, declared baldly: "Dome Canada Limited announced today that it has arranged for a $100 million loan. The lenders are the Canadian Imperial Bank of Commerce, the Bank of Montreal, the Royal Bank and the Toronto-Dominion Bank.

"This loan is expected to be repaid during the third quarter of this year."

The purpose and terms of the loan were obviously considered pieces of information for enterprising shareholders or journalists to uncover. However, when Dome Canada received its first PIP grant ten days later, another release was issued declaring that of the $110 million payment "$100 million has been used to fully retire the bridge financing that was arranged by the Company and guaranteed by Petro-Canada on June 25."

196

The PIP grants which had been touted as the brilliant innovation that would give Canadian companies an advantage over the bigger, wealthier foreign oil companies were now being used as corporate life jackets.

In a further modification that seemed designed to help Dome, PIP regulations were revised so that payments would be made monthly rather than quarterly. The publicly stated rationale was that since Beaufort expenditures were heavily concentrated during a period of about 100 days in the summer, then 3 months was a long time to wait for payment. In fact, it looked like yet another move designed to keep Dome afloat.

Empire on the Block

One of the most necessary — that is, according to the banks — but thankless tasks now facing Dome management was the disposal of assets. The banks were angry at Gallagher and Richards because they believed they had been slow in considering disposals. Gallagher had never been a great fan of acquisitions, but then he didn't like selling off new additions to the Dome family either. Both Gallagher and Richards found it difficult to adapt their hard bargining style both to their chastened situation and the decline in the oil market. They had always negotiated from a position of strength. They found it difficult to accept bargaining almost in desperation.

Richards' staff at least tried to demonstrate willingness to the banks. In an attempt to show that Dome really was doing its best to raise cash, one of Richards' aides made a stage-managed entry into a room-full of Canadian bankers and announced the company had just sold the corporate jet for $11 million. He had to return an hour later to report that the cheque had bounced!

Since virtually all Dome's assets were now pledged to the banks, whatever sale-price Dome negotiated for them disappeared immediately into the vaults of the company's disgruntled lenders. Peat Marwick now had a hand in preparing information on, and expediting, the sale of assets. "Data Rooms" were set up in Calgary, Denver and Toronto where prospective buyers could view documentation on the various parts of the empire now on the block.

On June 28, Dome arranged to sell the fleet of tankers owned by the Branch Lines Division of Davie Shipbuilding, the Quebec-based company it had acquired the year before. The sale, completed in July, brought in $44 million, of which $25 million was paid in cash and went straight to the banks.

The purchase of Davie, Canada's largest shipyard, for $38.6 million had been portrayed as the first step in plans to construct one or possibly two world-class shipyards, primarily to supply equipment for the Beaufort effort. At around the time of the NEP, Dome had been talking of shipyards in Canada capable of building 200,000 ton deadweight tankers. Later, Gallagher had spoken of a requirement of 25 such ships, all specially reinforced to withstand ice, at a cost of $350 million each. As much as $10 billion, said Dome, would be spent on goods and services for the Beaufort in Quebec alone. Ottawa's Department of Regional Economic Expansion (DREE), had been declared to be "enthusiastic" about the plans, which were unprecedented in scope. However, in retrospect, they appeared part of an almost megalomanic vision.

The international properties — primarily HBOG's producing lands in Indonesia and its acreage in Australia, Egypt, Brazil and Italy — attracted a good deal of attention. Engineering consultants Gaffney Cline were hired to prepare an independent evaluation of the properties. They came up with a price of $600 million to $700 million, valuing Dome's 87.5% stake (the other 12.5% had been acquired by TransCanada as part of the family deal on HBOG assets) at between $525 million and $612 million. However, that valuation was impossible to realize on the market.

When word had come to Jack Gallagher in London at the end of March to return to Toronto for crucial meetings with the banks, he had been pitching the idea of Dome International to the British oil company London & Scottish Marine Oil, known as LASMO. LASMO executives had indicated that they were far more interested in outright purchase of the properties than in the deal Gallagher was proposing. Now they were able to snap them up at what looked like a bargain price.

On August 10, Dome announced that it had sold the overseas properties to LASMO and BP Development Ltd., which was also based in London, for $340 million. The final price would, in fact, be $328 million.

For Dome, the deal was hardly attractive. Not only was the final sale price some $200 million below Gaffney Cline's valuation, but $119 million of the proceeds had to go to the Bank of Nova Scotia to retire a previous HBOG debt, while the remainder had to be placed in escrow with the other four Canadian banks. To top it all, the sale was responsible for most of the $100 million loss on disposal of assets that was to dent yet further Dome's already miserable 1982 results.

The next largest block of assets for sale was Dome's properties in the U.S. Fifty companies had expressed an interest by mid-June, and eight had participated in the Data Room program at Dome's U.S.

headquarters in Denver. However, no acceptable bids were made. Although the U.S. assets were not sold, Dome was forced by SEC regulations to write down the value of the properties to reflect the decline in market conditions. That took another $214 million out of 1982 profits.

In the North Sea, Dome had its 22% stake of Sovereign Oil & Gas, acquired when Dome had bought out Siebens, and a $125 million semi-submersible drilling rig that it had commissioned the year before. Some interest was shown but again no acceptable offers were made.

A consortium of Canadian companies looked at acquiring Dome's stake in TransCanada PipeLines. However, according to one of the companies involved, they were put off by TCPL's debt load and by the heavy price it had paid for its chunk of HBOG. Again, no offers were made.

The other assets on the block consisted mainly of Cyprus Anvil and other mining properties. Allowing HBOG to purchase Cyprus Anvil the previous August now proved to be a massive mistake. Although no official announcement had been made, Cyprus' mine at Faro in the Yukon had been closed down on June 4. Dome had $326 million tied up in Cyprus, which also had $135 million of long-term debt. Cyprus was a total disaster.

Everywhere the story was the same: the assets that Dome had acquired were turning out to be worth less — in some cases, much less — than the company had paid for them. The situation was greatly aggravated by the fact that Dome had borrowed virtually all the money for its purchases. If Dome now had to sell all the assets to repay its debts, it stood to reason that it would run out of assets to sell before it had paid off its debts. That was another definition of bankruptcy.

But that fact also explained why the banks were so tetchy. If the likely sale price of all the company's assets didn't equal the volume of its debts, then bankruptcy would leave the least secured of the banks without hope of repayment.

The disastrous sale of assets served to emphasize further that Dome had no possible financial future without swapping a large chunk of its debt for equity. But since the equity would effectively be there to take the financial bath because of the lower value of the company's assets, it was hardly likely that the public would line up for it. It had to come from the banks and/or the government.

Between the banks and the government, meanwhile, the underlying wrangle continued about just who was bailing out whom. Were the banks bailing out Ottawa's chosen instrument or was Ottawa bailing out a company that had been massively overindulged by the banks? Pierre Trudeau, for one, was obviously not impressed with the banks' stance. Late in June, he appeared on a taped television show and declared that any action on Dome's behalf "mainly has to be taken by the banks, which have been heavy lenders to the oil company."

For political reasons, it would have been almost impossible for Trudeau's Liberals to allow Dome to go under. At the same time, in order to bargain with the banks, they had to convince them that, in the last resort, they *would* allow Dome to founder. Within the cabinet, most ministers saw Dome as a burden they had to bear. Some, like Jack Austin, a believer in powerful interventionism, seemed to see it as an opportunity. If the government was to put up money, then it should demand equity and seats on the board. This, in Austin's opinion, would be a way of providing direct — and in his view, beneficial — influence on the business sector.

The bankers' public stance was that they, too, were willing to allow Dome to fail, since their security was sound. Provided there was an "orderly disposition of assets," they claimed, the loan defaults would not hurt them. However, the behind-the-scenes negotiations both between themselves and with Ottawa told a quite different story. As information about Dome's situation dribbled out into the public arena, a whole crop of new problems suddenly began to emerge in the international financial market. As the bankers came under increasing pressure, their relations with Dome became marked both by panic and rage.

A Ripple of Panic

In early July there had been a minor panic when Gary Lauk, an NDP member of the B.C. legislature, suggested that the Canadian Imperial Bank of Commerce might be in trouble because of its association with Dome. The panic arose not so much from the statement but from the fact that some people appeared to believe it.

In a very carefully worded press release issued on July 8, Dome declared: "Dome Petroleum has denied recent news reports of the Company's alleged inability to make interest payments on major borrowings from the Canadian Imperial Bank of Commerce. The news reports appear to have originated from statements made yesterday in the British Columbia legislature. Such statements are regarded by the Company as totally inaccurate and irresponsible.

"The Company has confirmed that it has met all interest payments not only to the Canadian Imperial Bank of Commerce but also to all other lenders and expects future interest payments to be made in accordance with the terms of its loan agreements."

The statement was, of course, carefully worded because it kept emphasizing interest payments. What the company had no chance of meeting were its principal payments on debt. In fact, just a week before the press release, Dome had been forced to seek the extension of certain principal payments because it couldn't meet them.

Dome's 10Q for the quarter ended June 30, 1982, contained the first explicit admissions that it was seeking to reschedule its debts.

"Since June 30, 1982," the 10Q said, "certain of the principal payments of certain of the Company's obligations, which have become due, are currently being extended on a short-term basis pending the outcome of discussions regarding the timing of their payment.

"The Company has determined that it is not reasonable at this time to expect that the above obligations will be repaid as scheduled. Consequently, discussions are underway with various lenders, the Government of Canada and other parties whereby the Company will attempt to come to an agreement on the rescheduling of principal payments on a portion of its debt."

For a banker, rescheduling a lender's debt is considered if the company is considered to have a long-term viability, *or* if its collapse will damage the bank as much as the lender. It goes back to Lord Keynes' classic, and increasingly quoted, remark, that if someone owed a bank a thousand pounds and couldn't pay, he was in trouble; if he owed it a million pounds and couldn't pay, then the *bank* was in trouble.

This situation, unique for the major Canadian banks, led to a severe deterioration in their relations with each other. Once again, it was the T-D's Thomson who was the centre of controversy. He continued to cling to the stance that the T-D could do no more for Dome. However, time was running out, and it was the banks who had set the clock. There had to be some form of agreement by the end of September, because Dome obviously couldn't repay the $1.4 billion due at the end of the month. Mulholland was adamant that if there was no agreement, then he would put Dome into receivership. He believed that Thomson's stance amounted to little short of blackmail, and that the T-D's chairman just didn't believe Mulholland would go through with his threats. Mulholland assured him that he would. In September, close to the deadline, all the CEOs were at a meeting in the Toronto office of Osler Hoskin & Harcourt with Mickey Cohen and other government representatives. Again, it was the Dome Mines guarantee — backed by the T-D — that was the cause of contention. The other three banks were demanding that the guarantee be extended as part of a bailout package. Thomson said that Dome Mines would never agree to the extension of the guarantee. So Mulholland said they'd ask Dome Mines themselves whether it would or not. And if they agreed to the extension, asked Mulholland, would the T-D continue to back it? "No," said Thomson. Bob Utting, the Royal's vice-chairman, gave an indignant huurrumph, like a bullfrog. Russell Harrison of the Commerce looked shocked. "I can't believe what I just heard," he said. Thomson reiterated that under no event would the T-D continue its guarantee. "Let's get this straight Dick," said Harrison. "The only question before us now is whether the T-D is going to belly up to the bar or not."

Thomson became flustered and announced that he had a dinner engagement to attend. He packed up his papers and left. There was a stunned silence. "This," said Harrison, "has very serious implications for the banking system."

The government, meanwhile, could afford to take a more sanguine view of the whole situation. It had already laid out its principles that any cash injection should be shared equally by Ottawa and the banks, and had not shifted from that. In some quarters, meanwhile, the government seemed to be taking a scarcely concealed delight in the banks' situation.

Trudeau: A Derisive Tone

Early in September, Trudeau, rubbing the banks' noses not merely in the Dome situation but in the international banking crisis of which they were a part, said in a radio interview: "A lot of people around the world made a mistake, including our renowned and very responsible banks ... You're asking me if we're going to bail [Dome] out? ... The answer is no. We're not going to bail it out. We're hopeful that the parties themselves will find some solutions and, as you know, we're helping them to look for one."

Trudeau's tone towards the banks was almost derisive. The day after the interview was aired, an official from the Prime Minister's Office was at pains to point out that: "What the Prime Minister was ruling out was that the government would act alone to aid Dome."

In a hastily prepared press release that showed equal measures of fright, annoyance and wishful thinking, Dome also declared: "Dome Petroleum stated today that the Prime Minister's recent remarks are in no way incompatible with the Company's understanding of the federal government's position. Dome has stated on repeated occasions that discussions are taking place with the government and the banks regarding Dome's financial position.

"The discussions with the government and the banks do not involve a bailout or anything else for nothing but are for the purpose of designing a joint venture program to solve Dome's temporary financial problems.

"Dome, despite its near-term cash shortage, has the potential to be a strong, economically viable company with an important and valuable contribution to make to the Canadian economy."

Pierre Trudeau's remarks also dented Dome's share-price, causing it to drop 45¢ to $3.65 the morning after the broadcast, yet another low for the year, before reviving to $3.95 at the end of the day.

Despite Trudeau's scorn, Dome's attempt to don a brave face and the banks' bickering, one fact was now obvious: the time had come to dictate a solution to Dome. For Russell Harrison, the man designated to do the dictating, the final process was to be uniquely difficult. Dome refused to go down without a fight, while his fellow bankers continued to scrap with each other right down to the wire. Meanwhile, the solution itself was to prove far from final.

17
Negotiations
Atop a Trapdoor

"The common shareholders should get down on their knees and thank God that we came to an agreement."

RUSSELL HARRISON
CHAIRMAN AND CHIEF EXECUTIVE OFFICER
OF THE CANADIAN IMPERIAL BANK OF COMMERCE

On September 23, 1982, the directors of Dome Petroleum filed into the somewhat drab boardroom of Dome Mines in Toronto's First Canadian Place. There they would hear officially the fate decided for their company by the banks and the federal government. The Dome side was led by Jack Gallagher, his smile this day a mere reflex action, a strangely inappropriate sparkle in Dome's sea of debt. He was followed into the boardroom by Bill Richards, Dome's pugnacious and impatient president, the chief architect of Dome's financial plight, but still a man who didn't know the meaning of the word "surrender." Then came Bruce Matthews, the erect chairman of Dome Mines, who may have felt that he had already seen more than enough corporate intrigue and financial disaster in his connections with the Argus empire and Massey Ferguson; Norman Alexander, the Winnipeg investment consultant with the amiable manner and shock of white hair; Rene Amyot, the Quebec City lawyer and chairman of Air Canada and most recent addition to the Dome board; Marshall Crowe, the tall, stooping former senior public servant who had been chairman of the National Energy Board and who was now an energy consultant; Fraser Fell, the Toronto lawyer and vice-chairman of Dome Mines; Mac Jones, Dome's principal Calgary lawyer; Wick Sellers, the Winnipeg-based president of a management and investment company; Mac Taschereau, president and chief executive of Dome Mines; and finally the somewhat frail figures of the two men who had known the company since its inception, John Loeb, octogenarian honorary chairman of giant U.S. investment conglomerate Shearson/American Express, and Bill Morton, the Boston-based investment manager.

Also present were several members of Dome's young executive elite

— George Watson, Steve Savidant, Don Gardiner, Colin Kenny — as well as Allen Lambert, a director of Dome Mines and a former chairman of the Toronto-Dominion Bank, whom Gallagher had invited to attend, and Bob Helman, Dome's principal U.S. lawyer. Four men represented the bank/government side: Russell Harrison, chairman of the Canadian Imperial bank of Commerce, Rowland Frazee, chairman of the Royal Bank, Mickey Cohen, now deputy minister of finance, and finally Brian Levitt, a young corporate lawyer from the Toronto firm of Osler Hoskin & Harcourt. The four men came in and circled the boardroom table, shaking hands with each of those present. It was a sombre occasion for all of them as they took their seats beneath the pictures of the three men who had chaired the board of Dome Mines since the end of the First World War: Jules Bache, the U.S. industrialist and investment banker; Clifford Michel, the prominent Wall Street banker and founder of Dome Petrolum; and finally Bruce Matthews, who was there in person to witness Dome's present corporate plight.

It is hard to imagine what Bache and Michel would have thought about the scene taking place beneath them. Bache would probably have found it incomprehensible. Before his death in 1976, Michel had seen the beginnings of the upsurge of Canadian energy nationalism in the early 1970s but if that Wall Streeter were to have returned from the grave he would have found it difficult to grasp what had happened to the company in just six years. Indeed, the recent saga of Dome would be difficult for virtually anybody not acquainted with the pecularities of Canadian business and politics to understand. Dome was in some ways a uniquely Canadian situation, a company pampered by the federal government and indulged by a powerful, elite banking system to the point of not just self-destruction but at least short-term damage to the entire economy. Meanwhile, it wasn't merely the Canadian banks who were caught with egg on their faces. The Citibank consortium had put up the last — and perhaps rashest — loan of all. They would claim that it was better secured than the other loans, but any bank that closes a $2.1 billion loan to a company three weeks away from technical bankruptcy without realizing that the terms on a major portion of the company's other loans had been changed, had more than a little reason to be embarrassed.

Where both Bache and Michel would have found cause for sorrow, and possibly anger, and where Matthews now found cause for discomfort, was in the degree to which Dome Mines had been dragged into Dome Petroleum's problems.

Dome Mines still held 27% of Dome Petroleum's shares, but Dome Petroleum in turn now owned 40% of Dome Mines. That relationship had caused Dome Mines to be drawn into Dome Petroleum's increasingly desperate struggle for survival. It would have its part to play — and price to pay — in the corporate package that would be hammered out over the ensuing week of intense and frustrating discussions with the banks and government.

In fact, Dome already knew the outline of the rescue package. At a dinner the previous evening, a dinner which Gallagher described to colleagues as "rough," Harrison, Frazee and Cohen had outlined the joint proposals for Dome's bailout to Dome's chairman. The rest of the Dome board, executives and advisors had dined separately, in an atmosphere like that on the eve of a battle. Wick Sellers declared that it was *not* the Last Supper, but there was little humour at the meeting.

For weeks, Richards, Savidant, Kenny and others had worked on a "shadow term sheet," a best guess at what the government/bank proposals were likely to be. What Harrison had told Gallagher the night before was close to that guess, but the deal still looked depressingly tough for Dome. The government and banks collectively were prepared to inject $500 million of cash each in the form of convertible debentures. However, these debentures were convertible at just $2.00 a share, which meant that after the debentures were converted, Ottawa and the four banks would hold a majority of the company's equity, and effectively control it. To make sure they did, they made clear that they would demand a majority of seats on the Dome board.

That was the formal message delivered primarily by Harrison in the Dome Mines' boardroom the following morning. It was given, according to one of those present, in the tone of a lecture. Harrison was very eager for Dome to realize that the banks and the government weren't delivering a negotiating position. This was it. Cohen and Frazee also made a number of comments. Cohen's stance, on behalf of the government, was that any deal with the banks had to be "shoulder to shoulder," with the banks matching Ottawa's cash injection. Ottawa was keen to avoid accusations that it was bailing out the banks. Cohen was very concerned that Dome be a viable company, with sufficient funds to drill its enormous landholdings. He didn't want the government merely to inject money into a corporate shell, whence it could be extracted by the banks. Therefore, although Dome's loans would be rescheduled — another critical part of the package — they would be rescheduled in such a way as to allow Dome sufficient funds to continue ongoing corporate activities.

Finally, the Dome team was told that the Citibank consortium would be asked — as part of the package which it had had no part in negotiating — to take $500 million of the Canadian banks' secured loans.

207

Some of the Dome people thought that sounded pretty optimistic. But then it wasn't their problem.

After the bank/government position had been outlined, Russell Harrison then dropped his bombshell: neither Richards nor Gallagher would be permitted to attend subsequent meetings.

This was thought to be partly an emotional decision; the banks were still furious with Dome's senior management for cajoling them into their present uncomfortable position. But it was also considered by the Dome side to be a tactical move. By separating the other directors from Gallagher and Richards they were undoubtedly weakening the board's bargaining strength. However, the bankers also believed that with Gallagher and Richards present, it would be impossible either to have realistic discussions or get the full severity of Dome's situation across to the corporation's board. It was not the time for Gallagher's visions or Richards' inveterate optimism. It was the time for cold harsh reality. The exclusion of Gallagher and Richards was also an undeniable statement about the banks' lack of confidence in Dome's senior management. To have come out and declared that Gallagher and Richards had to be fired would have created potential legal problems. Excluding them from discussions about the fate of their company spoke volumes.

Gallagher responded quietly for Dome and said they'd think about the proposal. Harrison, Frazee, Cohen and Levitt then departed and the Dome board and employees were left to mull over their fate. The meeting in the Dome Mines' boardroom went on for the rest of the day, after which the whole Dome team retired to the King Edward Hotel, which would be their command headquarters for the next week. There, around a large table in a room connected to Bill Richards' suite, they held numerous meetings, plotting ways in which they could minimize their losses.

Into the Lions' Den

The following morning, Dome's independent directors, that is, the non-executive members of the board, were due to meet with the opposition at Commerce Court to deliver their answer. An hour before the appointed time, a call was received from Russell Harrison, demanding that they come over *right now*; he had something he wanted to say. The Dome directors walked the two blocks to the great silver tower of Harrison's headquarters and there Harrison made it very clear that he didn't want them to think there would be a lot of negotiating. They weren't in a position to negotiate. He just wanted their acceptance.

So they went back to the King Eddy and Richards and Gallagher told them to hang in there, which, for a week, was what they did. Their negotiating position was, of course, terribly weak. In the words of one Dome director: "If it wasn't like Grant versus Lee, it was pretty close." For most of that week they trekked, sometimes several times a day, between the King Eddy and Commerce Court, feeling perhaps a little like Christians with a week's engagement in the lions' den. The King Eddy sat on the edge of one of the greatest concentrations of banking power in the world, so that even when they didn't meet in the Commerce, the Dome people found themselves in bank towers. Dome Mines' office was in the Montreal's headquarters while Dome's lawyers, Fasken & Calvin, were in the T-D Centre.

During the day, and often throughout the night, the Dome staff would prepare briefing documents and background papers. For the Dome side, Fraser Fell, the quiet-spoken, bald and bespectacled lawyer, was chairman of the directors' committee and a key figure. Other directors would come and go, or be consulted by phone.

The threat hanging over the Dome directors was the massive payment the company had to make to the four banks at the end of the month. Unless that was rolled over, Dome would go into receivership. Bill Richards later congratulated one of the directors, comparing his situation to negotiating while standing on a trapdoor with the noose around one's neck and the executioner's hand on the lever. The fact that they were negotiating at all increasingly enraged Russell Harrison. More than once during that week he would lose his temper. At one stage he accused the Dome directors of just not trying hard enough, although later he apologized for that remark.

The directors were trying to get a conversion price for the bank/ government debentures of $5 a share, two and a half times what they'd been offered. That enraged Harrison. "You guys aren't in the real world," he shouted. "You're broke!" But of course what made Harrison so angry was that he knew, as the Dome side knew, that they were all effectively trapped in the same situation. It jarred his banker's principles to the very marrow to think that the only reason he was here now negotiating with Dome was the sheer size of their financial imprudence — and of his own, and the other three banks' indulgence.

The negotiations spanned a weekend. During that weekend, the Dome team had a visit from Jean Chrétien, who had taken over as energy minister when Marc Lalonde had been promoted to deputy minister of finance. Most people believed that Lalonde still pulled the strings at Energy, and the fact that Lalonde's deputy minister, Mickey Cohen, still retained the Dome portfolio was, to say the least, an unusual situation. Nevertheless, Chrétien came and told the men from

209

Dome that "the boss," as he called Pierre Trudeau, wanted a deal done.

In the end, Dome won some concessions, although the eventual deal still looked like a tough one. They managed to force the initial conversion price up to $2.50 a share, and to have a gradually escalating conversion price in subsequent years. There was also an agreement that Dome shareholders would have the right to subscribe for $500 million of new shares. The banks and government had little objection to alternative sources of cash, although neither thought it realistic that shareholders could be counted on to put up more cash after the hammering most of them had taken.

Anger with the T-D

The Dome directors felt they had given it their best shot. But then, at the eleventh hour, the whole agreement almost fell apart, not because of Dome's stance, but becauseof the continuing feud between the banks, in particular between Thomson and Mulholland. Dome Mines and the T-D had been persuaded after much arm twisting to continue to provide the $250 million loan guarantee for Dome Petroleum as part of the Agreement in Principle (AIP). Under the new arrangement, the guarantee would be extended to July 31, 1993, and the T-D would continue to provide the stand-by credit to cover it. However, on the morning the AIP was to be signed, Mulholland discovered that the T-D had also made another agreement with Dome Mines. Under the AIP, each of the banks committed to take $125 million of Dome Petroleum debentures convertible into Dome shares. Mulholland learned, however, that the T-D had gained Dome Mines' agreement that Dome Mines should buy the T-D's share of the debentures if the T-D requested it. In return, the T-D agreed to reduce Dome Mines' obligations under the guarantee. In Mulholland's mind, the T-D was attempting once again to weasel out of its obligations by passing the buck to Dome Mines.

Mulholland demanded a meeting. The bank and government representatives met in Commerce Court and Mulholland told them flatly he would not sign the AIP with the T-D–Dome Mines provision. Now Harrison got mad at Mulholland. The chairman of the Commerce had found the preceding week an enormous strain. He couldn't believe that Mulholland would allow the whole thing to collapse now. But Mulholland got mad right back, declaring that if they thought the Montreal would go along with an eleventh-hour switch like that, they'd better think again. There was pandemonium as all the lawyers reassembled. Only Mickey Cohen reportedly looked on with an air of scientific detachment. In the end, the T-D's "put" to Dome Mines on the Dome Petroleum debentures remained as part of the agreement. However, it was effectively negated by the insertion of another clause declaring that such an arrangement would be subject to the approval of the other three banks and the government.

From Dome Mines' point of view, its situation was hardly improved. Indeed, it lost further freedom under other provisions of the AIP. Its 25.5% stake in Dome Petroleum was to be placed in a voting trust controlled by the government and the four banks. The shares of Dome Mines owned by Dome Petroleum were in turn to be placed in a separate voting trust controlled by Dome Mines. But since these shares were already pledged as collateral for Dome Petroleum loans, Dome Mines could do nothing with them without the banks' approval. Under the AIP, therefore, Dome Mines would virtually lose its independence.

The deal was eventually signed on September 29 in the boardroom on the 56th floor of Commerce Court. Present were the four bank CEOs — Harrison, Thomson, Mulholland and Frazee — who were now finding it difficult to sit in the same room together, Jean Chrétien for the federal government and Jack Gallagher as the main signatory for Dome. Once the signing had taken place, the irrepressible Gallagher made a little speech, noting how difficult the situation had been, how he appreciated the motivations and the approach of the government and the banks and how he was sure they had all had the best interests of the company at heart. The bankers endured this display of Gallagher charm because they regarded it as his final curtain call. The AIP clearly implied that the ballgame was over for Gallagher. But even now, Gallagher wasn't acting as if he was about to vanish into the dugout for the last time.

Bill Richards also took an amazingly sanguine view of the outcome of the negotiations. However, for some of the younger Dome employees, particularly Richards' young lions, the result was much harder to take. Bill Richards' assistant, Steve Savidant, was almost banging his head against the wall with frustration that the company couldn't get a better deal. Even those who had entered the final week's negotiations in the King Eddy with the attitude that there was a job to be done, and that anything salvaged would be a plus, were now thoroughly depressed.

After the official signing, a huge squad of lawyers got together to hammer out a press release on the decision. Not a word of the release went unchallenged and the process took several hours. Then, at last, the journalists who had dogged the steps of the Dome directors and hung around the corridors of the King Eddy, sometimes even attempting to force their way into meeting rooms, had their story: the story of Dome's billion-dollar bailout.

The proposal had three principal elements:

- A capital injection of up to $1 billion, one half of which was to be provided by government and one half of which was to come from the four banks. The injection would be through the purchase of convertible debentures.
- An opportunity for existing shareholders to subscribe for $500 million of debentures on similar terms.
- The extension of the term of "a substantial portion" of Dome's existing debt to at least ten years.

Under the proposal, the debentures, which would bear interest at prime plus 1%, would not require interest payments in cash. Payments would instead be made in Dome shares. The conversion rate to common shares for the debentures was to be $2.50 a share for the first 18 months; $2.85 for the next 12 months; $3.35 for the next 12 months; $3.90 for the next 12 months; $4.50 for the next 12 months; and $5.00 for the next 12 months.

In addition, the government, the banks and Dome shareholders subscribing for the debentures would also receive pro rata detachable warrants to purchase up to 50 million additional shares at $2.50 a share.

Interest on Dome's debt would continue to be paid currently and principal would be rescheduled to reflect cash flow. Most important, the government had insisted that Dome would "maintain a balance between ongoing prudent capital expenditures and debt repayment."

From the government's point of view, another key element was that Ottawa had an option to purchase all of Dome's frontier lands at an independently appraised price if Dome's capital expenditures on those lands was "below that considered by the government to be in the national interest." If Dome was only to survive as a financial cripple, Ottawa wanted to make sure that its condition didn't adversely affect the whole country's energy future.

Moreover, the agreement made it abundantly clear that Dome would never again be the freewheeling corporate force it had been under Gallagher and Richards. Under the covenants attached to the debentures, Dome's annual operating budgets, and all its "significant" capital expenditures and asset dispositions would require the approval of the four Canadian banks and the government. Equally as important, the government and banks also held the right of approval on both the composition of the board of directors and on senior management appointments.

212

At a press conference in Calgary, Jean Chrétien declared that the refinancing package for Dome would not only ensure that "this important player in the oil and gas sector" would continue to grow and prosper, but also that the refinancing scheme would bring about an increase in Canadian ownership. He stressed that the majority of the company's ownership would remain in private hands and that the government would not play a major role in the day-to-day operations of the company.

Dome's release declared that the company believed "the implementation of the agreement will resolve its cash flow problems and permit [Dome] to resume its role as a strong and active participant in the development of Canada's oil and gas potential."

Post-Agreement Turmoil

The cosy and positive tone of the releases from Dome and the government contrasted sharply with the enormous turmoil aroused by the agreement. The cries of protest came firstly from the shareholders, and secondly from the foreign banks. When the news reached the market, Dome shares slumped. On the Toronto Stock Exchange, they fell $1.87 to $3.25. On the AMEX, they sunk U.S.$1.44 to U.S.$2.75.

Under the proposal, it was calculated that the number of Dome shares would be more than trebled if the banks and the government subscribed for, and then converted, their full $1 billion of debentures. There was also a belief that the government might well buy the banks' debentures and wind up with majority control of Dome. Some in the cabinet, particularly Jack Austin, progenitor of Petro-Canada, were thought to have "Petro-Canada II" in mind.

Shareholders, lacking a full understanding of the depth of Dome's problems, believed — and were confidentially encouraged to believe by Dome management — that they had been raped. Such accusations were acutely annoying both to the government and the bankers. Shortly after the bailout, Russell Harrison granted an interview to Paul Taylor, an energy reporter with the *Globe and Mail*. During the interview Harrison told the reporter: "The common shareholders should get down on their knees and thank God that we came to an agreement. If we hadn't done this their shares would have been worthless now." Harrison, wrote Taylor, "brushed aside suggestions that the deal [was] bad for the shareholders." He expressed shock at the suggestion by some analysts that the shareholders would have been better off if Dome had been allowed to go into bankruptcy.

"It would have been the biggest bankruptcy in the history of the

213

world. A Canadian company with $7 billion in debt goes bankrupt — with every major bank in the world involved. I shudder to think of it. Do you realize what that would have done to Canada?" he indignantly asked the young reporter. "The credit of the Canadian banking system — and the Canadian government itself — would be in question."

Harrison concluded that the shareholders would be "out of their minds" not to go along with the refinancing arrangement. "Their only hope rests with us controlling the company."

Jean Chrétien expressed similar sentiments to journalists a couple of days later when he was on his way into a meeting of the cabinet's Priorities and Planning Committee at Meech Lake, Quebec. Speaking of the shareholders, he asked: "They would have preferred to have zero? … A collapse of the company would have been meaning [sic] zero for the shares."

A couple of days before, a Toronto stockbroker had filed a $5 billion class action lawsuit in the Ontario Supreme Court against the government and the banks involved in the refinancing. The suit had asked for recovery of damages for property trespass and conspiracy in the expropriation of capital property of the common shareholders. Chrétien's response to this was: "Anybody can go to court. They cannot blame me. I'm not a director of Dome."

A week or so after Harrison's remarks to the *Globe*, Bill Mulholland reiterated the extent of Dome's problems, although he delivered what looked like a mild rebuke to Harrison. Asked during a CBC interview whether he felt as Harrison did that shareholders should get down on their knees and thank God for the bailout, Mulholland replied: "Well, I don't have Mr. Harrison's gift for colourful expression I'm afraid. And I have learned from sad experience not to expect gratitude, so I wouldn't have said that. I would have said they should take sober account of their alternatives."

Asked how devastating the alternatives would have been, Mulholland responded: "Well, I'll put it to you as succinctly as I can. That agreement was signed Wednesday night at 7:00 and the time limit was Thursday [September 30] at close of business if things weren't fixed. On Friday at 8:30 in the morning we had our meetings scheduled out here with a team of lawyers with all the instruments drafted to put a receiver in and take control of the assets on which we had liens and there was really no choice because our counsel advised us that the management of the bank simply would be remiss in its responsibilities to its shareholders if we didn't act. Obviously, we didn't want to do that, but that's what would have happened and we missed that by about little more than 24 hours. Now what that would have meant in practical terms is essentially the dismemberment of Dome. It doesn't mean that everything necessarily stops or goes up in smoke or something, but it means that various pieces of the company are separated off or probably sold to new owners. The integrity of the organization is certainly destroyed, probably some loss of values because too much is being sold at the same time, the fire sale syndrome which is never the most advantageous way to do it. And whatever vitality and vigour is imparted to the economy in this part of the world probably would have been set back a couple of years, if not dissipated. The consequential economic cost of that would have been very, very great. Much greater than the primary cost."

Asked about the impact of the Dome affair on the reputation of the Canadian banks, Mulholland said: "I think a number of us perceive that it is very important in the broader image of the country abroad that this be properly resolved in an orderly, fair way and a competent way and it be done with dispatch and not allowed to drag on longer."

However, as Mulholland said those words, he was already well aware that apart from the Canadian shareholders, there was another much more important group who certainly did not perceive the refinancing solution to have been resolved in either a fair or competent way: that was the group of foreign banks whom the Canadian government and banks had decided — without consultation — would have to shoulder part of the refinancing's burden. Mulholland knew because he had flown to New York to meet with representatives of the Citibank consortrium as soon as the Agreement in Principle had been signed. The New York bankers didn't like the proposed deal at all.

There were a number of meetings with foreign bankers to explain the AIP. None of them went well. The prevalent attitude among the Citibank lenders was that after being conned both by Dome and the Canadian banks, they were now expected to save their bacon.

Shortly after the signing, and after Mulholland's trip to New York, another team led by the Bank of Montreal went down to meet with creditors in Manhattan's Hotel Pierre. The men from the Montreal laid out the terms of the AIP without any word on the background to the crisis or why the AIP was necessary. A couple of weeks before, the same New York bankers had heard a presentation from Dome telling them how well things were going. They wanted answers but the Canadian bankers were reluctant to give them. The Canadian banks wanted the commitment of money, not questions. At one stage, there was an outcry when Peter Waters from the Bank of Montreal tried to cut off further questions. The American bankers were infuriated by the Canadian banks' high-handed attitude. Canadian bankers just weren't used to being closely-questioned. Further questions were in fact allowed, but the meeting eventually broke up in confusion and with considerable acrimony.

A few days later, the same banking group flew to London for a meeting on Park Lane with Dome's European bankers. Again the meeting was rough. The Europeans wanted to know about the government's role in all this: wasn't Dome a chosen instrument? Why, asked the representative of a recently nationalized French bank, didn't the government simply take over the whole thing?

When Citibank had fully analyzed the Canadian banks' proposal, they sent a brief telex to the Bank of Montreal. "Lenders who are adequately secured," it said, "have no reason to participate."

The AIP was obviously still a long way from being resolved. It was not in Dome's corporate nature to fail to exploit this confused situation.

18
Corporate
Acrobatics

*" ... the first time they dangled you over the pre-
cipice was pretty scary, but after they'd done it a
few times and they hadn't dropped you, then the
whole routine became a little ho-hum."*

BILL RICHARDS

The Agreement in Principle was the strange fruit of six months of
wrangling between the banks and the federal government and between the banks themselves. It was clearly seen by Ottawa and the
banks as a solution to be dictated to the rash and impecunious Dome.
The final week of negotiations had obviously been a source of frustration for the banks, as Russell Harrison's occasional outbursts and
subsequent public comments had indicated. The document, as Harrison indicated, should rightly be the subject of a *Te Deum* on the part
of the shareholders. All that remained of the formalities was to receive
approval from grateful shareholders and from Dome's foreign bankers, who were expected to do the "decent thing" and share the burden
of the bailout.

The incensed replies of the foreign banks had obviously come as a
great surprise to the Canadian bankers. Their reaction had ensured
that there was little hope of reaching a formal agreement by the end
of the year, as originally planned in the AIP. But in any case, there
were other problems with the AIP. The unstated assumption of the
AIP was that Gallagher and Richards would find some way of grace-
fully bowing out, and that changes would be made to the board, so
that the transition of Dome to a new, less ambitious and more acquiescent creature could be made smoothly. Under these circumstances, however, there was little chance that Gallagher and Richards
would be in any great hurry to put the proposals to the shareholders.
In addition, they both rapidly came to view the AIP as the provider
of a valuable breathing space instead of the stunning corporate defeat
that it initially had appeared to be for them both.

The banks and the government looked upon the AIP as an unfortunate but definitive solution. Dome's senior management quickly

came to regard it as a safety net above which, to the detriment of the bankers' bloodpressure, they were soon practising their traditional style of corporate acrobatics. Richards subsequently told the author: "We signed the agreement and we recognized the necessity of it. I can't say I was in a state of euphoria. And we recognized that it was something that was going to buy time. ... I've always felt that within the four corners of the Agreement in Principle there was a lot of room for us to work. Therefore it wasn't that I felt as if I was signing with our fingers crossed."

However, the banks soon believed that that was *exactly* what Dome had done. To them, it appeared that Gallagher and Richards had made the agreement and then immediately posed themselves the question: how do we get around this?

In finding loopholes in the AIP, Jack Gallagher decided to outdo his president. His performance was undoubtedly to hasten his inevitable departure from Dome's executive suite. Richards, while quietly asserting that there was "lots of room to move within the four corners of the Agreement," adopted a far more acquiescent attitude towards the banks. Moreover, although traditional bankers recoiled at this scruffy, pot-bellied little man who had preached the joys of inflation to them and led them all on an enormous dance, they held an inevitably ambiguous view of him. They reluctantly realized that he was effectively the cement that held Dome together. Like the Universe in the mind of Buddha, Dome was — contrary to popular perceptions — the creation of Bill Richards' mind. Only he knew how the whole thing worked. Only he knew where all the financial corpses were buried. Most of the bankers were still emotionally eager for punishment to be meted out to Gallagher and Richards. Harrison was said to feel a little softer about Jack, and the T-D's Thomson was still something of a fan of Bill, but in the end they all realized that their top priority was getting paid back, and whichever of the two was more likely to help that process had far more chance of corporate survival, at least in the short term. Only Mulholland was mad as hell at both of them and insisted that they both be ejected as soon as possible.

Ho-Hum over the Precipice

Richards was striving to establish that he *could* change his spots. In a mid-November speech he told an audience of engineers that the management virtues of yesterday were the vices of today. He stressed that management had to develop and apply the qualities of caution and restraint. There had to be tight control of both capital and operating and capital costs. Richards, it appeared, had undergone the greatest conversion since St. Paul on the road to Damascus. Nevertheless, he didn't fail to put in a disguised plug for his own talents. "There was never a time," he noted, "when stable management with steady nerves was more required." Moreover, asserted Richards, there was a ray of hope for industry in falling interest rates. He claimed that the decrease in interest rates during the final quarter of 1982 would mean an additional cash flow to the Canadian petroleum industry of $750 million. He said that one-third of that amount would come to Dome. What he was effectively trying to get across was the impression that things had changed, the outlook was brighter. If Dome was to avoid the AIP, or at least to modify it and so lessen its impact, it would be necessary to raise money in the market. However, a public share sale would require investors to believe that Dome's situation was improving, and they would take a lot of convincing.

When the AIP had been signed, it had been assumed that the agreement could be formally put into effect by the end of the year. It soon became obvious that such a signing would be out of the question. However, the banks had only agreed to hold over the repayment of the debts due on September 30 until the end of the year. As the end of the year approached, it became obvious that the banks would have to postpone payment again.

On December 28, the four Canadian banks agreed to roll over the $1.4 billion due on January 1 to February 28.

Through 1983, the rolling over of Dome's ever-mounting current debt was to become an almost monthly feature. Moreover, the repeated rollovers indicated a shift of initiative back to Dome. Since the major cause of delay was lack of agreement between the major Canadian banks and Dome's other lenders, the banks had little choice but to continue to roll over their debts. Moreover, Dome management's sense of urgency also inevitably decreased as the debt was rolled over time and time again. As Bill Richards said: "The first time they dangled you over the precipice was pretty scary, but after they'd done it a few times and they hadn't dropped you, then the whole routine became a little ho-hum." By mid-year, Richards would suggest that anyone who talked about the $2 billion plus that Dome owed immediately was "boring."

The situation seemed almost bizarre. Dome was in a desperate financial crunch even without considering the huge debt rollovers. And yet Bill Richards was going around telling people that the company was on the mend. In fact, Dome would receive its worst financial accounting blows in the fourth quarter of 1982, after the AIP had been signed. Although they had not been sold, Dome was forced to write off $213.6 million from the value of its U.S. properties. There was also a net loss of $100.4 million on the sale of the overseas assets to LASMO and BP Development. This brought the company's total net loss for the year ending December 31, 1982, to $369.3 million, compared to net income of $199.1 million in the previous year. Most horrendous, of course, was the fact that Dome still had a long-term debt of more than $6.5 billion and that $2.23 billion of it was due during 1983. Ironically, however, Dome's debt load was now almost its only bargaining tool. Indeed, if its debt had been half the size it was, the prospect of liquidation might have been much more attractive to the banks.

Shareholders, meanwhile, were obviously unhappy with the AIP since it had caused Dome's shares to dip close to the $2.50 conversion price outlined in the deal. A group called the Dome Shareholders Protection Committee was set up by consultant John Duby, a former Rhodes Scholar and university professor who had leaped to prominence several years earlier when he led a successful shareholders' coup at United Canso Oil & Gas, thereby wresting control from the wealthy Buckley family of New York. However, the Dome shareholders had very little leverage, and much of the rationale for the group's existence seemed to disappear in the second quarter of 1983 as Dome's share price moved up to $6. Nevertheless, from the perspective of Gallagher and Richards, the shareholders were extremely important because it was only by eliciting further funds from them that the AIP could be avoided.

In order to test the investment waters, Calgary consultant Gordon Engblom was sent by Dome on a secret mission to speak to three leading Toronto financial analysts and three in New York. Engblom was asked to find out what investors thought of the AIP; whether they thought it would be changed; who investors blamed for Dome's plight, the management, the banks or Ottawa; and whether investors thought that Dome management had misled them.

The analysts were generally unenthusiastic about Dome's chances for a major public financing. They also felt there was a perceived problem with the company's executive leadership.

Within the company, meanwhile, the relationship between Gallagher and Richards became increasingly strained.

In the wake of the AIP, Dome had set up an "implementation group" that met every morning to discuss progress on the bailout. Its principal members were Gallagher, Richards, their two executive assistants, Don Gardiner and Steve Savidant, John Beddome and George Watson, who, although still only in his mid-30s, had been taking on an increasing amount of the company's financing burden.

"Implementation group" was a perfect title to quiet the bankers'

220

and government officials' fears. However, "escape committee" would have perhaps been a more appropriate designation. The problem was that Gallagher was being less than subtle about the group's intentions, and he was taking actions and floating ideas outside the group, activities which were felt to be counterproductive.

Gallagher had always been inclined to think aloud, spinning off lots of "what if" schemes to people both inside and outside Dome. To some bankers — and Dome directors — this inclination clearly indicated that he had little or no intention of going along with the AIP. In the months after the agreement, he floated a number of plans: that Alberta producers should take most of Dome's shares in TransCanada PipeLines; that part of Canmar should be sold to European or Canadian interests; that money should be raised via a joint deal with Dome Mines and its subsidiary Campbell Red Lake. He even toyed with the idea of using long-term Arab money.

From within Dome, the objection to these schemes wasn't necessarily that they were impractical, but that news of them often came to Richards from outside sources, or from one of Dome's directors. Richards felt that Dome should be seen to be speaking with a unified voice. The company already had massive enough credibility problems.

OPEC Crumbles

Meanwhile, the petroleum market situation, both in Canada and throughout the world, was getting worse rather than better. Both markets and prices were depressed, which damaged the outlook for Dome and the entire industry. OPEC's power had been crumbling since the first half of HBOG had been acquired in mid-1981. By the time the second half of the deal was completed on March 10, 1982, the organization was in danger of disintegration. The takeover of HBOG, like the thrust of the National Energy Program, only made sense in a world where oil prices continued to rise in real terms. Throughout the summer of 1982, as the federal government and the Canadian banks wrangled over a bailout package for Dome, the OPEC situation deteriorated further. Major oil companies were trying to isolate Nigeria from the OPEC herd as a way of breaking the cartel, while Iran was doing its best to break up OPEC's solid front by deep discounts on its oil sales. OPEC's 64th meeting in May was marked by brave words and hollow self-congratulations about how well OPEC was holding onto control of the market. But while the oil ministers of the OPEC countries talked about the necessity of maintaining price levels and keeping down production quotas, some of their national oil companies were dumping oil surreptitiously onto the world market. By July, it was openly admitted that Iran, Nigeria and Libya had all broken ranks. Others had done so less openly. For the first time since 1975, when ten oil ministers had been kidnapped by six pro-Palestinian guerillas in Vienna, an OPEC meeting was suspended.

In the weeks after the AIP had been signed at the end of September, 1982, all the oil-producing Persian Gulf states were publicly talking about leaving OPEC. To add to the confusion, Mexico was talking about joining it. Saudi Arabia, through its oil minister, Sheik Yamani, was showing more and more irritation at the need to support the OPEC benchmark price of U.S. $34 a barrel. On December, 20, 1982, yet another OPEC meeting broke up after failing to agree on production quotas or price differentials. A nonsensical "agreement" announced that total OPEC producction in 1983 would be 18.5 million barrels a day. It was nonsensical because although everybody went along with the overall ceiling, nobody went along with their individual production limit. Iran was seeking to increase its production quota from 2 million to 3.2 million barrels a day, Venezuela from 1.5 million to 2 million barrels a day, Iraq from 1.2 million to 2.2 million barrels a day, and Indonesia and Nigeria from 1.3 million to 1.5 million barrels a day each. Saudi Arabia, meanwhile, by far OPEC's largest producer, was refusing to reduce its official production quota from 7 million to 5 million barrels a day.

As 1983 opened, fears that OPEC would collapse greatly exacerbated fears about the future of the world banking system. The world's largest banks had bet *en masse* that oil prices would keep rising in real terms. They had lent huge amounts to developing oil producers like Mexico, which was already in severe financial trouble. A further collapse in oil markets could precipitate the global collapse that everybody feared but few publicly acknowledged. Back in Canada, Dome, with debts rivalling those of some developing countries, was very much part of the same crisis.

In the first quarter of 1983, the long-threatened cutting of official prices began. Britain, Norway, Nigeria and the Soviet Union all dropped their prices. Then, in the third week of March, OPEC finally slashed its benchmark price from U.S. $34 to U.S. $29, the first official price cut in the organization's history. Throughout all the oil producing countries, projects were being shelved and imports slashed. Even Saudi Arabia — with an output by now of a mere 3.3 million barrels a day vs. a production peak of almost 10 million barrels — was thought to be facing a potential budget deficit of $20 billion.

The link between these problems and the Canadian oil industry was the agreement made between the federal government and Alberta in September, 1981. Both that agreement and the National Energy

Program that preceded it had been predicated on a continuing rise in world oil prices and a regulated pursuit of those prices by oil and gas prices in Canada.

A key provision of the 1981 agreement had been that the upper price limit on oil found before 1980 would be 75% of the world price. In 1982, to ease the industry's financial problems, Ottawa had agreed to give 75% of the world price immediately to all oil discovered after 1974. However, it had not been foreseen that "old" oil, that is, oil discovered before 1974, would be pressing on its 75% limit within fifteen months of the federal-Alberta agreement. If that ceiling were maintained, the projected cash flows, on which Dome's future depended, would inevitably come down. Moreover, even if domestic prices were allowed to go to world levels — which, for political reasons, the federal Liberals would oppose — prices were still likely to wind up below the levels foreseen both in the NEP and the federal-Alberta agreement.

Alberta and the industry nevertheless pressed the Liberal government to move to world prices. Even Bill Hopper, chairman of Petro-Canada, joined their chorus.

In February, 1983, Jean Chrétien suggested that some flexibility in pricing might be possible and that even world pricing might be considered. However, this scheme was ultimately squashed within cabinet by Marc Lalonde. Moreover, in March, just ahead of OPEC's cut in its benchmark price, it was suggested that the Canadian price should be rolled back to prevent it going above the 75% level. Needless to say, this suggestion produced a sharp response from Alberta.

Canadian natural gas policy was also in severe difficulty. Again under the federal-provincial agreement, Ottawa had promised — as an incentive to Canadian gas consumers to use more domestic gas — to keep gas prices at 65% of the heating equivalent value of oil prices. To maintain this promise the federal government was forced to forego part of its Natural Gas and Gas Liquids Tax, one of the new taxes introduced under the NEP. In the very important U.S. market meanwhile, scarcely half of approved exports were being sold because Canadian gas prices — which in this case were directly linked to world oil prices — were considered far too high.

To top everything, under another feature of federal policy — and felt by the industry to be perverse — relatively cheap Albertan oil was still shut in while imports were subsidized by consumers. In January, 1983, for example, according to Albertan Energy Minister John Zaozirny, 10.5 million barrels of oil were imported into Canada while 5 million barrels of domestic oil, worth $200 million, went unproduced.

On June 30, 1983, after intense discussions, the Alberta and federal sides announced yet another new agreement on oil and gas pricing, the third major change since the Liberals had come to power in 1980. This new agreement, however, was generally welcomed by the industry for its pragmatism and flexibility, even though the Liberals resisted calls to go to world pricing.

Under the agreement, old oil prices were allowed to stay at $29.75 a barrel where they had moved on January 1, 1983. Thus they could stay above the 75% ceiling, but would not be allowed to go higher unless the world price moved upwards again, whereupon they would be allowed once more up to 75% of those levels. The $4-a-barrel increase planned for July 1 under the federal-Alberta agreement was scrapped. On gas pricing, increases would continue more or less as planned, although in 1985 and 1986 the Albertan government would absorb the cost of paying producers more. The federal government also announced that it would help subsidize transportation costs through the TransCanada PipeLine. A few days later, Jean Chrétien also announced that the federal government would go along with an "incentive pricing" scheme for gas exports, where if more than half of contracted volumes were sold, additional volumes could be sold at a discount of $1 a thousand cubic feet (MCF).

Financial Twilight Zone

OPEC's depressed outlook, lower projected levels of Canadian oil and gas prices, low gas exports and shut-in oil, all darkened the prospects for Canadian oil companies. Nevertheless, the AIP and subsequent wrangling between the banks had moved Dome into a kind of financial twilight zone in which Bill Richards could play, as the January, 1983 edition of *Fortune* magazine suggested, the "cock-eyed optimist," while Jack Gallagher openly talked about escape from the AIP.

In the middle of February, Dome made a major presentation to its European creditors in London, pointing out that the company had instituted numerous internal measures to improve cash flow and address the weakness of the company's capital structure. Capital expenditure had been slashed to a quarter of pre-1982 levels. Staff cuts, salary reductions and inventory reductions were saving the company about $100 million annually. The company planned to sell part of its stake in TransCanada PipeLines as well as its U.S. properties. Dome's main problem as an ongoing concern, however, was that it had little or no money to develop its asset base. It planned, so the London creditors were told, to use two principal tools in an effort to breathe financial life into its assets; project financing and farm-outs. Under

224

project financing, installations were financed on the basis of their own future revenue streams and thus, to a considerable degree, separately from the rest of the company's operations. Farm-outs involved Dome attracting other oil companies to drill on its lands in return for a portion of those lands.

"Going into 1983," said a secret briefing document issued by the company, "Dome finds its financial position slowly improving. Operating revenues continue to grow, although not as quickly as originally hoped, since there continues to be some further deterioration in the general environment for the Canadian oil and gas industry. Net cash flow is, however, substantially better than 1982 as a result of the dramatic decline in interest rates." To the rest of the world, meanwhile, Dome attempted to portray an image of "business as normal," which, under the circumstances, was somewhat difficult. Dome continued forcefully to promote its western LNG project, the multi-billion dollar scheme it had hatched for shipping liquefied natural gas to Japan. However, this megaproject again seemed somehow out of kilter both with Dome's financial situation and the tenor of the economic times. Under the plan, first announced at the end of 1980, Dome proposed to build a world-scale liquefaction plant, storage facilities and shiploading installations in the Port Simpson area of British Columbia. These facilities would have a total cost of $2 billion. Gas from Alberta and British Columbia would be liquefied and pumped aboard five specialized LNG carriers, with a total value of $1 billion, to be shipped to Japan. There, under a contract negotiated with Nissho Iwai Corporation, five Japanese utilities would take some 3 trillion cubic feet of Canadian gas over a 20-year period.

However, there were continuous rumours in the first half of 1983 that the project might run into problems. For a start, the price of the LNG was related to world oil prices and the export price of Canadian gas, both of which were dropping. This in turn meant that the price received by Canadian gas producers might be unacceptably low. From Japan, meanwhile, there were reports that the Japan National Oil Company was balking at guaranteeing the loans to finance the project. Nevertheless, as this book went to press, regulatory hearings within Canada on the scheme were going ahead while Dome, typically, was brushing aside all suggestions of problems.

Nevertheless, Dome couldn't disguise the horrendous financial problems still facing the company. Quite apart from the billions of dollars of principal repayments hanging over its corporate head, it estimated that its interest and preferred share dividend payments alone for 1983 would be a massive $822 million. Moreover, whatever sale of assets was achieved, the money would have to go to the banks.

From the Canadian government's point of view, the timing of the implementation of the AIP — or indeed whether it was implemented at all — was of less pressing importance than it was to the banks. There was also thinly disguised irritation on the part of the banks to persistent rumours of Dome's desire to renegotiate its bailout package. Bill Mulholland, for example, in response to a question about Dome attempting to find an alternative refinancing package, said during a press conference early in 1983: "I don't know anything in particular about it. There is the occasional newspaper article. So far as I know nothing more than that is eventuating. Dome can have any kind of package it wants, really. All it has to do is pay off its debt."

Energy Minister Jean Chrétien was also showing irritation at Dome's attitude. When Gallagher and Richards suggested to him that they wanted to avoid the AIP, he told them: "If you can find the money, my friends, good luck." In a subsequent press interview he said: "If you ask me if I feel they need the money, I guess so. But I don't know and I basically don't care if they want to sink."

One element of the whole situation that increasingly galled the banks was the apparent failure on the part of Gallagher and Richards to acknowledge that their days were numbered. Pressure was applied to the board to bring that fact home to them. But the board, in any case, already realized that the time had clearly come to exercise its authority. Within the free enterprise ethos, corporate failure demanded that management pay the price. Moreover, it wasn't meant to be up to the management to demand the terms on which they would pay it. The time had come for corporate heads to roll, and the ethos said that the first to roll had to be that of the chief executive, Jack Gallagher. Smilin' Jack thought otherwise.

19
Gallagher's Final Days

*" ... I'm not made temperamentally in a way that
allows me to stop."*

JACK GALLAGHER

Jack Gallagher had grown used to having his own way with his board of directors, the investment community and the banks, and he saw this acquiescence simply as their concurrence in the validity of his visions. He had been both hurt and surprised at the speed and ferocity with which his former allies in Ottawa and at the major banks had turned upon him. But he still believed he could always count on his board to support him.

Although Gallagher admitted that he had allowed the day-to-day leadership of Dome to move away from him in recent years, he felt that since the crisis had come to a head early in 1982, he had applied himself diligently to its solution. In his eyes, Dome was still very much Jack Gallagher's company, and he felt he had a responsibility to see it through its present difficulties. After all, he told himself, it wasn't as if he'd steered the company into its present mess. He did, of course, recognize his own fault in the whole affair by allowing the "younger men" their head in the HBOG takeover. Gallagher would point out to colleagues and acquaintances that he had never been a fan of growth through acquisition. Unfortunately, he also now took to openly blaming Bill Richards for Dome's difficulties. For Gallagher, the conclusion was obvious: if anybody had to go it had to be Bill. It was very difficult for him to grasp the fact that the banks were increasingly inclined to see him as a major part of the remaining problem. His statements about Richards were hardly helping the relationship between them or the internal cohesion of the company. The two men's young assistants, Steve Savidant and Don Gardiner, became crucial to keeping the lines of communication open. Moreover, Gallagher's statements did little for his own popularity. There was small doubt that what he said was true: Richards *had* been the architect of expansion, and Gallagher *had* been sucked along in the wake. It was equally

227

true, however, that Gallagher had hung on to the title of chief executive officer, and with it ultimate responsibility for the fate of the company. By blaming Richards he was not only breaking the rules of corporate responsibility but also those of gentlemanly corporate conduct.

It was felt that Gallagher was discussing Richards' departure with far too many people both inside and outside the company, although he appeared at times to agonize over the prospect of ditching Dome's president.

Meanwhile, Gallagher's continuing obsession with the Beaufort seemed somehow strangely inappropriate at this time. Following an October Liberal fund raising dinner in Calgary, Gallagher had gone up to Jean Chrétien's room for a chat. Gallagher told Chrétien that he really must come up to the Beaufort. "Sure," said the amiable energy minister, "I'd really like to come sometime." And Gallagher said no, not sometime, tomorrow morning. There would be a plane waiting for him at 8 A.M. But Chrétien said he couldn't, he had to be in Ottawa in the morning. Then Gallagher almost began to plead with him: they were testing a well at that very moment; would Chrétien come up if they found oil? But Chrétien said no, he had a meeting with the Prime Minister the following day. Gallagher looked hurt and disappointed. Later Chrétien would comment that he was pretty sure Dome would have struck oil if he'd gone up, "even if they had to bring it up in the airplane!"

This kind of encounter was doing very little for Dome's already shaky credibility. In addition, Gallagher's tendency to throw off numerous proposals to escape the AIP was also considered imprudent, and, in many cases impractical.

"If"

For Christmas, 1982, Gallagher sent out greeting cards with Kipling's poem "If" printed on them. The gesture was full of pathos, for it not only said a lot about how Gallagher perceived his present position, but the poem also summed up his entire life's philosophy, the philosophy of a gambler.

If you can keep your head when all about you
    Are losing theirs and blaming it on you;
If you can trust yourself when all men doubt you,
    But make allowance for their doubting too:
If you can wait and not be tired by waiting,

> Or, being lied about, don't deal in lies,
> Or being hated, don't give way to hating,
>   And yet don't look too good, nor talk too wise ...

Gallagher believed that the banks and government had "lost their heads" over Dome and were now blaming him; that the public misunderstood his role in the mess. But he could wait. He knew all about waiting; he had been waiting for the big petroleum find all his life. Now he believed he was close to it in the Beaufort. His fondest dream was that the proverbial gusher would arrive, like a *deus ex machina*, and solve all Dome's problems.

As for lies, Gallagher may have always been an optimist, but he had never been a liar, and hatred was an emotion totally alien to him. His highest priority had, in his mind, always been people. That was one of Dome's problems; it had grown away from him, grown too big. He couldn't know the people any more and it hurt him to think that any of his employees might blame him for their personal problems. Self-image was very important to Gallagher, although he believed he had never pretended to be a plaster saint, to "look too good" or "talk too wise."

> If you can dream — and not make dreams your master;
>   If you can think — and not make thoughts your aim,
> If you can meet with Triumph and Disaster
>   And treat those two impostors just the same:
> If you can bear to hear the truth you've spoken
>   Twisted by knaves to make a trap for fools,
> Or watch the things you gave your life to, broken,
>   And stoop and build 'em up with worn-out tools ...

Dreaming and thinking; those had been the skills on which Jack Gallagher had built his reputation. In particular, his vision of Beaufort exploration had been transformed into hundreds of millions of dollars worth of steel and technology in the Far North. But somewhere along the line the dream had begun to turn into a nightmare. Gallagher had certainly basked in the apparent corporate triumphs of Dome Canada's creation and the Conoco tender offer, but now the brunt of the other "impostor," disaster, seemed to be falling on him alone.

Now it seemed that the development of Dome Petroleum and the pursuit of big oil — the things Gallagher had given his life to — lay broken. Nevertheless, he was determined that however "worn-out" his tools looked, he would stick around to see his empire back on an even keel.

If you can make one heap of all your winnings
    And risk it on one turn of pitch-and-toss,
And lose, and start again at your beginnings,
    And never breathe a word about your loss:
If you can force your heart with nerve and sinew
    To serve your turn long after they are gone,
And so hold on when there is nothing in you
    Except the Will which says to them: "Hold on!" ...

That seemed the most poignant stanza of all. Its first four lines could be carved on the gravestoines of all the really dedicated oilmen. They were the greatest gamblers, in a game where the odds were always against them. Ever since Dome's first deep wildcat at Buckinghorse thirty years before had been drilled, and come up dry, Gallagher had built up the company despite disappointment after disappointment. In the end, the biggest gambles had been taken at the instigation of Bill Richards, but now everyone was blaming these on Gallagher.

Jack was now in his late 60s, a time when "heart and nerve and sinew" in many men might be gone, but he still had his will, the will that told him to "hold on." The problem was that such a situation was unprecedented. A couple of years before, the idea of "holding-on" at Dome would have been unthinkable for Jack; Dome *was* Jack Gallagher. But now they were trying to tell him it wasn't so; that Jack Gallagher's Dome was a disaster; that Dome could only survive as a very different creature.

If you can talk with crowds and keep your virtue,
    Or walk with Kings — nor lose the common touch,
If neither foes nor loving friends can hurt you,
    If all men count with you, but none too much:
If you can fill the unforgiving minute
    With sixty seconds' worth of distance run,
Yours is the Earth and everything that's in it,
    And — which is more — you'll be a Man, my son!

Gallagher had always had a unique ability to talk to crowds. As a salesman of his Beaufort vision he was skilled at reducing geology to terms the ordinary person could understand. But he could also "walk with Kings." He had met with, and impressed, a dozen heads of state and senior politicians from all over the globe. But his fondest image of himself was as a man with the common touch; a man who always had time for a word for employees, or a chat with people on airline flights. All men counted with Jack, but ultimately "none too much," for Gallagher was at heart a very private man whose major concern

230

was his family, his wife, Kathleen, and his three sons, James, Thomas and Frederick.

Gallagher felt that he had filled the "unforgiving minutes" of his life with work. So recently, it seemed, the "earth and everything that's in it" — the geologist's dream — had been his.

But the banks, in particular, no longer saw Jack the way he saw himself. Some considered his Christmas card to be a blatant tug at the heart-strings, and they were determined not to be taken in by the Gallagher charm again. They were becoming more and more furious with his attempts to skirt around the AIP and his failure to accept the fact that they wanted him to go, and go quickly. One angry banker told the author: "Jack Gallagher was out to lunch because without the banks' agreement, Dome couldn't sell five cents-worth of equity. He also seemed to have adopted the view that the longer Dome stalled, the more chance there was of renegotiating the agreement." In the words of a director of one of Dome's corporate family: "They finally had to do a job on Gallagher. Jack just didn't realize he was an obstruction. He was in wonderland. He was a great visionary, but not a great financier."

The people who had to "do the job" were Dome's board of directors. For some of them, it was the hardest job they had ever faced.

Stiffening the Board

During Dome's troubles, the Dome board had come in for a good deal of criticism. They had been accused of exercising very little effective control over the company's enormous expansion and its acquisition of massive debt. They had also been accused of selling out the shareholders through the Agreement in Principle. Now the banks were accusing them of not axing Dome's top management quickly enough.

It was certainly true that Gallagher and Richards had held total sway over the board in earlier years, but that was hardly surprising. The board was there to look after the shareholders and the share-price had soared until the summer of 1981. Moreover, Gallagher and Richards were uniquely persuasive and forceful. It was inevitable, given these factors, that the board would adopt a rubber-stamp mentality. The only director who had seriously balked at Gallagher's and Richards' executive style and Dome's expansion had been Mac Taschereau, the president of Dome Mines. He had, in fact, offered several times to resign but his resignation had been turned down because it was felt that the president of Dome Mines had to be on the Dome Petroleum board. Moreover, it wouldn't have looked good.

231

Shareholder anger over the Agreement in Principle seemed misplaced, and was based on a misunderstanding of the weakness of Dome's bargaining position. However, the pressure for management changes wasn't coming from the shareholders — the board's first theoretical concern — it was coming from the board's peers in the banks. What made it all the harder for the directors was that many of them respected and admired Gallagher. They wanted to make his departure as painless as possible. But Gallagher was willing himself, as in Kipling's poem, to "hold on." Bill was the problem, he told some of the directors; Bill should go.

Nevertheless, in February, Gallagher was persuaded that he had to make an announcement about his retirement from the position of chief executive. He agreed to the issue of a press release on February 23 that stated: "Dome Petroleum Limited announced today that Mr. J.P. Gallagher, Chairman and Chief Executive Officer of the Company, has requested its Board of Directors to appoint a committee of Directors to seek from within and outside the Company suitable candidates for Chief Executive Officer (CEO) of the Company. Mr. Gallagher has indicated to the Board that he proposes to retire from the position of CEO at the Annual or Special Meeting of Shareholders, which it is anticipated will be held in the second half of this year to consider implementation of the Company's Financial Plan with its bankers and the Canadian Government."

The release said nothing about Gallagher's chairmanship, and he still remained the dominant voice in the committee to select his successor. Meanwhile, he remained chief executive until the special shareholders meeting, which he would now presumably be even more reluctant to hurry into being. For the banks, that wasn't good enough.

The matter finally came to a head at a board meeting in the Toronto offices of Fasken & Calvin in early April. Gallagher had, in fact, been told at a private dinner the night before that he would have to step down. It was an emotional meeting, but until the last he tried to avoid his ouster. Between that dinner and the board meeting the following afternoon he had lobbied several of the directors. At least if he had to go, he told them, then it was only fair that Richards should go too. The wording of the February press release, suggesting that the search for the new chief executive would take place within Dome as well as outside the company, had led to speculation that Richards might be in the running for the chief executive post. In fact, given the bankers' attitude to Dome's president, that notion was little short of ludicrous. Nevertheless, it worried Gallagher. People didn't like him for saying it, but he just couldn't get the notion out of his mind that all this was Bill's fault. Why was it that he had to pay and not Bill?

The unpalatable answer was that Bill was still perceived as useful; Jack was not. It was a terribly hard truth for Gallagher to bear.

The fateful meeting finally started at about 3:30 on the afternoon of April 7. Gallagher and Richards were asked to leave the room. They went off to separate offices while their fate was discussed. After more than an hour they were invited back. Richards' wings were clipped first. He was told that John Beddome would be appointed executive vice-president and chief operating officer of the company. That meant Beddome would run its day-to-day operations. However, Richards was left with the title of president. Then Gallagher was told that he would have to give up the title of chief executive immediately, although he clung tenaciously to the title of chairman. It would be his for a little more than two months.

The following day, a press release was issued. It declared: "Mr. J.P. (Jack) Gallagher announced today that he has decided to retire from the position of Chief Executive Officer of Dome Petroleum Limited effective April 8, 1983, in order to effect a more gradual transition in a change to the senior management position of the Company. Mr. Gallagher has agreed to continue as Chairman of the Board of Directors of Dome Petroleum."

At the same board meeting it was decided that in the interim period until a new chief executive was appointed, an executive committee of the board, headed by Wick Sellers, would act as CEO. There was also a significant changing of the guard within the board. Bruce Matthews, who was also stepping down from the chairmanship of Dome Mines, resigned, and his place was taken by Allen Lambert, the former head of the Toronto-Dominion Bank who already sat on the Dome Mines board and who had joined the Dome board in its negotiations over the AIP.

Within Dome there was embarrassment following Gallagher's push from the executive suite. Some of the senior people avoided him. But in Jack's mind he wasn't finished yet. He was still chairman of Dome Petroleum and he was still chairman and chief executive of Dome Canada. He still felt he had a role to play.

In early April, Gallagher also received adverse publicity because of revelations in the company's 10K filing for 1982 with the Securities and Exchange Commission. The report disclosed that under a preexisting agreement, Gallagher had consented to make himself available as a "consultant" after his retirement, and that the company, subject to certain unstated conditions, had agreed to pay him a monthly fee of approximately $27,500. The 10K also revealed that the agreement provided for the payment of these fees in a lump sum ($2.64 million on December 31, 1982), plus interest, if his employment was terminated by the company "prior to his proposed retirement other than

233

for certain specified reasons." These consultancy fees, or the lump sum payment, were related to the salary that Gallagher had forgone since 1967. Some of Dome's board members, however, were irked that they hadn't known about the arrangement. It was widely known, and well-publicized, that Gallagher drew no salary. His principal benefit from the company had been assumed to be the large interest-free loans that Dome executives received to buy company shares (see Appendix B). Now the word around the oilpatch was that Jack Gallagher had somehow worked himself a sweetheart deal, an assertion that offended Gallagher.

Gallagher Goes Public

To "put the record straight" both on the circumstances of his departure from Dome and the AIP, Gallagher requested an interview on CBC's "Morningside" radio show. The interview, with the show's host Peter Gzowski, was aired on the morning of April 22. Asked about "the conditions of his departure" by Gzowski, Gallagher replied: "I had indicated to our board three years ago that I was approaching 65 and that I wanted to step aside as CEO of Dome, and at that time the board said if you leave, we leave. So I carried on and I didn't want to leave in the down period of Dome. But as we now feel that we have bottomed out and are on the way up, the time is ripe. I intended to stay on as chairman, and conduct the shareholders' meeting in the mid-summer or early fall. I am also still CEO and chairman of Dome Canada which is the exploration arm of Dome Petroleum and so it'll be the type of job that I enjoy."

Whatever the board and banks said, Gallagher still felt he should continue as chairman. Meanwhile, he had obviously decided that being chief executive of Dome's "exploration arm," Dome Canada, wasn't such a bad fate. In response to Gzowski's question as to whether Gallagher felt any bitterness towards the remaining management, Gallagher said: "Oh no, not at all. No, I'm still part of that company. Just because you step aside as CEO means you're not following everything on a day-to-day basis, but I'm still in there at eight in the morning and I'm still there till six at night. And on weekends."

The problem, of course, was that the board had told him about as bluntly as it could that they didn't want him there between eight and six. Or on weekends.

Gzowski took a gentle tone with Gallagher, leading him into the verbal furrows he knew so well, the views and statistics he'd expressed a thousand times — on Dome's creation, his early days in the Far

North, his views on Senate reform, the potential of the Beaufort. But Gallagher obviously wasn't his old smooth self. There was a hint of desperation and self-justification that had not been there before. Of the consulting agreement, involving the $2.64 million lump sum payment, Gallagher stressed that it was the result of a forced savings plan on his part; it was not "a payoff."

Gzowski touched on a critical point — and one that Gallagher certainly wanted brought up — when he said: "But it strikes me as I read your life story and realize what you did for that company and where you stood on that company's most interesting and perhaps dramatic financial years that if Dome is in trouble now financially, it's largely because of huge overexpansion, Hudson's Bay, etc. It seems to me you're the man who voted against much of that expansion. I think from time to time you were the only voice saying let's not grow that fast and yet, you're the person who is now stepping out. The people who are staying in are the people who wanted to expand that quickly ... that seems — I don't understand how business works — but it seems curious to me."

Gallagher seized his chance. " ... I enjoyed growing slowly," he said. "I like to grow solidly. I like a hands-on operation. I enjoy knowing all the people. And therefore, up until the last two or three years, that's the way we grew. You can become a large company but you grow solidly from within. That's been my style and you are correct in saying that philosophically I was not in tune with some of the younger people in the organization who wanted to grow a little more quickly, therefore, philosophically, I was not in favour of growth by acquisition, mainly because people get hurt when you acquire another company. I didn't resist because I was 65 years of age. I wanted to step aside. I felt that the younger people would be carrying on. I'm not saying they were wrong and I was right, because if the market ... "

Here, Gzowski, whom Gallagher seemed to be playing like a violin, was obviously overcome by the unfairness of it all. He interrupted: "But they were wrong and you were right."

"No," responded Gallagher, full of magnanimity now he had exonerated himself, "but if the market had gone the other way they would have looked great. We got caught in a downdraft. But you're very correct, philosophically I enjoyed being a little smaller. When you're a large company you catch all the flak."

The interview finished with a little of Gallagher's undying northern vision. Said Gzowski: "Jack Gallagher, you're just not about to give up on your vision are you?"

Gallagher responded, with a defiant tone in his gentle voice: "No, why should I, Peter?"

Gallagher later had copies of the transcript circulated.

Less than a month later, Gallagher attended the annual dinner of the Independent Petroleum Association of Canada (IPAC). IPAC had always been the voice of the smaller, Canadian oil companies, and Gallagher had been one of its founding members. IPAC's other founders were there, including Carl Nickle, Ed Galvin and Bill McGregor, all of whom had founded their own oil companies and become multi-millionaires. But until recently, Jack Gallagher had appeared by far the most successful of them all. There was a feeling on this night that they were all witnessing the end of an era. But Gallagher was still resisting being pushed, and still believed there was a role for him to play. That was obvious at the annual meeting of Dome Canada a week later.

There, beneath the rococo mouldings and chandeliers of Calgary's Palliser Hotel, Gallagher, looking as sprightly as ever, faced the Dome Canada shareholders. On his left stood a great white screen, waiting to be filled once again with the Beaufort vision. Some representatives of American banks who were present could hardly believe it, but Gallagher went into his full, hour-long, Arctic slide-show, the red dot from his hand-held flashlight, like some technological warrior's laser-sword, darting about the maps of his favourite geographical area at the top of the world. Gallagher appeared to be in fine form. When asked at a press conference afterwards if he intended to stay on with Dome Canada, he said: "Yes, I'm not made temperamentally in a way that allows me to stop."

However, the time had now come for Gallagher to step down from Dome Petroleum. Within the company, the plan had been to combine the annual and special shareholders meetings some time in the fall, but Gallagher had declared that he wanted to chair the annual meeting. If Gallagher intended to chair that meeting, the board decided that it would have to be brought forward. Suddenly, on May 31, it was announced that it would take place on June 28.

The Last Meeting

Annual meetings are times for a company's management and board of directors to account to shareholders for their stewardship. In the past Dome's had always been the Jack Gallagher show. This year's would be different: a carefully stage-managed, carefully packaged series of presentations that tried to put the best light on the most disastrous year in the company's history. But by far the most important feature for the shareholders was that this meeting would see the passing of Jack Gallagher's era at Dome.

236

June 28 was obviously a very sad day for Jack Gallagher as he made his way to the huge convention hall of Toronto's Harbour Castle Hilton Hotel. While the shareholders and their proxies assembled, the directors filed in and the press took their seats, Gallagher stood symbolically alone near some sound equipment to one side of the hall, going through the notes of his speech.

Gallagher had usually conducted these proceedings alone. Today, he sat on a rostrum with Harry Eisenhauer, Dome's corporate secretary, Wick Sellers, Bill Richards, John Beddome, and an empty seat which would, by the end of the morning, be taken by his successor. As he opened the meeting, he sounded tired and spent. His smile was absent. Nevertheless, for the next hour and a half he would stoically play his role in a carefully scripted event whose finale would be his departure. The official business of the meeting went without incident, apart from an aged shareholder who leaped up to declare that he wanted to give Dome some more money to help it out of its problems. At the end of the presentations of Gallagher, Richards, Beddome and Sellers, and before the official question period, Gallagher announced that he would be standing down as chairman following the meeting. Then he announced that his place would be taken by John Howard Macdonald, a name known to very few people in the hall. Macdonald was group treasurer for the giant Royal Dutch Shell Group in London, England. A 55-year-old chartered accountant, Macdonald would, said Gallagher be "ideally suited to take over the reins of your company at a time when its problems were essentially financial." Gallagher then invited Macdonald up to say a few words. In a broad Scottish accent, Macdonald thanked Gallagher, said he was heartened by preliminary discussions with the government and the banks and declared, with unmistakable firmness, that he wanted to lay to rest the idea that the Canadian banks would be appointing any directors to the board of Dome. Then he took his place at the end of the rostrum, and Wick Sellers ceremoniously produced a place-card with his name upon it.

Gallagher conducted the question period and then delivered a few encouraging remarks. Dome would survive, said Gallagher. "We're leaner, we're tougher, and, we'll certainly be more careful and I think probably a better company in the long run."

Then Wick Sellers moved to the podium. Sellers, in his role as chairman of the Chief Executive Committee had, earlier in the meeting, perhaps indicated a little too clearly that he was now effectively running the company. Richards and Beddome, he had said, reported to him, and of course through him to the executive committee. Sellers was not considered a corporate heavyweight by his peers but he had clearly had his eyes on the CEO position for himself. He had also been one of the spokesmen who had told Gallagher that he had to step down. As such, he had hardly endeared himself to the man who had first brought him onto Dome's board back in 1976.

Sellers affected a tone of deep sincerity as, in his well-modulated voice, he began: "With the indulgence of the shareholders, let me interrupt this meeting in order to express some thoughts about a man who has received a great deal of public attention over the past few months."

The lights dimmed. The giant screen to the left of the podium was filled with slide after slide of Jack down through the years. "This entire company," Sellers continued, "is experiencing a fundamental change in management which will profoundly affect the fundamental nature of Dome in years to come. As we move confidently towards the future, we should reflect on the powerful and positive influence which this man has had not only on our company and on its people but on the very roots of the industry of which we are part. The achievements of Dome are in reality the reflection of the significant achievements of one John Patrick Gallagher, known fondly by many of you as Smilin' Jack."

The ancient shareholder, who had by now interrupted the meeting several times, set up a doleful, but indisputably genuine chorus in the background: "We're sorry to see him go. We're sorry to see him go."

Sellers continued: "There will be those of you who may dwell upon our company's present difficulties, and I don't mean to minimize them, but to do so at length is to forget that in a very short period of 30 years, Jack Gallagher has brought this company from insignificance to a position of vital importance to our country and to our oil and gas industry. No one, particularly Jack, would suggest that he has done it alone, for many have contributed to the building process. But it has been his vision, his optimism, his foresight and I suggest his extraordinary good luck which have provided the dramatic leadership essential to the growth of this company."

The pictures of Gallagher continued to follow each other: Smilin' Jack in a casual cardigan; Smilin' Jack with Charlie Dunkley, who had faithfully served Dome for 25 years and was now back in Calgary wondering how everything could have gone so wrong; Smilin' Jack with John Masters of Canadian Hunter, one of the newer lords of Canadian oil; and most of all, just full-face shots of that dazzling smile. Twenty feet to the left of the screen, Jack Gallagher sat in the dark without a smile, and with tears in his eyes, listening to words that must have sounded hollow.

"For those of you who have experienced the unforgettable Gallagher handshake and felt the positive effects of his remarkable smile, you know that Jack Gallagher leaves you with an indelible impression of caring about you personally and who is genuinely interested in your thoughts and ideas."

The peroration continued to its inevitable conclusion, a phrase Wick Sellers had been rolling around now for several weeks: " … Jack Gallagher I'm sure will go down in the history books truly as one of the great, great Canadians of our time."

It was as if Cassius rather than Mark Antony had delivered the euology over the body of a Caesar not dead but mortally wounded. The directors who had forced Gallagher to resign had all been "honourable men." They had dispatched Gallagher because they believed it was for the corporate good — or at least it was what Dome's bankers demanded, which amounted to the same thing — but some of them had obviously dispatched him with much heavier hearts than others. John Loeb was one director conspicuously absent from this last meeting presided over by his old friend Gallagher.

When Sellers had finished his speech and the lights came on once more, the audience stood as a single entity to applaud the fallen chairman. When the ovation stopped, Gallagher quietly thanked Sellers and brought the meeting to a close.

At a subsequent press conference, Gallagher sat looking sad and was unusually silent while Wick Sellers made perhaps inevitably vacuous noises about Dome's bailout negotiations. At the end of the conference came the indelicate question everybody from Dome had hoped would not be asked: was Jack Gallagher pressed to resign? Gallagher hesitated and then replied that three years ago he had wanted to resign. Then he just shook his head. "And was there no pressure from the banks?" persisted the journalist. "No pressure from the banks," said Gallagher, and then Doug Evans, Dome's PR man, leaped in and closed the conference.

20
Richards
Bows Out

"The first standard is to survive. Our judgment was that if we had to rely on the tender mercies of the banks, then we weren't going to survive. We weren't going to fail because we didn't avail ourselves of every opportunity that was presented. You do what you have to. If you like it that's nice, but if you don't you still do it."

BILL RICHARDS

After the 1983 annual meeting, it appeared that Gallagher was at last out of the picture. Nevertheless, he still held the titles of chairman and chief executive of Dome Canada, which he regarded as the "exploration arm" of Dome Petroleum. He would also, he said, remain an "active" Dome director. Richards, meanwhile, seemed to maintain only a highly tenuous position in the Dome Tower. But although his wings had been publicly clipped, he still held the title of president. For some of the bankers, who were used to a discreet world where the strings of corporate "pull" were not meant to show, and where a nod was as good as a wink, this blatant unwillingness to depart had proved frustrating to say the least.

At the same time, bad feelings persisted between the bankers. The feud between Bill Mulholland and Dick Thomson continued to fester. Negotiations with foreign bankers and the sorting out of the pyramid of security packages that Dome had compiled during its lending binge dragged on.

Although he had officially left Dome Petroleum, in July Gallagher was still pointing out that he was the largest shareholder on the board in order to imply his continuing clout. He was also making trips to London to suggest that Dome's situation was improving and that a private financing was possible, while Richards meanwhile still sat atop the Dome Tower plotting escape routes.

A private financing was, of course, attractive to the bankers. They had no desire to take the debentures under the AIP and would much rather that an equity injection come from Dome shareholders. But the

241

roles Richards and Gallagher continued to play made some of the bankers almost apoplectic with rage.

Nevertheless, at least one part of the banks' problems with Dome management — in fact the major one — had been solved: inexorable behind-the-scenes pressure had led to the appointment of a new chairman and chief executive, John Howard Macdonald, the little Scots chartered accountant from the Shell Group in London.

Macdonald's appointment had come as a surprise. In the months following the setting up of the Chief Executive Search Committee in February, half a dozen names had been through the public rumour mill: Bill Daniel, the head of Shell Canada; Jack Armstrong, the retired chief executive of Imperial Oil; Peter Gordon, head of Steel Co. of Canada, Stelco; and Alf Powis, head of Noranda Mines. Wick Sellers had clearly been interested in the job. He had moved from Winnipeg to Calgary in his role as chairman of the committee that was fulfilling the function of chief executive officer, and he had given up his chairmanship of the Canada Development Corporation. Perhaps the two most intriguing suggestions for the CEO job had been Gerry Maier, the former chairman of HBOG, who was now president of Bow Valley Industries, and Bill Mulholland, the chairman of the Bank of Montreal. In fact, the Dome directors' committee had cast their eyes over a much larger list, and had eventually come down to a short list of half a dozen names.

Wishing to appear amenable to the bankers upon whom Dome's fate ultimately depended, the CEO selection committee had approached the chief executives of the big four banks to provide them with lists of likely candidates for the top job at Dome. The T-D had provided a list of suggestions. At least one of the senior bankers explained curtly that choosing a new CEO was not the banks' but the board's responsibility. The bankers, seeking scapegoats for their anger at Dome, had not neglected the Dome board. Blind to the lack of constraint they had themselves exercised, some of the bankers were highly critical of the ease with which Gallagher and Richards had ridden roughshod over their directors.

Before the Dome board made its final selection, however, it presented the candidates to a meeting of the four bank CEOs and senior government representatives. After being advised of the acceptability of the candidates, the name eventually chosen by the selection committee was that of Macdonald. The Scotsman had first been approached when he was passing through Canada on Shell business, and had later been visited in London by Fraser Fell, Allen Lambert and Norman Alexander.

Although Macdonald's first words at the annual meeting had made clear that the banks would *not* be appointing board members or management to Dome, the banks were obviously glad to have him at the wheel. Macdonald had 23 years experience with Royal Dutch Shell, the second largest, and probably the most respected, of the Seven Sisters. He had spent his last seven years as Group Treasurer, overseeing the financing of one of the world's largest corporate empires. In that position, he had come to know virtually every major banker in the world. (Asked after the annual meeting of Dome whether he had met with the Canadian CEOs, he had said: "I've known them all for years.") According to his colleagues, he possessed all those qualities associated with a Scottish chartered accountant; he was extremely shrewd, doggedly persistent, and personally taciturn. He reflected the belief firmly instilled into Dome's directors by their banking contacts that debt repayment had to take priority over exploration and development. It was also true that Dome possessed more talent on the oil and gas side than on the financial side. As to why he had considered taking such a difficult position, the answer was remarkably simple: Dome had offered him a remuneration package that he couldn't refuse. It was rumoured to be worth $1 million a year over its contract term.

A Role for Richards

Within the Dome Petroleum board, it was assumed that Macdonald would probably take over the chairmanship and chief executive position at Dome Canada from Gallagher, although that move ultimately rested with the board of Dome Canada, which was now more than ever eager to indicate its independence. However, the most fascinating speculation surrounded the future of Bill Richards with Dome Petroleum. Within Dome, Richards still received an enormous amount of respect and support, but feelings within the company were not now the prime consideration. One Dome board member told the author that he believed Richards had a "transitional role" to play. Another had suggested — before Macdonald's appointment — that Richards might continue in a long-term role if somebody strong was placed above him. Macdonald was undoubtedly strong. The issue was ultimately how a Scottish chartered accountant would get along with a man who held a mutable view of numbers, and who had viewed profit projections as marketing tools.

Nevertheless, within Dome there was no doubt that Richards had been a tower of strength since the Agreement in Principle. It seemed

243

almost incredible that, even in the depths of Calgary's post-AIP gloom, Richards had still managed to rally the troops. They were even playing practical jokes on the 33rd floor of the Dome Tower! Richards had taken to filching fat cigars from the office of Colin Kenny, the former Trudeau aide, and one evening when he crept into Kenny's office and opened the cigar box, lying inside was a mouse-trap. Richards just loved that.

"Attitude is very important and you also have the responsibilities of leadership," Richards had told the author in January. "Somebody told me one time that the president should always look like he's having a hell of a lot of fun. If you get consumed by worry and remorse, you're not terribly useful." He still seemed to believe that his indomitable will could pull it off. Of the AIP, he said: "It's just a facility. What we'd like to do is get the problem solved and get back to running an oil and gas company. ... The by-word now is self-help and what we hope is that we'll be successful enough in our efforts that we won't need that billion dollars."

About his personal survival, Richards professed not to be concerned. "My objective is to steer Dome through its problems. The personal outcome is not that important to me. There are lots of things to do in life. I feel very committed to the solution of the problem." But of course, for all intents and purposes, the problem was inseparable from Richards; if Dome failed, he failed, and failure was something he found almost impososible to countenance. "Inherent in the taking of risks," he had said, "is the possibility of failure. The first standard is to survive. Our judgment was that if we had to rely on the tender mercies of the banks then we weren't going to survive. Well, we had a strong determination to survive. We weren't going to fail because we didn't avail ourselves of every opportunity that was presented. You do what you have to. If you like it that's nice, but if you don't you still do it."

His words conjured up a scene from the film *Monty Python and the Holy Grail* in which a knight has his limbs severed one by one, but even when he's left on the ground as merely a trunk with a head, he refuses to give in. His opponent could only shrug and ride off. As a director of one of the Dome family noted: "They'll have to carry Richards out of the Dome Tower in a box."

By the late spring, however, the strain was beginning to become more obvious. The will persisted but Richards was looking tired and drained. In late May, he told the author: "The AIP was drawn up quickly, so the AIP has to be changed. ... One of the important things we have to do is change the psychology." But then came a slight crack, a chink in the battered armour. Richards admitted that at times he felt he had "the worst job in Canada." He also said he'd feel "indifferent about walking out the door."

Nevertheless, addressing the annual meeting, he gripped the sides of the lectern in typical forthright style and put his usual optimistic shine on Dome's financial position. He said that the company was stronger now than it had been six months before, and that HBOG's properties had been reappraised and its reserves had been discovered to be 15% higher than originally anticipated. He outlined dispositions and declared that the western LNG project was "the most important Canadian energy project in sight for the decade." However, he also revealed that the company would suffer a further write-down on its U.S. assets in the second quarter of 1983.

Richards said Dome's objectives were to improve financial strength; reduce debt; and minimize direct capital expenditures while still developing its assets. This latter objective would take place through asset dispositions, farm-ins, project financing and continued efforts to restrain capital and operating costs. Nobody could quibble with the soundness of Richards' program of restraint, but Dome's glowing future was strictly a provisional one. Dome had no future at all without a capital injection, and, equally important, the rescheduling of its debt. A key part of the AIP had been that the Dome management had to be agreeable to the banks, and Bill Richards was still considered far from suitable to many of them.

The week before the annual meeting, Bill Mulholland had made a swing through Calgary and Edmonton. There he had spoken to the press, and the issue of Dome had naturally been raised. Many observers thought that Mulholland had deliberately come west to clarify Dome's position in advance of the rosy picture he knew would inevitably be painted at the following week's annual meeting. In Calgary, on June 21, Mulholland laid it on the line. "The large part of Dome's debt," he said, "is demand, if we choose to make it demand. A refinancing of Dome outside the Agreement in Principle is probably unfeasible without a formal extension of the term of that debt. A formal extension of the term of that debt by the banks is not a practical possibility until (1) the Dome management is stabilized and the banks have confidence in it, and (2) the disciplines contemplated in the Agreement in Principle are in place and working."

"Stabilized" management, of course, meant changed management. The question was, how far were the changes meant to go? Mulholland obviously knew that Macdonald was coming because he had agreed with the appointment. But he also added: "You want to remember that the non-Canadian bank creditors, or at least the ones that have any semblance of organization, have said from the very beginning that they would not agree to Dome refinancing until the new management was in place and all of the talk that's going on in the press about disputes amongst the banks and all of that is largely nonsense.

"On the first day of acquainting foreign banks with this arrangement, and I can say so because I was personally present, the answer from their spokesman was that they were prepared to co-operate but they could not make any commitment until the new management was in place and that was the statement on Day One and that has been the consistent position ever since."

The question was: who among Dome management would the foreign bankers want removed? In particular, who could Citibank want removed? The answer seemed obvious: it would be the man they considered had "hoodwinked" them by neglecting to inform them of the shortening of the Canadian bank loan — Bill Richards. Gallagher, after all, claimed not to have *known* about the loan's shortening, although many found that hard to believe.

Mulholland was then asked about the desire of the shareholders to avoid the "dilutive" effects of the AIP.

"Let me put it to you this way, without intending to make any kind of commitments on either our or anybody else's behalf. Those arrangements provide a very strong incentive for the Dome shareholders to avoid those dilutive effects, as you put it, and, should they wish to do so, I would think it is not beyond the realm of possibility that the creditors would find that a very constructive development and would be willing to co-operate in that endeavour. *But, they aren't going to do it until those prerequisites have been met, which I mentioned a few moments ago."* (Author's italics)

In other words, the AIP provided an incentive to Dome shareholders to inject more money, but the banks wouldn't allow any such financing without the requisite management changes. That seemed to indicate that Bill Richards might come up with any imaginative private financing scheme he liked, but the banks wouldn't allow it until he had left.

Dome's president had been compared in the past to James Cagney, both in looks and corporate style. Some of the major Canadian bankers now viewed Richards as acting out a typical Cagney movie scene: he was holed up and daring the authorities to "come in and get him." The problem was that he was holed up in a house that belonged to them, or, at least, on which they held the mortgage. Some of them felt that they couldn't afford to go and blast him out. Also, quite unlike Cagney, Richards was declaring himself firmly committed to considerable home improvements. Would they blast out someone who could increase the value of their collateral?

Although the odds were massively against them — in fact, they really appeared to have no chance at all of survival — Gallagher and Richards continued to tweak the noses of the banks' chief executives to the bitter end. In the old days, when the Dome myth was still alive, some of the bankers must have lain sweating in the middle of the night when they thought of how much they had lent out to Dome. Now, when it appeared that the fundamentals of a settlement were in place, the nightmares had started again. What if Howard Macdonald went along with Richards' schemes? What if Gallagher and Richards managed to bring the shareholders into what the bank CEOs regarded as their "dream world" and the shareholders turned down the Agreement in Principle? Of course, the idea was ridiculous, because the banks could put Dome into receivership any time they wanted to. But what if, even now, Dome decided to call their bluff? For the bankers, the whole thing represented one of the biggest frustrations of their lives. There was only one path to follow, and yet Gallagher and Richards were still looking for side-alleys.

In the end, however, Dome's board was left in no doubt about the course of action they had to follow: Bill Richards had to go. By the summer of 1983, he almost certainly didn't care so much any more. He had been living under enormous pressure for two years, devoting every waking hour to the mammoth task of keeping Dome afloat. In fact, as he spoke at the annual meeting, the executive committee of the board may already have told him that his departure would have to coincide with Howard Macdonald's arrival.

However, the announcement of his departure was delayed for more than two months. On September 8, at a press conference in Calgary, Bill Richards announced that he would be giving up the Dome presidency and also his directorships of Dome, Dome Canada, Trans-Canada PipeLines, Dome Mines and Sovereign Oil & Gas.

Richards was less than ebullient as he delivered the requisite remarks of the loyal corporate man: "With the appointment of Mr. Macdonald, the company has acquired an executive of exceptional ability and qualifications. Under his leadership, I have every confidence that Dome Petroleum will prosper in the years ahead."

Then, with masterly understatement, he said: "This job hasn't exactly been a bowl of cherries for the past few years, but I feel we are past our financial crisis. As a result, I feel free to pursue things that have more interest to me. I plan to stay in the oil and gas business, on my own, and maybe even make some money."

The Dome share price rose 25¢ to $5.75 on the news. A week later, John Beddome would be appointed the company's new president. By the end of the month, Bill Richards would be gone. The bankers' will would be done.

Meanwhile, the bankers themselves were the objects of massive criticism for their rashness at home and abroad. It was a uniquely uncomfortable position for them.

The Bankers Beat Their Breasts

Remorse is not an oft-displayed public emotion on the part of bankers. The reason is simple: remorse indicates errors and errors shake confidence. The reaction of bankers to their toughest year — and with an even tougher year possibly to come — ranged from a mild and far from customary breast-beating to almost brazen denials of fault. Russell Harrison, chairman of the Commerce and the man who had received the most public heat throughout the Dome bailout, delivered what could only be considered an admirably frank assessment of the banking community's overall problems. Speaking to the annual meeting in January, 1983, he said: "If there is a lesson for us to learn from recent experience — and we are not above learning from experience — it is not that we should cease doing business. More to the point, it is that we should not do business merely for the sake of it, without sufficient regard to its relevance, its quality, its security and its profitability. Collectively, the entire world banking community in recent years has chased after asset growth without, in too many cases, due regard to the more important fundamentals of good banking."

In an address to his bank's annual meeting the same month, Bob Utting, vice-chairman of the Royal, even added a touch of humour to remorse, presenting what he called a "General Confession for Bankers." It went like this: "We have made loans we ought not to have made, we have left unmade loans we ought to have made, and there is no wealth in us."

Elsewhere, however, there appeared a somewhat one-sided view of the problems of the banks' customers. While attacking their number one target, the federal deficit, many bankers appeared to consider themselves blameless for the economic state of their customers. For example, Ted McDowell, vice-chairman of the Toronto-Dominion, spoke of the business community being "too busy embarking on a spending spree ... a spree that saw once-strong balance sheets weakened through pyramiding debt, as company after company contracted the fever and threw themselves into the acquisition game."

Nevertheless, McDowell did later in the same speech allow himself a small *mea culpa*, admitting that "in our bid to outperform our competitors, all of us in the industry allowed ourselves too much exuberance — too much dependence on continued prosperity at a time when many signals were out to caution had we noticed them."

Speaking of the international scene, Dick Thomson of the Toronto-Dominion accused some countries of "overborrowing." But of course there could be no overborrowing without the banks overlending. Robert Korthals, the T-D's president, even had the audacity to suggest: "When another bank makes a mistake, we want their customers to turn to us. The other banks are making lots of mistakes."

In fact, the T-D had performed relatively well, but for the banks as a whole, 1982 had been a financial disaster.

The four banks involved with Dome all showed enormous increases in their 1982 provision for bad loans. Dome, in fact, was not necessarily one of them. Due to the Agreement in Principle and the commitment to reschedule, its loans were still considered relatively "sound." However, the rush of bankruptcies at home and the international situation led to a staggering increase of 166% in "loan loss experience" to $1.77 billion in 1982. For the Bank of Montreal, the figure was $550 million, for the Royal, $530 million, for the Commerce, $488 million, and for the Toronto-Dominion, $198 million.

Due to a process of averaging loan losses over a five-year period, the actual provisions made — and hence deducted from profits — were smaller, a total of $1.1 billion for the four banks. Nevertheless, the impact on profits was considerable. In 1982, the pre-tax profit of both the Royal and the Montreal nose-dived, the Royal's by 49% to $330 million, and that of the Montreal by 47% to $239 million. The pre-tax profit of the Commerce fell by 18% to $358 million. Among the four, only the T-D showed a profit increase, of 6.5% to $327 million. To Bill Mulholland and Russell Harrison, the performance of their rival, Thomson, must have been particularly galling in the light of Thomson's reluctance the previous summer to assume what they considered to be his fair burden of the Dome bailout package.

Within all the Canadian banks, the loan loss experience and the extent of "non-performing" loans, on which no interest was being paid — estimated at about $8 billion — caused many internal changes. Bright young men who not so long before had been thrusting loan salesmen suddenly found themselves working in "special loan groups," the banks' equivalent of intensive care units. Asset growth came to a grinding halt.

Meanwhile, Mulholland, at his Calgary press conference in June, had tried to create the impression that there was little real disagreement with the foreign banks and that it was merely a matter of the departure of Gallagher and Richards before the AIP was put in place. Foreign bankers privately expressed their doubts about the orderly picture presented. American bankers told the author that it was a situation in which "nobody was steering." One described it as a "headless horseman," another as "an eighteen-ring circus."

249

Behind the scenes, relations were a good deal more tense than portrayed. A group of lenders brought together by investment dealer A.E. Ames (now part of Dominion Securities Ames) had made an unsecured $75 million loan to Dome. Dome had failed to meet a condition of the lending agreement relating to the coverage of its debt and the group had brought a law suit. Under the suit, Ames was seeking repayment, or, failing that, to become secured. The secured bankers were terrified that if the Ames group became secured, then *all* the unsecured lenders might be in a position to become secured. Thus Ames found itself being fought not so much by Dome as by the other banks.

There was also a major panic at the end of March, 1983, when a Japanese bank, Mitsui and Co., one of the members of a syndicate which had lent $130 million to Cyprus Anvil, refused to defer a principal repayment. As a result, Cyprus Anvil received a notice from its banks requesting payment of the $6.5 million principal due. This action required a piece of fancy footwork on the part of Dome. It transferred its 87.5% of Cyprus Anvil, via an elaborate corporate arrangement, to Dome Canada for a fee of $20, so that Cyprus Anvil's possible default would be isolated from its own affairs. In the end, Mitsui was "persuaded" by its partners, the largest of which was the Toronto-Dominion, to go along with a deferral of principal payments.

Mitsui's actions, however, had stirred the fear constantly present both for Dome and the bankers, that a smaller lender or creditor might simply refuse to play ball, in the hope that the larger lenders would effectively "buy him out." The principle followed by the major bankers was that "nobody leaves the room." But more than 50 banks and lending institutions were an awful lot of people to keep in one room.

For all the foreign lenders, the key point of contention was the $500 million of Dome's Canadian bank loans that the big four wanted them to take over. The foreign bankers, in particular the Americans, were adamant that they would do no such thing. By mid-1983, Dick Thomson of the T-D had infuriated Mulholland by publicly declaring that the $500 million might not be necessary. Mulholland who was thought to consider Thomson "weak-kneed," believed the T-D chairman was giving away an element of the banks' bargaining position.

Meanwhile, part of the key to Dome's survival lay with the corporate group that — like the banks — had been led on a helter-skelter ride by Dome, the company's family and friends. Like the banks, they were involved with Dome Petroleum up to their necks, and also like the banks, most of them had little chance of escape.

21
The Family
and the Future

*"It's not like yanking out an appendix. It's more
like open-heart surgery. You're hoping that nobody
jiggles the table."*
ANONYMOUS SENIOR BANK EXECUTIVE

Dome's "family" relationships now more than ever resembled some massive corporate soap opera, with eagerly sought financial divorce and convoluted new forms of incestuous relationships springing up everywhere. One member of the family, TransCanada PipeLines, was in the process of leaving the fold; Dow Canada found itself caught up in the messy aftermath of its participation in the HBOG takeover and was seeking a financial separation; but the two nearest relatives, Dome Canada and Dome Mines, found themselves more closely linked than ever to Dome Petroleum's future. Dome Canada's exploration expenditure was now vital to the exploitation of Dome Petroleum's massive land spread, while Dome Mines was thought to hold the complex secret to avoidance of the Agreement in Principle.

TransCanada, an extremely staid pipeline company when it was controlled by Canadian Pacific, had been sucked into the maelstrom of Dome's takeover activities. Between December, 1979, when it first entered the partnership with Dow Canada's Maligne Resources, and March, 1982, when it had acquired its 13% of HBOG, it had spent a little over $1 billion on oil and gas acquisitions related to Dome, a huge amount of money even for a company of TransCanada's size. Dome's problems had inevitably reflected upon TransCanada, and the most damaging rumour had been that the federal government wanted to obtain control of TCPL as part of a Dome bailout. TCPL was eager to squash these rumours.

It was clear, however, that Dome would have to dispose of its TransCanada shareholdings to raise cash. TransCanada's management eagerly looked forward to severing the relationship. On October 28, 1982, just a month after the announcement of the Agreement in Principle, Rad Latimer, TCPL's president and chief executive, in a speech to the Empire Club in Toronto, sought to clarify his company's situation.

"There have been mountains of publicity, speculation and comment about the Dome refinancing," he said. "The nub of it is that if anyone thought a magic wand would be waved when the banks and the federal government came in with their proposals, then they just misread the process. It is an extremely complex situation because there are a number of levels of investors with different kinds of security — people all over the place with valid interests in Dome. It is naive to think that all those interests would be satisfactorily dealt with when only two elements were sitting at the table. All that that represented was the first big step forward because it gave notice that the biggest stakeholders — the federal government and the banks — were determined to save Dome and keep it from going under. The process is now going on from there and it is going to be prolonged."

Then Latimer came to the heart of his message: "What should be clear, however, is that TransCanada is not involved in, or a part of, the solution. Meanwhile, there has been a great deal of speculation and curiosity over what happens to TransCanada PipeLines in all of this. One area of speculation that is particularly damaging is that the federal government is interested in acquiring TransCanada. I can say that from all the conversations I have had inside and outside government, there is no evidence to support such a notion. Rather, the federal government, the Alberta government and the banks appear very interested in finding a long-term, stable home for the TransCanada shares held by Dome Petroleum. And I think once the dust settles, there are several ways these shares can be distributed to Canadian investors in an acceptable way. TransCanada would welcome and support such an outcome and I have every reason to believe that it would be welcomed by any of the other interests in Dome. It would certainly be welcomed by the 23,000 other Canadian shareholders of TCPL."

Within a few months, Latimer's desires were fulfilled.

On March 1, Dome signed an underwriting agreement to sell 6 million of its TCPL shares, while Dome Canada would sell 5 million shares of its holding. Dome Petroleum's net proceeds from the sale were $146.8 million, those of Dome Canada $122.4 million. At the time of the underwriting agreement, Dome declared that Dome and Dome Canada had "agreed not to reduce further their direct or indirect shareholdings in TransCanada PipeLines Limited within 90 days from the closing date of this offering and have no present plans to do so." However, just two weeks before, at a meeting with bankers in London, Dome had told them that they had a plan effectively to sell the remaining TCPL shares at market prices. They did not outline the details of the plan, but they revealed that "although technically not a disposition, it has exactly the same effect." Whatever the scheme — code-named "Banquet" — it eventually fell through, and in July Dome offered the remainder of its TCPL shares under an underwriting agreement that would bring it another $116.3 million. Dome Canada, however, kept its remaining 5.3 million TCPL shares.

TCPL's Latimer was extremely keen to sever the relationship. However, Dome Canada's 11.8% block still represented the largest individual holding. Moreover, as this book went to press, Gallagher and Beddome were still on the TransCanada board. As a representative of Dome Petroleum, Beddome would, of course, not be expected to stay on beyond the next annual meeting in 1984. There was a wrinkle in the situation, however, because Gallagher also presumably represented Dome Canada on the TCPL board. Nevertheless, it seemed inconceivable to the business community that he could remain as a director of Dome Canada or TCPL for very long. Latimer was reported to be reluctant to have any directors from Dome Canada on his board, particularly if they were Dome Petroleum-related. Yet, Dome Canada's stake seemed to indicate that some representation was needed. In the summer of 1983, that issue remained to be resolved.

Meanwhile, while worrying about its ongoing relationship with Dome, TransCanada also had to face enormous problems related to the glut of Canadian gas and sagging gas markets, particularly in the U.S. Under a complex arrangement worked out in the fall of 1982 (see Appendix C), TCPL sought to solve these problems through Topgas, a $2.3 billion financing scheme that was the largest such corporate arrangement in Canadian history. The scheme, which provided a cash injection for gas producers as a *quid pro quo* for easing their contract requirements on TransCanada, also provided about $150 million for Dome Petroleum at a time when it could not have been needed more.

All in all, it appeared that TCPL would escape relatively unscathed from its relationship with Dome. The same could not be said, however, for Dow Canada and its resource subsidiary, Maligne Resources.

Dow in a Tangle

For Cliff Mort, the president of Dow Canada, the closing of Maligne's purchase of its stake in HBOG had been one of the most difficult, and ultimately thankless, corporate tasks he had ever faced. In order to persuade his U.S. parent to close the deal at all, he had had to work out a complex arrangement with Dome under which Maligne had the right to sell back approximately $74 million of properties a year to Dome for five years. The first "put" under such an arrangement occurred in November, 1982, although Maligne obviously knew by then that Dome was strapped for cash. Dome offered Maligne a promissory note backed up with Dome stock. Needless to say, Maligne was none too happy with the arrangement and turned it down. Subsequently Dome and Maligne struggled to work out some other way of fulfilling Dome's contractual obligation — which it plainly could not meet — and at the end of April, 1983, a deal was worked out under which Maligne would collect $75 million for the 1982 put — probably through the sale of the shares of Dome Mines that had been pledged as collateral in order to allow Maligne to buy its share of HBOG in the first place. However, it abandoned the four remaining puts. There were also other modifications in the business relationship between Dow and Dome.

What had started almost a decade before as a partnership that introduced a somewhat staid petrochemical subsidiary to the exciting world of petroleum exploration — a partnership which for a while had been enormously lucrative — had by now become a nasty taste in the mouth. Dow Canada, in the words of a Dow executive, was now under orders to do two things: "Get out of oil and gas, and don't do anything dumb."

But Cliff Mort, by now consulting in Calgary, wasn't the only executive within Dome's family circle to suffer because of Dome's desperate financial situation. Dome Canada and Dome Mines, too, had experienced major managerial shake-ups by the middle of 1983. For Dome Canada, the most important change was the departure of Bill Richards from its presidency. This event, however, didn't reduce the symbiotic relationship between the two companies. It was just meant to change the balance of the relationship.

Home Joins the Party

Now that Dome Petroleum was so severely strapped for cash, its relationship with Dome Canada — involving Dome Canada's comprehensive farm-in agreement on Dome Petroleum's lands — became of even greater importance. Dome Petroleum was in a virtual corporate coma, its capital expenditures having been slashed to a quarter of pre-1982 levels.Such a cutback meant that the company was engaged in little more than basic "asset maintenance." However, to maintain its land position, it had to drill wells. Dome Canada's commitment to drill on Dome's lands thus became critical. But even with Dome Canada spending virtually its entire exploration budget on Dome Petroleum lands, the pace of development was insufficient. Other major farm-ins were necessary.

Dome Canada's exploration agreement on Dome Petroleum's lands was still highly valuable. It gave Dome Canada access to perhaps the best land spread of any Canadian oil company. However, given the prevailing bad taste over the Canmar deal, the independent directors of Dome Canada needed to establish that they really were independent. At the end of December, 1982, Bill Richards was stripped of the Dome Canada presidency. On January 1, he was replaced by Louis Lebel, a well-known figure around the Calgary oilpatch (and also one of the rare oilmen associated with the Liberal party). A lawyer by background, Lebel had served from 1948 to 1980 with Chevron Standard, the wholly owned Canadian subsidiary of Standard Oil of California, the West Coast member of the Seven Sisters. There he had been a vice-president in charge of Chevron Standard's land and legal departments and also held responsibility for the company's government relations and public affairs. His civic involvements had included a term as chancellor of the University of Calgary, and chairmanship of the Canadian Petroleum Association. The other key addition to the Dome Canada board was Jack Stabback, the former head of the National Energy Board who was now senior vice-president of the Royal Bank's Global Energy and Minerals Group.

A number of exploration agreements involving Dome Canada were announced in 1983. On March 10, with much hoopla, Dome Petroleum and Dome Canada announced a five-year exploration program in the Beaufort involving five separate agreements with a total of 38 companies. The total cost of the program was estimated at almost $1 billion, of which Dome Canada was responsible for about $720 million. In fact, the vast majority of that amount would come not from Dome Canada but from the Canadian taxpayer, since most of the expenditures would be eligible for federal PIP grants at the maximum rate of 85%. That meant that Canadian taxpayers might wind up paying some $600 million of the $720 million Dome Canada tab.

In July, 1983, this arrangement was modified. A three-year agreement involving an estimated $1.47 billion was announced that brought Home Oil, the natural resource arm of Toronto-based Hiram Walker Resources, into the exploration agreement between the two Domes.

Under the agreement, Home and its 88.5%-owned subsidiary, Scurry-Rainbow Oil, agreed to pay 40% of exploration and development costs on Dome Petroleum lands in return for a 20% interest in the lands surrounding the exploratory wells. Dome Canada would pay the remaining 60% of costs. In the Beaufort, Home and Scurry-Rainbow agreed to pay between 15% and 35% of Dome Petroleum's costs to earn between 7.5% and 17.5% of the lands involved. Dome Canada would pay the other 65% to 85%.

For Home Oil, the advantage of the scheme was the access that it

255

gave the company to Dome Petroleum's enormous land spread. For Dome Canada, the splitting of the farm-in meant that it could participate in more wells and that it now also had access to the exploration expertise of more than one company. For Dome Petroleum, it meant that more money would be spent on its lands, with a corresponding increase in reserves, production and cash flow. However, the deal, which was reported to be consistent with the previous five-year Beaufort agreement, was again to be paid for mostly by the Canadian taxpayer. The majority of the program was still in the Beaufort, with projected expenditures of $1.1 billion out of the $1.47 billion total. Once again, most of this would be subject to grants at the maximum PIP level of 85%.

For Dome Canada shareholders, of course, PIP grants were an enormously valuable boost to exploration expenditures. However, questions remained about the equity and the economic rationality of the enormous amount of tax money being ploughed back into the Beaufort. PIP grants had been introduced to give Canadian companies the edge in enormously expensive, long-term frontier exploration. But now, with international oil prices collapsing, they seemed to be subsidizing expenditures in an area most oil people regarded as simply uneconomic. Even Jack Stabback, Dome Canada's newest director, had declared in a speech in May, 1983, that: "While it is desirable to delineate and ultimately produce from the frontiers, there is little doubt that the industry's expenditure plans would be far different if the PIPs did not exist. One has to wonder whether it is appropriate that over 50% of Canada's exploration expenses are being devoted to frontier exploitation."

Meanwhile, despite the enormous subsidies to its exploration program, Dome Canada shares were still languishing well below their offer price of $10. Jack Gallagher, speaking at the Dome Canada annual meeting at the end of May, declared that there was not sufficient risk capital in Canada "to take care of the after-market (that is, trading in a company's shares after their initial issue) for a non-dividend paying resource stock." He was thus effectively acknowledging what more level-headed observers had said from the time of Dome Canada's flotation: that far too many shares had been issued of a company that could only be held by Canadians. For that situation, nobody could bear responsibility but Dome Petroleum, the underwriters of Dome Canada, and the federal government that had given the new vehicle its blessing.

To rectify the situation, Gallagher suggested a new sliding-scale capital gains tax that reduced by 10% a year on all resource investment held for more than one year. "If you like the idea," Gallagher told the Dome Canada meeting, "suggest it to your member of Parliament because your stock is suffering today due to a limited after-market, not due to poor exploration results."

Gallagher didn't suggest — and perhaps didn't realize — that the shares were also languishing because of continued concerns over Dome Canada's vulnerability to exploitation by Dome Petroleum and that his own continuing status as chairman and chief executive would lead to excessive investment in the Beaufort. Gallagher's delivery of the full "Northern Vision" slide show did little to allay fears.

Dome Mines Dances On

Dome Mines continued to be the member of the Dome Petroleum family most inextricably linked to the Dome crisis. By mid-1983 it was also seen as a potential route by which Dome Petroleum might escape its financial fate. Dome Mines remained firmly linked to Dome Petroleum not merely through their major shareholdings in each other and their overlapping directorships — which had now been strengthened with the appointment of former T-D chairman Allen Lambert to the Dome Petroleum board — but also through the contentious guarantee of Dome Petroleum's HBOG loan, and the even more contentious commitment by Dome Mines to take out the T-D's Dome Petroleum debentures if the AIP was put into effect.

The accounting impact of the relationship was all too readily apparent with the release of Dome Mines' 1982 results. Although the mining side of the business remained profitable, Dome Mines had to take its relative share of Dome Petroleum's losses into account. This resulted in a net loss of $74.6 million for the year.

By mid-year, Dome Petroleum was openly talking of a plan to dispose of a large part of its 30.9 million shares of Dome Mines, with a theoretical market value of between $600 and $700 million. However, there were major problems in such a disposition. For a start, the market almost certainly could not bear a disposition of this size in one lump. Then came the question of whether the disposal would only be saleable to Canadian investors, which would further restrict its scope. The shares were, in any case, all pledged under various loan agreements, so the banks' agreement was necessary. Finally came the uncertainty for potential buyers of the continuing relationship with Dome Petroleum — in particular the loan guarantee and commitment to the Toronto-Dominion on debentures under the AIP.

Concurrently, Dome Petroleum was talking about a private share offering of between $500 million and $700 million, but was also noting that Dome Mines would have to take a share of this offering in order

257

to maintain its percentage ownership of Dome Petroleum. Obviously, not everybody went along with these plans for Dome Mines and its future. In June, Mac Taschereau unexpectedly resigned as president of Dome Mines. The publicly stated rationale was that Taschereau had disagreed with a plan to inject "additional executive expertise" into the company. Specifically, this related to lawyer Fraser Fell taking over as chairman from the retiring Bruce Matthews but also assuming the title of chief executive officer, which had until then been held by Taschereau. Taschereau's departure was a very clear signal of the requirements for a new chief executive. His main job was not to run a mining company; it was to engage in fancy financial footwook with the Miners' long-time dance partner, Dome Petroleum.

22
The Hangover

" ... no amount of external criticism of banks can come close to matching what is available on the inside."

BOB UTTING
VICE-CHAIRMAN OF
THE ROYAL BANK OF CANADA

"I think people are taking their frustrations out on us a little. ... When you go through the letters, it often turns out that we haven't handled the situation all that badly. ... For instance, a lot of them say: 'Gee, you really are better than you sometimes say you are.' It is probably true that we don't spend as much time saying that we're good."

ROBERT W. KORTHALS
PRESIDENT OF
THE TORONTO-DOMINION BANK

As this book went to press in the late summer of 1983, the Dome situation remained in a strange kind of limbo. Almost a year after its signing, the Agreement in Principle had still not been put into effect because it had still not been presented to Dome's shareholders. However, at least one of its provisions, the installation of a new chairman and chief executive officer, and of a new president, had — after a long and painful struggle — been achieved. In a way, the AIP had been a success: it had bought time and given all parties a chance to reflect on an intensely emotional situation. There was now an almost universal desire to find private financing alternatives to the injection of government and bank capital which would have left these two groups as Dome's major shareholders. Nevertheless, many uncertainties over such a financing remained: there were still enormous complexities involved in the sale of Dome's stake in Dome Mines, and there were still barriers to a major public offering of Dome Petroleum shares. However, Dome's situation, largely due to the decline in interest rates, had improved considerably. Its internal organization had been trimmed down and its financial control tightened up. But because Dome's survival still depended not merely on a major injection of new funds but also on a rescheduling of its bank debts, Dome could do virtually nothing without bank approval. Meanwhile, Dome would be subject to renewed problems if interest rates were once more to rise.

Assuming an equity injection and a bank rescheduling could be achieved, what questions did the great Dome drama raise? Who was at fault and who should pay? What would Dome's legacy be for Canada's corporate sector? How had Dome affected the country's status not only in its own eyes but in those of the world?

This book has tried to emphasize the importance of the international oil upheaval, domestic politics — in particular the Liberals' National Energy Program — and fiercely competitive bank lending in setting the scene for Dome's unprecedented expansion. These elements combined to create a collective infatuation with petroleum investment, a mad rush in early 1981 to acquire oil and gas assets for corporate gain and the national interest. In this atmosphere, it seemed only appropriate that the fastest growing and most imaginative company in Canada should make the biggest and most daring takeover. It was that takeover that brought Dome to the point of bankruptcy.

Dome's fight to survive clearly showed that the driving force behind its expansion had been not the man in the public eye, Smilin' Jack Gallagher, but Dome's president, Bill Richards. For a great many years, Gallagher's velvet glove and Richards' iron fist had formed a formidable combination. But when their management ways parted, the glove appeared elegant but ineffectual, the fist naked and ruthless.

There could be no denying that, in their very separate ways, Gallagher and Richards were, and are, exceptional men. A person's life, unlike the curate's egg, can be "good in parts." For the vast majority of their working lives, Gallagher and Richards were skillful, innovative, hard-working and successful. They aggressively promoted the search for petroleum; they conceived and built major new projects; they created many thousands of jobs. Their talents of persuasion, originality and aggression were well served by the economic and political times. But when the times changed, their talents turned into liabilities.

An assessment of Richards' career, of how it might be viewed in the sweep of Canadian corporate history, was, of course, difficult because his career was far from over. Richards was the sort of man who would inevitably rise again. He undoubtedly ranked as a great entrepreneur. With employees and friends, he had always been a much more caring and sensitive man than his corporate persona would have indicated. But for corporate rivals he was a nightmare. Many accused him of not playing by the rules. But for all its dynamic image, he regarded the oilpatch as a far too cozy place. He rejoiced in rocking

260

the boat. He always said exactly what he thought, in distinct contrast to the multinational executives who, when they spoke publicly at all, had been trained to chew each word a thousand times before making utterance. He had little personal ego — as his scruffiness endearingly showed — but his corporate ego was massive. One of his mottoes was: "My way or the highway." But Bill's way ultimately led into the morass of HBOG.

The crucial personal mistake made by Jack Gallagher was that he stayed on too long, and, in particular, held onto the position of chief executive when that function had, in effect, passed to Richards. Much earlier in his career he had spoken of retiring at 50, and possibly joining the United Nations. Later, when he had evolved his ideas about Senate reform and the imbalance of provincial representation, it seemed that he would dearly have liked some more direct political role. But it had just been too difficult to leave, particularly after the excitement of the Beaufort started in 1976. The Beaufort was a benign vision, but Gallagher's persuasive abilities and the political climate had caused it to be taken to almost economically dangerous lengths.

However, neither Gallagher's nor Richards' spectacular rise, nor their precipitous fall, would have been possible without the government and the banks. Ottawa had always held a somewhat schizophrenic attitude towards Dome, but the banks were the vehicles for the company's overindulgence.

A Damaged Reputation

The banks can offer little defence for their basic imprudence in lending such large volumes of money to oil companies — and in particular Dome — on the basis of assumptions that proved incorrect. They were driven, as this book has tried to show, by an obsession with asset growth that led to the abandonment of traditional measures of financial prudence.

In March, 1983, the Canadian Broadcasting Corporation screened a documentary about the Bank of Montreal. The bank had obviously agreed to open its doors to the CBC because it thought the program would be about its aggression and success under Mulholland. But in the middle of the filming, the whole banking situation began to turn sour. The result was a picture of a confused bank caught up in a situation over which it had frighteningly little control. Towards the end of the program, Ed Marcaldo, previously the bank's star international money salesman, had been challenged on the question of the bank's prudence. His response had been almost pleading: "If your banker came up to you and wanted to lend you money that you had no productive purpose for, would you take the loan? ... and if you did take the loan and it didn't work out very well would you blame the banker for giving you the money in the first place?"

Mercaldo spoke more truly than he perhaps intended, for his reply begged another question: what were the banks doing lending money to people who had "no productive purpose" for it?

In the words of one of the shrewder oilmen who managed to emerge still rich from the crisis of 1982–83: "[The banks] were greedy and didn't do their homework." Some of the bankers claimed that this wasn't the case. Sure, they were competing heavily with each other, but usually they were criticized for *not* competing with each other. How, they asked, could they win? But such excuses were weak. No bank could expect sympathy for jumping from ultra-conservatism to imprudence. Moreover, they attracted further criticism for their subsequent jump in the opposite direction, that is, for the speed and ferocity with which they turned on their former star customers. A great deal of this reaction appeared to be purely emotional. Some of the bankers who believed they had been duped by Gallagher and Richards took it very personally.They wanted retribution.

What added to the bankers' annoyance — and also provided some justification for their hard line — was that they had not merely exposed themselves to an unprecedented degree to one company, but that they had exposed themselves to two men who refused to play by the rules. They were angry at themselves for not only allowing a rogue element into the system, but a rogue element that had undermined the system's very existence.

But the area in which the bankers looked their worst was in their relationships with each other. They indulged in the sort of acrimony and bargaining tactics expected from the merchants of a casbah rather than from models of the Canadian establishment. They had exposed themselves as mere mortals, and sometimes petty ones at that, fluctuating between panicky pleading and macho brinkmanship. In so doing, they had undoubtedly damaged the reputation of the Canadian banking community both at home and abroad.

"Two years ago," a New York merchant banker told the author, "the Canadian banks looked like the finest institutions in the world. Now if I was at the Chase or at Citibank, I'd never worry about the Canadian banks again. They're moneylenders, yes, but bankers, no." Said another: "The whole display was comic. It was just like Gilbert and Sullivan."

American banks were hardly in a position to cast the first stone at others' bad lending practices, particularly when it came to the Third World's sovereign debt crisis. Unfortunately, the Canadian banks were deeply mired in those problems too. Although the sense of foreboding that had hung over the Toronto IMF meeting of the year before had subsided, the magnitude of the problem had not declined. It would hang over the world banking system for the remainder of the century.

Banking's Catch 22

Who would pay? At best, Dome might cost the banks nothing should a private financing be pulled off. However, bad loans elsewhere, typified by continuing record provisions for loan losses in 1983, would inevitably be paid for by the banks' other customers, who would receive less for their deposits and pay more for their loans and their service charges. To many observers, that was the most unfair aspect of the whole business. Richard Lafferty, the Montreal-based investment dealer and long-time thorn in the side of the banking establishment, declared in a June, 1982, submission to the Commons Standing Committee on Finance: "A strong argument is being made by the banks and others that the banks are entitled to earn a fair return on their assets. This is nonsense. The penalty for misjudgment in the marketplace is a loss and not a subsidy from the rest of the marketplace because an individual group became greedy or negligent in its judgment."

But there was a Catch 22 here: if a bank suffered financially, then it was really the soundness of its depositors' money that was at stake. It was as counterproductive to attempt to punish banks as it was to punish countries. Those who did stand in line for punishment, however, were the executives responsible for the bad lending. Ultimately, in loans as large as those to Dome and sovereign countries like Mexico, the buck could only stop at the very top. So the question was: how big was the buck? Did Dome *really* endanger the banking system?

Three of the major banks — the Montreal, the Commerce and the T-D — had a combined total of well over half of their equity capital at risk to Dome. In the event of a bankruptcy, they pointed out, the money would not simply have gone down the drain. Much of it would have been recovered through an "orderly liquidation" of Dome's assets. However, it is difficult to see how the liquidation of a multibillion dollar corporation like Dome could have been carried out in an orderly way in a relatively small, capital-hungry market where presumably only Canadians would have been permitted as purchasers, and moreover where there were so many often conflicting collateral claims on assets by lenders. Ultimately, of course, the federal

263

government — for the reasons mentioned above — could not countenance a major chartered bank failing. However, the bankers could not deny they allowed a situation to develop where a collapse was *believed* to be possible. That they had overlent to Dome was clear from the single-lender ceilings recommended at the end of 1981 by the Inspector General.

It is also important to remember that the greatest danger to the system occurred not after Dome was forced to appeal to the government at the end of March, 1982, but before the Citibank loan was signed on March 10. If the Citibank loan had fallen through, either because of Dome's financial plight or through knowledge of the shortening of the Canadian bank loan, then a much more serious crisis would have resulted. Dome would not have been able to complete the purchase of HBOG. More important for the banks, it would not have been able to dispose of parts of HBOG to family and friends and, as a result, reduce Dome's Canadian bank debt by some $1 billion. Citibank, in its obvious ignorance, did a great favour to Dome, the Canadian banks and ultimately the taxpayers of Canada, who would then surely have had to subscribe additional bailout funds for a much larger corporate mess.

The bankers' public stance was that they were certainly not guilty of corporate error great enough to warrant dismissal. Indeed, they never even addressed the possibility. In theory at least, their fate rested with the boards of their banks, which in turn raised another basic issue of the Dome affair — the role of corporate directors. If boards of directors were meant to be the ultimate custodians of shareholders' interests, how well did they perform?

Careless Custodians?

In fact, in most cases the boards of directors in the Dome affair emerged looking like mere bystanders, which made them less than innocent. The intelligence or integrity of individual board members was not the problem. The problem was that boards in large companies, or in those with an impressive track record, inevitably become rubber stamp mechanisms for management. Board "clubbiness" isn't a capitalist conspiracy; it's human nature. This was particularly true of the boards of Dome Petroleum and Dome Mines. Until the crunch, the members were close colleagues of Richards and Gallagher, and faced with the two men's mesmerizing presence — and outstanding track record — a passive stance was hardly surprising.

However, if the system was to have any vitality and meaning, if anything more than obeisance was to be made to the concept of free enterprise, then serious questions had to be asked of the board members of a company that got into such deep trouble. Moreover, responsibilities had to be accepted. At some stage — and sooner rather than later — the Dome Petroleum board had to be pruned and revitalized. Meanwhile, even more searching questions might have been asked by Dome Mines' shareholders, who had seen their company deeply embroiled in the Dome mess while a majority of their board members were also board members of Dome Petroleum.

Most of these two boards were made up of honourable and intelligent men, but as with the case of Admiral Byng, sometimes heads have to roll, both *pour encourager les autres* and to demonstrate to the world at large that business is not entirely a cliquey conspiracy, that it can clean its own house.

As for bank boards, the Dome situation highlighted that they more than any — when it came to banking decisions — were mere rubber stamps, rendered all the weaker by their unwieldy size. Their function was not so much to guard shareholders' interests — that, they believed, was being taken care of by management — but to provide business for the bank and give expert advice on different areas of corporate life. But this latter function would have to come under sharp scrutiny in the case of Dome. There could be little doubt that the senior oil people who inhabit bank boards would have questioned Dome's original HBOG loan, although they would never mention this outside the bank's boardroom, where goings on are almost hermetically concealed. However, there is also little doubt that by the time they saw the loan at a board meeting, it was a *fait accompli*.

And the federal government, too, had little to be pleased about in the Dome situation. It was Ottawa's disastrous National Energy Program, and the equally disastrously misguided agreement with Alberta in September, 1981, that put the official stamp on price projection fantasies. It was the NEP that told Canadian companies to go out and take over the perfidious foreigners. Mickey Cohen, who emerged from the bailout negotiations with his reputation intact, was reportedly shocked at the argumentative behaviour of the bankers. But despite personal recriminations, the bankers were ultimately concerned with protecting their shareholders' and depositors' money. Cohen could take a less acrimonious line because he was committing public funds to Dome.

If interest rates stayed down, economic activity picked up and private funds were found for Dome, then there might yet be some cause for congratulation in the handling of the Dome bailout; it would then be the bailout that involved no bailout. Nevertheless, it was important to remember than Dome would probably remain the single biggest corporate customer of the Montreal, the T-D and the Commerce for many years to come. Its corporate bulk, meanwhile, would hang over the entire Canadian oil industry. Most informed observers believed that for the Dome situation to be resolved fully, and for the company to revert to "normal," might take an entire decade. Bankers and their lawyers would spend years merely sorting out the myriad covenants to Dome's mountainous loans.

For Canada as a whole, whatever the outcome, Dome represented a uniquely painful experience. For a few short years, a country starved of superstars had two that looked ready — and seemed able — to take on the world. Alberta, with its regional insecurities and its historical resentments, had a company courted both by Ottawa and the world's bankers. For investors, Dome had seemed like the Canadian dream: secure speculation. As Peter Newman wrote in *Maclean's* in November, 1982: "The Calgary company was to have been the centrepiece of Canada's march to industrial maturity and energy self-sufficiency. Instead it has become a symbol of mismanagement and failure on a grand scale — the *Titanic* of Canadian business."

In the summer of 1983, Bill Richards had struggled to earn his place in history as the man who kept the corporate *Titanic* afloat. But in reality, it was being kept afloat by the banks, who could not afford to let it sink. That Richards appeared to control the wheelhouse, while they buoyed it beneath the waterline, had been an intense frustration. Richards knew that it would require a peculiar act of vindictiveness to sink a ship in order to drown the captain. But both he and the banks had also known that his days were numbered, and that Dome's new course would be charted by Howard Macdonald. Commercial icebergs remained, but no longer would Dome go out looking for them. It would be a slower and straighter course, and a very different ship.

Appendix A

A BRIEF HISTORY
OF HUDSON'S BAY OIL & GAS (HBOG)

HBOG's complex history stretched back to its formation in 1926 as the result of an agreement between the Hudson's Bay Company (HBC) and an American oilman, Ernest Whitworth Marland. Marland was an anglophile wildcatter who indulged his twin passions for oil and all things British by introducing fox-hunting and polo to the Oklahoma oil lands. His attraction to the Hudson's Bay Company came into the same category. He admired HBC as one of the romantic and venerable British trading companies, but also because it held an abundance of the most important raw material of the oil business — land.

Under the charter granted by Charles II in 1670, the "Governor and Company of Adventurers of England trading into Hudson's Bay" were granted possession of the "territory, lymittes and places" of Rupert's Land, an area the size of Europe drained by Hudson Bay and stretching from the Rockies to the Great Lakes.

In 1869, two years after Canada's confederation, the Hudson's Bay Company sold Rupert's Land to the new country for $1.5 million, but retained title to 5% of it, some 7.5 million acres spread between Winnipeg and the Rockies. Land is divided in Canada into townships, that is, grids composed of 36 mile-square sections. In general, the formula agreed upon between Canada and the Hudson's Bay Company gave the Bay section eight, and three-quarters of section 26, of each unoccupied township south of the North Saskatchewan River between Winnipeg and the Rockies. In each fifth township it got all of section 26. Since so much acreage had been given to the railways, the HBC was also given additional acreage north of the North Saskatchewan River to make up its 5% allotment.

This land was initially sold off by the Company to settlers complete with the rights to any minerals that might lie beneath it. However, after 1889, HBC followed the practice of retaining mineral rights, not primarily for petroleum but in the hope of finding gold and other precious metals. These rights were disputed between 1909 and 1925 in a case that finished up in the House of Lords. There, the highest court of the empire decided that the Hudson's Bay Company held rights to all minerals *except* gold and precious metals, which belonged to the Crown.

It was the Company's petroleum rights that led Marland, while organizing a gasoline marketing subsidiary in England in 1926, to seek out Charles Vincent Sale, the Hudson's Bay Company's newly appointed Governor. The result was an agreement under which a new company, Hudson's Bay Marland Oil Company, was formed with the exclusive rights to explore on HBC lands. The Hudson's Bay Company held one-sixth of the new company, with an option to increase this holding to 25%, which it eventually exercised in 1952.

A couple of years after Hudson's Bay Marland was formed, Marland found himself in financial trouble and was forced to sell out in the U.S. His company was merged by banking giant J.P. Morgan with Continental Oil Company (Conoco), a mid-western oil producer and marketer. Conoco, a West Coast independent oil producer, had been absorbed into John D. Rockefeller's all-embracing Standard Oil Company in the mid-1880s. It had become independent once more when the Standard Oil Trust had been broken up in 1913. Following the Conoco takeover of Marland's company, Hudson's Bay Marland was renamed Hudson's Bay Oil & Gas. Its parents were now Conoco and the Hudson's Bay Company.

After an initial burst of exploration, HBOG was to remain virtually dormant for the next 20 years, until the find at Leduc, Alberta by Imperial Oil in 1947. HBOG became active again, although it did not earn its first profit until 1956. The following quarter-century saw it become a powerful force in Western Canadian oil, and also a significant presence in other countries. By 1968, the book value of its assets, at $247 million, was higher than that of the Hudson's Bay Company. Its net earnings, of $27 million, were almost twice as large.

Appendix B

EMPLOYEE OWNERSHIP OF DOME PETROLEUM STOCK

One of Dome's key strategies for involving its staff in its fortunes was via a wide range of schemes to purchase — and be given — shares of the company. That was the prime reason why Dome employees held so much stock of Dome. By far the largest stockholder among management was Jack Gallagher. Then came Bill Richards. Following Dome's 1981 stock split, Jack Gallagher held 5.3 million and Bill Richards 1.4 million shares. At the height of the market frenzy in the summer of 1981, when Dome stock was hovering around $25, Gallagher's stake was thus worth $132.5 million, and that of Richards around $35 million. All directors and officers together held 10.8 million shares, worth $270 million, while there were several million shares owned by the rest of the staff. Bill Richards used to like to tell the story about the lady who retired from the filing department with $100,000 from her Dome stock.

Employees *could* go into a company pension plan, but were encouraged to invest in the company through a profit sharing plan instead. Originally the plan was one in which the company and the individual both made contributions to buy Dome shares, but the scheme eventually became non-contributory. There were advantages to not being in the pension plan, since the company then made a higher rate of contributions to the profit sharing plan on the employee's behalf. Shares were also given to employees annually on the basis of length of service.

For executives, there operated between 1972 and 1981 a generous scheme called the Key Employee Stock Incentive Plan, under which company trustees bought previously unissued shares of Dome at the market price on behalf of the "key" employees. Employees were lent the money to purchase the shares interest free, and were not required

269

to repay the loan for ten years. But they were also prevented from paying for, and collecting, the shares except at delayed intervals, thus providing them with a powerful incentive to stay with the company — at least when the share-price was rising. However, the November 1981 federal budget rendered the interest foregone on the loans taxable. Equally important, the share-price in 1981 went into reverse, and in 1982 went into a nosedive. No shares were issued under the plan after 1981, and in June, 1982, large amounts of debt associated with the scheme were extinguished as the shares languished below the price at which the trustees had bought them. For Jack Gallagher alone, $4.6 million of such debt was extinguished.

In place of the scheme, the company introduced a stock option plan. This granted employees options to purchase shares for periods of up to ten years at the market price on the day before the option was granted. In 1982, options on 1,363,000 shares were granted at a price of $3.50. No option was exercised. On February 22, 1983, a further 328,500 options were granted at $3.75. Of these, 25,000 went to Bill Richards and 24,000 to John Beddome. Since the Dome price subsequently rose above $6 in the first half of 1983, these options looked well worth exercising.

Also, in order to entice "ordinary" employees to stay with the company during its dark days, 1,352 Canadian employees were granted options on 6 million shares at close to the market low of $2.75. By mid-1983, the value of these options had doubled.

Appendix C

A NOTE ON TOPGAS HOLDINGS

The slump in demand for natural gas in the late 1970s and early 1980s — particularly in the U.S. market — presented a potentially major problem for TransCanada PipeLines (TCPL) because of the nature of its contracts with its Albertan gas suppliers. These contracts contained "take-or-pay" provisions under which the pipeline had to make payments on a contracted volume of gas whether it took the gas or not. It would then take delivery of the paid-for gas at a later date. However, the decline in gas markets to below contracted levels had led to a dramatic increase in the volume of payments TCPL had to make under its take-or-pay contracts. By the end of 1981, these totalled over $1 billion, despite the fact that in 1980, TCPL had renegotiated its contracts so that the take-or-pay provisions now came into effect only below 80% of contracted volumes. If the contracts had not been renegotiated in 1980, then it was estimated that TCPL's obligations under take-or-pay for 1982 alone would have been a massive $931 million. Although the financing charges on the cash borrowed to make take-or-pay payments were ultimately borne by Albertan producers under the "Alberta Cost of Service," determined by the Alberta Petroleum Marketing Commission, nevertheless, TCPL decided that some new arrangement was necessary. The company forecast that take-or-pay provisions would grow by leaps and bounds, thus turning TCPL into an effective banker for the whole industry, so it approached the major producers and the major representative associations of the industry with a proposal for a new arrangement.

A scheme was eventually agreed upon whereby the minimum level of contracted sales to TCPL — below which take-or-pay payments were required — would be reduced in return for an immediate injection of cash to producers. When the scheme was originally proposed, there was some concern that it was yet another piece of Dome's "fancy financial footwork," particularly since Dome, as a major gas producer, was also a major beneficiary of the new agreement. In fact, however, Dome had been itself skeptical about whether TCPL could pull it off.

The objectives of the scheme were to eliminate existing take-or-pay payments from the books of TCPL and liquidate the associated financing; to virtually eliminate the need for further take-or-pay payments; to provide a cash injection for the industry; and to decrease the financing charges borne by the producers. All these objectives would be achieved through a new entity, Topgas Holdings Limited, a new Alberta company incorporated by the managing banks, the chief of which was Citibank. Under the arrangement, TCPL would receive approximately $1 billion from Topgas in return for the gas for which it had already paid but not yet received. Meanwhile, the producers would receive some $1.3 billion related to take-or-pay obligations for the 1980–81 and 1981–82 contract years. In return, the producers agreed to further reduce the level at which take-or-pay started to 60% of the contracted volumes for the 1981–82 contract year, and to agree to a fixed repayment schedule for ten years starting in November, 1984. Under the arrangement, TCPL wound up with a stronger balance sheet, the cash to pay off $663 million in bank loans and $318 million to finance future pipeline additions; the producers wound up with over $1 billion; and the banks wound up with a loan at prime plus $7/_8$% and collateral in the shape of gas production.

Nevertheless, within just a few months of the conclusion of the Topgas deal — a deal that was meant "to virtually eliminate the potential for further take-or-pay payments by TransCanada" — it became clear that slumping export markets would mean that TCPL would not even be able to take the 60% of volumes contracted for in the 1982–83 contract year. The prospectus for the sale of the second tranche of Dome Petroleum's TransCanada holding, dated July 12, revealed: "The Company anticipates that nominations for the contract year ending October 31, 1983, will be below this threshold and consequently it will incur take-or-pay obligations for the year not exceeding $400 million." Theoretically, most of this cash was meant to come under take-or-pay export contracts which TCPL itself had with U.S. purchasers, but there was a move on the part of these U.S. pipeline companies to defer their contractual payments as TCPL had in turn done with its Canadian gas suppliers. Once again, the cost of any additional financing on the part of TransCanada would ultimately be borne by Canadian gas producers, but the situation was still one of considerable uncertainty.

272

Tables

Table 1

Dome's Lenders

Virtually every major bank in the world — American, French, German, British or Japanese — appears in this list, which is, of course, headed by four of Canada's big five banks. It is also interesting to note that four of Canada's major trust companies appear among the non-bank institutions that lent money to Dome.

	Outstanding principal as at December 31, 1982 ($ Million)
Canadian Imperial Bank of Commerce	941.9
Toronto-Dominion Bank	986.2
Bank of Montreal	928.6
Royal Bank of Canada	287.8
Credit Agricole	84.4
First Interstate Bank of California	84.4
The First National Bank of Chicago	84.4
International Westminster Bank Ltd.	84.4
Manufacturers Hanover Trust Co.	84.4
Morgan Bank of Canada	84.4
NBC	84.4
Security Pacific National Bank	63.3
Marine Midland Bank, N.A.	42.2
National Bank of Detroit	42.2
Bank of British Columbia	21.1
The Bank of New York	21.1
Continental Bank of Canada	21.1
European American Banking Corp.	21.1
The Fuji Bank Ltd.	21.1
The Industrial Bank of Japan, Ltd.	21.1
Security Pacific Bank Canada	21.1
The Sumitomo Bank, Ltd.	21.1
Credit Suisse	117.2
Citibank	194.0
Bank of America National Trust & Savings Assoc.	89.4
Chase Manhattan	109.7
Chemical Bank	94.4
Continental Illinois	214.2
Midland Bank	77.4
Credit Lyonnais	96.4
Société Générale	71.4

continued

Bank of Tokyo	21.1
Banque Nationale de Paris	35.3
Barclays	45.3
LBI (Canada) Ltd.	35.3
Treasury Branch-Musketeer Kaiser	29.7
Berliner Handel Sund Frankfurter	12.7
Deutsche Bank	25.3
Dresdner Bank AG	25.3
The Long Term Credit Bank of Japan, Ltd.	12.7
Swiss Bank Corp.	59.1
H.M. the Queen in Right of the Province of Alberta	10.0
Canada Permanent Trust Co.	50.0
Canada Trust Co.	25.0
Royal Trust Corp. of Canada	18.0
National Trust Co. Ltd.	5.0
Saskatchewan Co-Operative Credit Society Ltd.	5.0
The Mutual Life Assurance Co. of Canada	2.0
Marubeni	107.0
10.5% Prudential Debentures	175.2
Arctic Petroleum Corp.	175.0
Lynco Notes	6.1
1st Mortgage Rev. Bonds	3.7
Public bonds, debentures, etc.	611.6
Other and foreign exchange	94.2
Total	6705.5

SOURCE: Dome Submission to Creditors.

Table 2

The Citibank Consortium

Citibank
Bank of America National Trust & Savings Assoc.
Chase Manhattan
Chemical Bank
Continental Illinois
Credit Agricole
First Interstate Bank of California
The First National Bank of Chicago
International Westminster Bank Ltd.
Manufacturers Hanover Trust Co.
Morgan Bank of Canada
National Bank of Canada
Security Pacific National Bank
Marine Midland Bank N.A.
National Bank of Detroit
Midland Bank
Credit Lyonnais
Société Générale
Bank of Tokyo
Bank of British Columbia
The Bank of New York
Continental Bank of Canada
European American Banking Corp.
The Fuji Bank Ltd.
The Industrial Bank of Japan, Ltd.
Security Pacific Bank of Canada
The Sumitomo Bank, Ltd.
Midland Bank Canada

Table 3

Breakdown of the Big Four's Loans to Dome

As of the end of 1982
($000,000)

Canadian Imperial Bank of Commerce

Dome Energy Ltd. (HBOG takeover)		260.1
Musketeer (Kaiser acquisition)		144.5
Dome Investments:		
TransCanada PipeLines	265.8	
Dome Canada	165.0	
Other	100.0	530.8
112572 Canada Inc.		5.5
Alerk		1.0
		941.9

Toronto-Dominion Bank

Dome Energy Ltd. (HBOG acquisition)	260.1
Musketeer (Kaiser acquisition)	216.0
Dome Oils Inc.	95.0
Cyprus Anvil	130.0
Canpar FRN's Dome (Siebens)	86.7
Canpar FRN's Provo (Siebens)	124.0
Canpar FRN's Provo (Siebens)	74.4
	986.2

Bank of Montreal

Dome Energy Ltd. (HBOG acquisition)	260.1
Musketeer (Kaiser acquisition)	144.5
Natural Gas Liquids Plant A	200.0
Natural Gas Liquids Plant B	124.0
Income Debentures	200.0
	928.6

Royal Bank of Canada

Dome Energy Ltd. (HBOG acquisition)	260.0
Goliad	2.5
Orion Bank Ltd.	25.3
	287.8

Total–Four Banks	3144.5

SOURCE: Dome Petroleum presentation to bankers in London on February 14, 1983.

Table 4

The Big Four's Continued "Exposure" to Dome

As the following table shows, although loans to Dome represent a comparatively tiny proportion of the banks' overall assets (primarily loans), they represent a large portion of the banks' capital, the relatively slim financial base on which the banks' inverse pyramid of debt is built. In relative terms, the Toronto-Dominion remains the most exposed to Dome while the Royal has the least exposure. In fact, these figures, representing the position at the end of 1982, are not the height of the banks' exposure to Dome, which occurred between the original loan for HBOG and the disposition of HBOG assets to Dome's corporate family and friends. During that period, total indebtedness to the big four was some $1 billion greater. It was during this period that William Kennett, Inspector General of Banks, told the banks' chief executives that no single loan should exceed 50% of capital, that it should be a rare occurrence for a loan to go that high, and that any loan exceeding 20% of capital was to receive his special attention.

	Dome Loans	Total Assets	Capital	Dome Loans as % of Assets	Dome Loans as % of Capital
		($ Million)			
CIBC	941.9	68,300	2,380	1.4	39.6
T-D	986.2	45,000	1,753	2.2	56.0
Montreal	928.6	62,000	2,029	1.5	45.8
Royal	287.8	88,500	2,883	0.3	10.0

Table 5

How Dome Dominated Stock Market Activity

Dome Petroleum became an increasingly powerful stockmarket force in the latter half of the 1970s. In 1980, the year of the NEP, the value of trading in Dome Pete stock, at $3,462 million, was second only to that in Gulf Canada, whose offshore east coast interests had become the centre of attention. However, in 1981, the year in which Dome's popularity peaked, it dominated trading. Under assault by Dome, meanwhile, shares of HBOG came second in trading value. Two other members of the Dome family, Dome Mines and the newly created Dome Canada, also featured in the top 20. In 1982, when things fell apart, more Dome shares were traded than in 1981, but slumping share-prices led to a large decline in the value of trading. Once again, Dome Mines and Dome Canada made the top 20, as did the preferred shares that were given to HBOG minority shareholders.

1980 — Year of the NEP

Rank		Million Shares*	Turnover Rate	Value of Trading ($ Million)	1980 Prices High	Low $	Close	Change in Year
1	Gulf Canada	188.3	83%	5,389	38.62	19.87	23.37	+ 5%
2	Ranger	97.8	163%	1,329	27.50	6.50	22.50	+162%
3	Bow Valley	72.1	208%	1,400	27.00	11.00	20.00	+60%
4	Inco	56.1	74%	1,628	38.25	21.37	24.12	−12%
5	Alcan	49.7	61%	1,746	45.00	26.75	40.00	+46%
6	Dome Petroleum	48.1	97%	3,462	93.25	52.25	71.50	+32%
7	Husky	45.9	59%	738	20.87	9.62	20.50	+99%
8	Imperial Oil A	44.0	287%	1,860	57.50	30.37	32.87	−26%
9	B.C. Resources	37.6	39%	262	9.25	5.75	5.87	−17%
10	Hiram Walker Res.	29.9	43%	900	35.75	23.25	30.75	−16%
11	Noranda Mines	29.7	26%	825	33.62	22.12	30.00	+34%
12	Canadian Pacific	28.6	40%	1,276	52.62	34.50	43.50	+11%
13	Bell Canada	25.1	15%	489	21.25	17.62	20.00	− 2%
14	Inter-City Gas	23.1	119%	467	26.37	10.50	15.37	−21%
15	CP Enterprises	22.0	16%	573	33.00	17.87	25.25	+33%
16	Hudson's Bay Oil & Gas	21.4	28%	647	38.50	21.50	24.62	− 4%
17	Carling O'Keefe	20.8	96%	198	12.50	5.75	8.50	+24%
18	Norcen Energy	19.0	72%	503	40.00	28.00	31.00	− 3%

278

				Value of Trading ($ Million)	High	Low $	Close	Change in Year
	Northern Telecom	18.1	35%					
20	Seagram	17.2	49%	1,078	77.00	40.00	70.12	+46%

* Stock splits in 1980: Gulf Canada 5-1, Ranger 3-1, Bow Valley 3-1, Alcan 2-1, Hiram Walker 1.375-1, CP Enterprises 2-1, Hudson's Bay Oil & Gas 4-1.

1981 — Year of the HBOG Takeover

Rank		Million Shares*	Turnover Rate	Value of Trading ($ Million)	1981 Prices High	1981 Prices Low $	1981 Prices Close	Change in Year
1	Dome Petroleum	183.2	73%	3,306	$25^3/_8$	$11^1/_4$	15	+ 5%
2	Gulf Canada	90.1	40%	2,265	$31^1/_2$	$16^3/_4$	$18^1/_2$	− 21%
3	Hudson's Bay OG	65.3	86%	2,609	$51^3/_8$	21	$50^7/_8$	+106%
4	Ranger Oil	43.9	73%	637	23	8	$9^3/_8$	− 58%
5	Inco	39.4	51%	880	$28^1/_2$	$15^1/_8$	$17^1/_8$	− 29%
6	Hiram Walker	37.5	54%	1,072	$35^1/_2$	$20^3/_8$	$23^1/_4$	− 24%
7	Alcan Aluminium	36.1	44%	1,303	$47^1/_2$	$23^1/_2$	$27^3/_8$	− 32%
8	Noranda Mines	30.6	24%	733	$26^3/_8$	$19^3/_8$	$22^1/_2$	− 25%
9	Bell Canada	27.8	16%	516	20	$16^7/_8$	$19^1/_4$	− 4%
10	Canadian Pacific	27.7	39%	1,254	55	$36^7/_8$	$41^7/_8$	− 4%
11	Nova Corp.	25.5	24%	288	$14^3/_8$	$7^1/_4$	$9^1/_2$	− 27%
12	Bow Valley Ind.	24.8	70%	494	$25^1/_2$	$13^3/_4$	$19^1/_8$	− 4%
13	Husky Oil	23.4	30%	381	22	$9^1/_2$	$10^5/_8$	− 48%
14	B.C. Resource	22.7	24%	105	6.63	3	3.95	− 33%
15	Imperial Oil A	22.5	15%	736	$38^1/_4$	$24^1/_2$	$25^1/_2$	− 22%
16	Mitel Corp.	22.2	60%	749	$48^7/_8$	$18^1/_4$	28	+ 33%
17	Abitibi-Price	20.4	99%	637	$32^1/_4$	$19^1/_8$	$20^7/_8$	− 15%
18	Dome Canada	19.2	22%	155	$11^1/_2$	4.60	7	*
19	Dome Mines	19.0	25%	472	$30^3/_4$	$18^1/_8$	$18^1/_4$	− 30%
20	Cadillac Fairview	17.8	22%	219	$18^1/_4$	$7^1/_2$	$13^7/_8$	+ 81%

* New issue Stock splits in 1981: Dome Petroleum 5 for 1, Domes Mines 4 for 1, Nova Corp. 3 for 1, Cadillac Fairview 3 for 1, Pez Resources 3 for 1, Corona Resources 4 for 1, Lochiel Exploration 2 for 1, Surf Oils 3 for 2.

continued

1982 — The Year Things Fell Apart

Rank		Million Shares*	Turnover Rate	Value of Trading ($ Million)	High	Low $	Close	Change in Year
1	Dome Petroleum	200.6	81%	1,123	15	2.55	3.30	−78%
2	Gulf Canada	68.8	30%	997	$18^5/_8$	$10^3/_4$	$14^5/_8$	−21%
3	Mitel Corp.	56.2	150%	1,446	38	$15^7/_8$	$37^1/_4$	+33%
4	Alcan Aluminium	47.5	56%	1,229	$35^1/_8$	$20^3/_8$	$34^1/_2$	+26%
5	Inco	45.0	53%	573	$17^1/_2$	$9^7/_8$	$14^5/_8$	−15%
6	Bell Canada	37.7	20%	732	$24^1/_2$	$16^5/_8$	$24^3/_8$	+27%
7	Ranger Oil	37.4	61%	280	$10^1/_4$	5	$7^7/_8$	−21%
8	Dome Mines	29.3	38%	368	$19^1/_4$	$6^1/_2$	$19^1/_4$	+ 6%
9	Nova Corp.	29.1	25%	202	$9^5/_8$	$5^1/_4$	$8^7/_8$	− 7%
10	Dome Resources A pfd.	26.2	206%	997	$57^7/_8$	47	$56^3/_8$	+16%
11	Canadian Pacific	26.0	36%	793	$41^7/_8$	$24^7/_8$	$35^7/_8$	−14%
12	Hiram Walker Resources	23.3	33%	408	$23^1/_2$	$13^7/_8$	$19^3/_4$	−15%
13	Imperial Oil A	21.4	14%	553	$33^3/_4$	$15^5/_8$	$28^3/_4$	+13%
14	Husky Oil	20.3	26%	152	$10^7/_8$	4.75	8.25	−22%
15	Genstar	20.1	65%	352	$23^3/_4$	$8^7/_8$	$20^1/_4$	−13%
16	B.C. Resources	20.0	21%	60	3.95	2.38	2.69	−32%
17	Turbo Resources	19.7	92%	29	4.70	0.55	0.74	−84%
18	Noranda Mines	18.4	15%	303	$22^7/_8$	$11^3/_4$	$19^1/_2$	−13%
19	Canadian Imperial Bank of Commerce	18.2	45%	268	$33^1/_8$	$16^1/_4$	$32^3/_4$	+13%
20	Dome Canada	18.2	21%	82	$6^5/_8$	3.25	4.15	−32%

*Includes trading on Canadian and American exchanges but not London.

SOURCE: *The Financial Post 500.*

Table 6

How Dome Dominated the AMEX

Dome dominated the American Stock Exchange in both 1981 and 1982, but under very different circumstances. In 1981, it was hitting its peak. By the end of 1982 it had dropped almost 90%.

10 Most Actively Traded Issues on the AMEX for 1981

1981 Posi-tion	1980 Posi-tion	Trading Volume Year 1981 (Shares)	Year End Selling Price (U.S. $)	Issue
1	6	57,831,800	12-3/4	Dome Petroleum Ltd.
2	1	32,862,700	15-5/8	Gulf Canada Ltd.
3	3	28,644,600	7-7/8	Ranger Oil (Canada) Ltd.
4	—	26,931,500	19-7/8	Houston Oil Trust
5	43	25,253,500	43	Hudson's Bay Oil & Gas Ltd.
6	34	23,050,200	6-3/4	Int'l. Banknote Co., Inc.
7	19	20,913,600	33-1/4	Wang Labs., Inc.
8	195	16,912,600	9/16	Cyprus Corp. (The)
9	21	14,734,200	2-3/8	Champion Home Builders Co.
10	2	13,716,200	45-1/8	Houston Oil & Min. Corp.

10 Most Actively Traded Issues on the AMEX for 1982

1982 Posi-tion	1981 Posi-tion	Trading Volume Year 1982 (Shares)	Year End Selling Price (U.S. $)	Issue
1	1	116,901,500	2-11/16	Dome Petroleum Ltd.
2	7	39,968,200	29-1/2	Wang Lab., Inc.
3	3	23,144,100	5-7/8	Ranger Oil (Canada) Ltd.
4	9	22,820,500	5-1/4	Champion Home Builders Co.
5	2	21,903,800	11-3/4	Gulf Canada Ltd.
6	4	19,689,300	12-1/8	Houston Oil Trust
7	14	15,537,100	29-3/4	Amdahl Corp.
8	6	12,891,300	4-1/8	Int'l. Banknote Co., Inc.
9	13	11,638,700	1-1/4	Tubos de Acero de Mexico, S.A.
10	15	11,372,200	15-1/2	Ozark Airlines, Inc.

SOURCE: The American Stock Exchange.

Table 7

Dome's Spectacular Decade

($ Million)

	1982	1981	1980	1979	1978	1977	1976	1975	1974	1973
Revenues (after royalties and revenue taxes)	2,999.7	2,204.2	1,143.6	945.5	627.3	518.7	384.7	234.7	171.7	71.9
Expenses										
Cost of product	730.5	581.6	418.5	328.1	292.1	254.3	213.0	123.2	80.1	24.0
Operating and general	1,078.1	726.2	173.5	184.8	94.1	74.5	45.0	21.7	16.1	13.7
Interest and financing[1]	649.0	499.9	150.1	111.6	46.6	29.4	18.1	11.1	12.2	7.0
Depletion, depreciation and amortization	313.0	163.4	82.9	62.6	30.9	24.7	18.1	13.7	11.5	7.1
Preferred share dividends of subsidiaries	163.5	24.0	18.2	22.9	2.2	—	—	—	—	—
Other[2]	403.6	—	—	—	—	—	—	—	—	—
Total Expenses	3,337.7	1,995.1	843.2	710.0	465.9	382.9	294.2	169.7	119.9	51.7
Income before income taxes	(338.0)	209.1	300.4	235.5	161.4	135.8	90.6	65.0	51.8	20.2
Provision for income taxes	93.9	78.2	84.3	95.9	47.5	33.8	36.0	23.9	23.6	8.5
Equity in earnings of associated companies	57.1	78.0	71.1	42.1	11.2	2.2	0.7	—	—	—
Minority interest	(5.5)	9.8	—	—	—	—	—	—	—	—
Net income (loss)	(369.3)	199.1	287.2	181.7	125.1	104.3	55.3	41.1	28.2	11.7
Cash flow	224.0	388.5	449.6	323.4	198.7	163.5	110.2	80.4	63.4	27.3
Debt[3]	6,844.0	6,628.4	3,025.8	1,771.7	797.1	520.5	372.4	239.8	110.9	94.5
Capital expenditures	860.0	3,747.9	1,635.1	1,003.8	312.0	(a)	(a)	(a)	(a)	(a)
Total Assets	9,916.6	10,208.7	5,078.7	3,130.5	1,713.4	1,197.7	875.7	613.7	414.0	293.4

[1] Does not include capitalized interest of $212.9 million in 1982; $215.1 in 1981; $142.4 million in 1980; $29.9 million in 1979; $12.6 million in 1978 and smaller amounts in earlier years.

[2] For 1982, consisted of $35.4 million unrealized foreign exchange loss, $213.6 million write-down of U.S. properties and $154.6 million loss on disposal of assets.

[3] Includes redeemable preferred shares. Figure for 1982 includes $2,228.5 million due within one year (the current portion of debt). Other years exclude the current portion.

(a) No comparable figures available.

SOURCE: Dome Annual Reports.

Table 8

The Dome Board's "Family" Holdings

Name	Common Shares of the Company[4]	Common Shares of Dome Canada[5]	Common Shares of TransCanada	Common Shares of Dome Mines
Norman J. Alexander	125,000[1]	30,000	4,000	—
Rene Amyot	2,500	1,000	—	230
Marshall A. Crowe	2,600	3,600	—	—
Fraser M. Fell	17,000	12,000	—	1,200
John P. Gallagher	5,382,220[1,4]	60,000	500	120
Maclean E. Jones	85,000	64,800	—	5,200
Allen T. Lambert	30,000	8,400	—	3,600
John L. Loeb	3,801,520[2]	—	—	—
A. Bruce Matthews	80,000[3]	10,000	—	31,200
William F. Morton	201,000	—	—	—
William E. Richards	1,457,316[4]	64,683	—	1,200
Frederick W. Sellers	6,000	12,000	150	—
Malcolm A. Taschereau	2,000	120	—	13,000
All directors and officers as a group (33)	13,545,233[4]	226,791	19,650	24,550

[1] Includes shares held by their immediate families. Mrs. Gallagher holds 2,500 Series A preferred shares of the company.

[2] Includes shares held by Mrs. Loeb, and 2,513,160 shares held by trusts of which Mr. Loeb is co-trustee, with shared voting and investment power.

[3] Major-General Matthews' holdings are taken from the proxy statement and information circular for the 1982 annual meeting.

[4] Includes shares which these individuals have the right to acquire under the Company's Key Employee Stock Option Incentive Plan as follows: Mr. Gallagher–440,000 shares; Mr. Richards–200,000 shares; all directors and officers as a group–1,602,500 shares.

[5] Includes shares which these persons have the right to acquire on exercise of warrants or conversion of debentures. Except for Messrs. Gallagher and Richards and all directors and officers as a group (and Mr. Amyot, who holds warrants only), such warrants generally comprise one-sixth of the total shares shown. Mr. Gallagher holds warrants as to 10,000 shares, Mr. Richards as to 4,000 shares and all directors and officers as a group as to 50,190 shares. Mr. Richards holds convertible debentures as to 40,000 shares and all directors and officers as a group as to 240,340 shares.

SOURCE: 1983 proxy statement and information circular for Dome Petroleum.

Table 9

The Men in the Hot Seats — Dome's Board of Directors

Name	Age	Became a Director	Business Experience (extends to past 5 years, unless otherwise shown) and Directorships
Norman J. Alexander	74	1967	Investment Consultant, Winnipeg. Director, Continental Illinois (Canada) Ltd.
Rene Amyot, Q.C.	56	1982	Chairman, Air Canada. Partner in the law firm of Letourneau, Stein & Amyot, Quebec City. Director of Dome Mines Limited (1981).; Sigma Mines (Quebec) Ltd. (1979); The Imperial Life Assurance Company of Canada; Logistec Corporation; and Rothmans of Pall Mall Canada Limited.
Marshall A. Crowe	62	1981	President, M.A. Crowe Consultants, Inc. (since 1978), Ottawa, an energy consultant. Director (since 1978) of Associated Kellogg Limited; Energy Ventures, Inc.; Gulf Interstate Company; and Sulpetro Limited.
Fraser M. Fell, Q.C.	54	1971	Partner in the law firm of Fasken & Calvin, Barristers and Solicitors, Toronto, with which he has been associated since 1953. Chairman of the Board and chief executive officer of Dome Mines Limited. Director Sigma Mines (Quebec) Ltd. since 1971. His directorships also include Aetna Casualty Company of Canada; The Excelsior Life Insurance Company; and Royal Trustco Limited.
John P. Gallagher	66	1951	Former chief executive officer of the company and chairman of its Board of Directors. A director of Dome Mines Limited (1976), TransCanada PipeLines Limited, (1978); Canadian Imperial Bank of Commerce, (1979); Chairman and Chief Executive Officer, Dome Canada Limited (1980).
Maclean E. Jones, Q.C.	65	1976	Partner, Bennett Jones, Barristers and Solicitors, Calgary. Director, Canadian Imperial Bank of Commerce; and Dome

Name	Year	Age	
			London Life Insurance Company (1983); and of Trilon Financial Corporation (1983). Director CIP Inc., Hiram Walker Resources Ltd.; Royal Trustco Limited (1983); Hudson Bay Mining and Smelting Ltd.; and Western International Communications Ltd.
John L. Loeb	1950	80	Honorary Chairman, Shearson/American Express, Inc., investment bankers (member New York Stock Exchange) New York.
A. Bruce Matthews*	1954	73	President, Matthews & Company, Inc., a private holding company. Chairman of the Board of Dome Mines Limited since April, 1976. Director, Third Canadian General Investment Trust Ltd.; Canadian General Investment Ltd.; and Economic Investment Trust Limited.
William F. Morton	1950	77	Investment Manager. Honorary Director (1978) Boston Safe Deposit and Trust Company and The Boston Company, and until 1978 a director of both these companies.
William E. Richards**	1974	56	President of the company, Calgary. A director of Dome Mines Limited (1978) and TransCanada Pipelines Limited (1978). Director of Dome Canada Limited since 1980 and president of that company 1980 to January, 1983.
Frederick W. Sellers	1976	52	President of Dionian Industries Ltd. (a management and investment company, Winnipeg). Director, Canada Development Corporation; Polysar Ltd.; and Monarch Life Assurance Company. Chairman of the Board of CDC Ventures Ltd.
Malcolm A. Taschereau	1978	54	Former president and chief executive officer, Dome Mines Limited. Former chairman and president, Campbell Red Lake Mines Ltd. and Sigma Mines (Quebec) Ltd. Director, Canada Tungsten Ltd. (1981). Prior to 1978, executive vice-president of Dome Mines Limited and an executive officer of Campbell and Sigma.

* Retired June, 1983.

** Resigned Dome presidency and all related directorships effective September 30, 1983.

Index